A N D R E A   C A G A N

MEMOIRS

OF A

GHOST

One Sheet Away

ISBN: 1505319625
ISBN 13: 9781505319620
Library of Congress Control Number: 2014921487
CreateSpace Independent Publishing Platform
North Charleston, South Carolina

Advance Praise for Memoirs of a Ghost

Above all I am deeply moved by Andrea's honesty. Her intentions on finding, resolving, and acknowledging the truth of herself are so movingly written and so compelling in their revelations—a template for silenced women.

—Olympia Dukakis, Academy
Award winner

Andrea Cagan has written a book that encompasses the *entire* range of female emotions. It's all here: touching, enraged, lonely, courageous, and loving. She goes off on tangents that are extremely heartfelt...follow her. The beauty is in her complex complications...drink it up! She writes "just like a woman...yes she does."

—John Densmore, drummer, the
Doors

Memoirs of a Ghost reveals Andrea Cagan as a writer of gift and style, of revelation and insight. She travels from ghostwriter to soul searcher, all with the touch of a wise seer.

—Lynda Obst, Academy Award–
winning producer
and best-selling author

I dedicate this book to Jill, my beautiful sister,
who has lent me her unwavering love and support,
throughout my life,
even when I was being a brat.

Contents

For a moment, I could imagine what it would be like to be a ghost—
To walk forever through a silence deeper than silence,
To apprehend but never quite reach the lights of home.

— Michael Cunningham, *A Home*
at the End of the World

PROLOGUE

There is no greater agony
Than bearing an untold story inside you.

— Maya Angelou, *I Know Why the Caged Bird Sings*

*E*veryone has a story to tell, a song to sing, a poem to recite, a picture to paint, a grievance to be voiced, a bloodcurdling shriek to be screamed, or a lullaby to be crooned to soothe the hard edges of existence. We speak our minds and tell our stories with feather quills and fountain pens, typewriters and computers; we paint them on sidewalks, dance them in the streets, chalk them on blackboards, sign them with our hands, pin them on refrigerator doors, emote them in late-night poetry circles, brag about them, hide behind them, snore through them, and use them to wake ourselves up. We struggle to escape from them as we climb mountains and weather tempests for the sole purpose of finding our way back to them once again.

We all have our own individual styles, and we tell our stories on monitors, on parchment, on paper, or on canvas. We see them reflected in the gusting of the wind, the falling of the rain, a punch in the stomach, a belly laugh, a snort, a holler, or a really good fuck as we search for a revelation, a key to a gateway, a code to try to unravel the mystery. We drum up the courage to truly be seen with a kick in the pants, a smack upside the head, an encouraging pat on the back, a drop of human kindness—anything that might wake us up and guide us on the long and arduous journey back home to where we first took up our stories and where we will finally leave them behind.

Everybody has a story that yearns to be written. It spills off of fingertips as it races along, page after page, fashioned from twenty-six letters and a throng of punctuation, overflowing with commas, colons, spaces, quotation marks, exclamation points, and four-letter curses. Sometimes the words are free and flowing, pouring out like honey, smooth and refined, filled with honor, respect, wisdom, and mindfulness, connected in perfection, protecting us along the way, and healing our souls. At other times, the words are covert, fearful, and aggressive, breaking through barriers, chugging out like muddy gushes of stagnated water, clotted with blood, polluted by repetition, refried, blackened and lifeless, stained with algae building up over time and blocking the inroads, linked together in anger, sharp as swords, stinking like old cheese with the sole intention to kill the spirit.

And still, we search for someone, anyone, who will listen to our stories as we take our turn in the relay race of life. Pick up the baton. Meet a deadline. Beat the clock. Get there late. Make the grade. Take the cake, and eat it up. Hide the truth. Speak it loud and clear. Round and round, we strive to unburden our souls as we display our battle scars, both tangible and invisible, evidence of how we suffered, bled out, died, and then resurrected ourselves.

Everybody has a story that screams out to be told, and I help them tell it. I am the ghost, the hidden one who sees all, confessor to the rich and famous, keeper of their secrets, and purveyor of their furtive messages, languishing beneath my white sheet of invisibility as I listen, I empower, I encourage, I tape, I transcribe, I organize, I refine, I cut and paste and dramatize everyone else's stories, helping them face themselves in ways they never thought possible.

Now the tables have turned as I remove the sheet, bring my attention to myself, and surrender to the healing I took birth for. My own story has been lying in wait for me, hidden among the white, ghostly folds, faithful and unswerving, always here for me since the beginning. No matter what I was doing or thinking, no matter where I was hiding or how I got there, no matter to whom I was listening and whose life

I was narrating, I was gathering fragments of my own story, following my inner creative thread, the connective tissue that has linked me to everything and everyone else since before I knew my name or even that I had one.

I have always been writing. From the moment I learned to read, I wrote. When I felt invisible, I wrote. When I cried or laughed, I wrote. When I left home to pursue my ballet career, I wrote through the loneliness. On one-night-stand bus tours, I wrote through the tedium. When I trained on bleeding blisters and sprained ankles, I wrote through the pain. When I swallowed the mind-altering drugs that defined the sixties, I wrote through the psychedelic passageways. When I cheated with a girlfriend's boyfriend, I wrote through the guilt. When I traveled the world to research the faith healers, I wrote through the confusion and the wonder. When I was battered and broken, I wrote through my suffering and collapse, and then I wrote through my grief and recovery. And when I met the loves of my life, I wrote about each of them, and I did the same thing when I left them or when they left me.

Now, here I am, still writing, finally telling my story, tapping the letters on the keyboard while I still can, while my fingers still move and my eyes still see, while my brain still works and my ears still pick up the sound waves that sometimes soothe and bless, and other times irritate and aggravate.

In my life, I have been a hopeful child, a dancer in the clouds, a singer in the shower, a mediocre poet, a grateful sister, a graceful ballerina, an orphaned daughter, an adored lover, a battered wife, an actor, a liar, a truth teller, a miracle maker, a creator of beauty, an editor, a critic, a ghostwriter, and always and above all else, a storyteller, which I claim now in the name of women the world over. Women who have been silenced and annihilated for generations and cannot tell their stories. Women who cannot remember their stories and remain bound in their own sheets of invisibility, whether they were once adorned in silken gowns and jewels or tattered rags. Women who lunch, and women who starve. Women who nag and bark orders, and women with blindfolds, gags, and earplugs, yearning to speak, to be heard, to be seen, to sing, to scream, to find a way to matter, to be visible in the worlds in which they live.

This is my book, my story, my running in place, my journey through the passages of life, my part in the relay race, my victories and forfeits, my glorious war cry, and my silent surrender to the healing of my soul. This is the ghost revealed.

It's my turn.

Chapter One

ONE SHEET AWAY

The pages are still blank, but there is a miraculous feeling

of the words being there, written in invisible ink and

clamoring to become visible.

— Vladimir Nabokov

I sank back against a soft mountain of pillows on my bed, my eyes glued to the television. It was eleven o'clock on a weeknight, fifteen minutes before the start of *The Late Show with David Letterman*, where one of my books was about to be featured. In 1998 a retired host of a popular afternoon network talk show had hired me as a ghostwriter to pen her memoir-type book about life after television, and this was her first promotional appearance.

After fifteen years of undying loyalty to the network, when she was let go for the heinous crime of getting too old, she did what was expected of her, bowing out gracefully, pretending that leaving was *her* idea, passing the baton on the air to the young upstart who would replace her, all the while assuring her fans that she was thrilled she could finally "spend more time with her family." As the big bosses not so subtly ushered her out and ushered in the younger woman, she had eased the sting by using her newfound spare time to continue sharing her life with her fans, this time in a book. I had helped her.

When she hired me, I'd been a ghost for several years, and I knew the ropes. While there is a degree of intrigue in the title "ghostwriter," I don't think any writer aspires to being a ghost. I can't imagine a child saying, with wonder in her eyes, "When I grow up, I want to be a ghostwriter, someone who does all the work and gets none of the credit." I certainly didn't see that in my future. I fell into it, not so much by choice but by serendipity, when I offered to help a friend (an athlete) finish his long-over-due book. He had ninety-five poorly written pages before he got stuck, and I worked for a full year with this man, rewriting every word in his manuscript, adding new points of view and a lot of flair and personal stories to his biography. It was early in my writing career, and when this pro athlete's book premiered at number one on the *New York Times* best-sellers list, a book party followed, laden with celebrities. I flew to New York to attend, but while he thanked everyone and their cousins for helping him, he overlooked me completely. As far as he was concerned, I wasn't there. His publishers knew about me, though, and apparently told their cohorts. That was when I went from being ignored and invisible to being sought after and invisible. Baby steps.

I welcomed the paychecks and told myself it was just for a little while as I began doing the heavy lifting for a variety of celebrity book projects, poring over intimate journals and notes, ordering someone else's chaos, organizing the past, lining up their chapters, figuring out where the gaping holes were in the continuity of their hectic lives, and transcribing taped interviews, the hard labor that I liken to doing the floors and windows in a celebrity's vast house.

These people lead huge lives that are not necessarily better or happier than anyone else's, but they're decidedly bigger, more nuanced, and far more complicated. There are a multitude of nooks and crannies in a celebrity's life to dust off in order to reveal the stories that got tucked away when other demanding activities overpowered the hidden pearls. That was my job—to unearth the gems that were strewn among the routine comings and goings of someone else's world, to find the humanity under the hair and makeup of people who were so accustomed to living public lives, they had forgotten where they had hidden away their small pleasures and internal struggles that connected them to the rest of us.

I looked forward to having the time and space to write my own stories, but being a ghost lasted longer than I expected. I just kept getting seduced by offers that were too well paid and potentially interesting to pass up. Each time I signed a contract to be a ghost, I thought it would be my last, as I researched my clients with gusto, sat at their dinner tables, followed them around in their day-to-day lives, and dug as deeply into their psyches as they would allow. I was the proverbial fly on the wall, silently observing their habits, learning about their likes and dislikes, all the while making sure never to get in the way. My job resembled that of a therapist, but there were some major differences. While I asked a load of questions, dug into the past, and promised them confidentiality, I was not required to fix or change anyone or to make sure they understood their own psyches so they might avoid repeating destructive patterns. Rather, I was hired to root out those patterns, expose them, and, when necessary, to help my subject remember things that he or she had deliberately stashed away and forgotten. In short, my job was to make order out of their chaos, and I found it deeply satisfying.

Making order from chaos

Once the book was written, after I'd made the necessary edits and changes, I accepted the fact that the process was the reward, and I stepped back like my job description dictated, while they did their TV talk-show appearances and magazine interviews and toured the country to speak about their books and themselves. I have to admit here that I was somewhat envious. Not so much of their place in the sun—that was too vulnerable and exposed for my taste. I had no interest in being recognized by strangers, traveling to a different city each day, sleeping in strange hotels, and having to look balanced and fashionably put together when I showed up for book signings. I had done a form of that when I was a ballet dancer, traveling on a bus from city to city, performing every night on a different stage, sleeping in a strange bed, fighting chronic exhaustion, and dancing on injuries. I was over it. What I envied were the thank-you letters and kudos that came with the publication of the book.

I noticed time and again, a recurring phenomenon. It seemed that the more adept I became at picking up another person's speech patterns and vocal rhythms and expressions, the more my own edges would dissolve and the more ghostly I would feel. When I started to feel like I barely existed at all, it was a sign that I had morphed successfully into someone else, which was necessary to be really good at my craft. Sometimes it scared me, though, especially when feeling like a ghost seemed more real than feeling like me. *What was I doing to myself?* I wondered. It seemed unnatural and eerie when I felt more like a ghost than a human being.

The truth was, however, that being a ghost, remaining in the shadows, and writing for a living actually suited me. In fact, being a ghost was hardly new to me. When I traveled from city to city with my ballet company, in an attempt to save money, only half of us checked in at the front desk of the cheap hotels where we stayed for a night. We called it "ghosting" when the other half snuck up in the elevator, stole into a room, and took the mattress off the box spring. We put it on the floor and we alternated sleeping on the box spring or the mattress, paying as if it were a single room. We were that broke.

I never got caught. None of us did, but there was always an underlying fear of being exposed. In fact, there was underlying fear in most aspects of being a performer, so being a ghostwriter had some safety in it. As much as I loved to write, I had no attraction toward living in a fishbowl, being stalked, or having an entourage with bodyguards and handlers in tow. And I had to ask myself—was my own story interesting enough to tickle a publisher's fancy? Maybe I wasn't charismatic enough to be that center-stage personality or desperate enough for recognition from audiences or hungry enough for the constant publicity. Maybe the clothes in my closet weren't hip enough or my nerves weren't tough enough to find myself on the "What Was She Thinking?" worst-dressed list in *People* magazine. Or being the subject of a Twitter war. Or being chased by photographers and stormed by large numbers of fans.

I was working with a legendary diva in her New York suite of offices some years back when we decided to meet her agent for lunch at the

Russian Tea Room on Fifty-Seventh Street, just up the street. When we got on the elevator together, she stretched her neck, squared her shoulders, and put on a very large pair of sunglasses. Once we exited the elevator and hit the street, she began walking with her head down, at a clip so fast I had to run a little bit to keep up with her. Halfway up the block, someone shouted out her name, and a crowd of people came rushing toward us. I felt a stinging pain on the top of my right foot and looked down to see that a woman had pierced the skin on my arch with her stiletto heel, drawing blood, in order to get closer to the star of stage and screen. I limped to the curb, bending down to rub my sore foot. I stayed at the perimeter of the crowd that was deepening by the moment as the adored one was swallowed up.

Still, she walked forward steadily, signing a few autographs, and when she reached the entrance to the Russian Tea Room, the maître d' who was standing at the door grabbed her arm to pull her inside. She let him know I was her guest as I scuttled in behind her, and we were ushered to a table that had been placed between a wall and a giant fern. Her agent was already there, and we joined him for a delicious lunch, some good conversation, and a few laughs. After lunch, the agent escorted us both back to the diva's Fifty-Seventh Street offices. Once we were safe and sound in her suite, the door locked behind us, I exhaled and asked her, "Is it always like this?"

"Like what?" she asked innocently. She had no idea what I was talking about.

"The way people rush you on the street."

"Oh, that," she said, looking a little bit sad. "I really should have a bodyguard, but I don't want to live like that." She was so used to it by now, she didn't even think about it anymore.

It was all revelatory to me; I really had no idea what it felt like, but I knew I would resent primping and making sure I looked perfect each time I went outside. I prefer to avoid the kind of relentless attention that shines on the people who hire me. I don't want every outfit I wear to be analyzed or every wrinkle in my face magnified; I would never pass muster. I don't do facial fillers and I don't like scheduling every hour in my appointment book with a different promotional activity. I need to be able to go outside without makeup, dress in my favorite sweats with a hole or two and a bunch of pulled threads, lie around on my bed, stare at the walls or the TV, and just breathe, luxuries that celebrities are generally forced to forego, since they are always under scrutiny from the media and their rabid fans.

Not everyone is cut out for that kind of life. As hard as it was to be sidelined and ignored once a book came out, I reached a degree of acceptance of my role, since I knew what I had to do from the moment I signed on the dotted line and began writing about someone else's life. And the truth is that I liked writing for celebrities. Their lives fascinated me—not so much the glamour or the pomp or the wealth. I was more interested in the unseen efforts and maneuverings it took to grow and maintain such demanding lives. I liked being one of a handful of people who got to know the person beneath the persona. The truth beneath the press release. The feelings beneath the plastered smiles. The wrinkles beneath the Botox. Whether someone attained mastery as an actor or a scientist, a musician or a dog trainer, a reporter or a professional athlete, a motivational speaker or a psychologist, he or she had to utilize the same single-pointed focus and stamina that necessarily accompanied mastery in any field, and those stories were infinitely interesting to me. They still are.

After being the ghost in the room for so long, I have learned that along with the difficulties, this job has its perks and dispensations. I get to write every day and hone my craft; I have phone numbers and immediate access to people who are largely inaccessible; I get a lot of attention at dinner parties; and I get to tell a close friend or two what I'm doing and with whom I'm doing it. Although the offers have come, I've never been interested in writing (or reading) unauthorized biographies, which I consider rude, invasive, largely untruthful, and generally mean-spirited. I just don't savor the idea of probing the life of a person who doesn't want to be examined.

Rather, I take pleasure in working one on one, looking for the key that will unlock someone's memory bank as I put in play my hard-earned interviewing skills, working him or her finely and subtly until I come up with the spot-on question that produces the nearly invisible tic or sigh, the mysterious smile or sudden frown on my client's face that alerts me that I've entered a hot zone. At that point, I need to tread carefully. A wrong move on my part could shut it all down and cause my subject to retreat and shove me out. On the other hand, if my approach is careful and smooth enough not to make waves while I tactfully deny my client an easy out, I just might gain access to a vein of rich information that will make a story come alive with authenticity and humanness.

On the night I was waiting for *The Late Show with David Letterman* to start, I believed the trajectory of my career was about to change, as my name would finally be displayed on the cover of a client's book. I had been a bona fide ghostwriter up to then—no name and very little credit, the silent partner who left no trace that I was ever there. I had endured all manner of last-minute unwelcome surprises, like a paranoid chanteuse removing all the juicy material from her memoir right before publication, throwing the book into the category of "dry as a bone," and there was nothing I could do about it. I had worked with a feuding couple whose "perfect" relationship, the topic of their book, was on such shaky ground that I would pray each night that they would stay together long enough to see the book published. I battled over words and sentences with a client, sometimes winning but always having to be the one to yield in the end. In other words, I had paid my dues, and I knew that I would continue to do so. But while I waited for the show to start, I was finally taking a step forward in my career to become a "With."

Surely you've seen biographies that are written about and supposedly by someone famous. But underneath the neon lettering of the star, in much smaller, duller lettering, it says, "With so and so." That's me. The With. The so and so who actually wrote the book. I really liked how this TV host's book had turned out; I'd worked hard on it, and tonight I was about to see my name on the front of a book, *With Andrea Cagan*, for the first time on national television.

At the stroke of 11:15 p.m., Mr. Letterman came walking out to the usual applause from his studio audience, buttoning his perfectly tailored jacket and performing a very funny monologue. I've always enjoyed him—his sense of humor tickles my funny bone—and I was excited when he announced my client as one of his guests, mentioning that she was there to promote her brand-new memoir. They cut to commercial, and when they returned, there she was, her long, wavy, auburn hair perfectly framing her face, wearing a designer dress and heels, sitting in the guest chair and holding the book in her hands. Our book. I smiled broadly. She may not have been the most forthcoming client I'd ever had. Her stories were usually ho hum and she was always in full makeup when we worked, so I guess she felt she needed to maintain her image, even when we were alone. But she had treated me well, and I'd come to appreciate her over the months that we'd worked together.

After such an extended career on the air, she bantered easily with Dave for a moment or two, and he asked her for the book, which she handed over. He opened it and read a couple of sentences that were famil-iar to me, of course, and they talked for a few minutes. Then he held the book up in front of him. But when the camera zoomed in on the cover, my name was gone. Someone had placed white tape over it so that it appeared there was no "With" at all. I had spent the last six months writing my butt off, thrilled that my name was about to appear on a cover, which my con-tract had stipulated, only to be taped into obscurity. They might as well have taped my mouth shut like political protesters do when they're trying to personify dehumanization. I felt profoundly betrayed.

When I got my breath back, I picked up the phone to plead my case to someone, but I hung it back up again. There was no one to call. My agent had no power over this infraction. If I reached the anchor's agent (it was already two thirty in the morning in New York), he would deny all responsibility, blaming it on the TV staff and assuring me that his cli-ent had had no say in the matter. And that was exactly what happened. When I did mention my upset a few days later to my subject's agent, he admonished me to say nothing to his client about it.

"It wasn't her fault."

"She could have stopped them from doing it," I countered.

"Don't bother her with trivialities," he warned me. "She's very busy. She has a book to promote."

I wondered if the mere thought or mention of me at this point felt like a haunting to the person in front of the camera. When one of my clients took her last look in the mirror before she went on the set to sit beside Dave or Jimmy or Ellen to promote her book, did she see me looking back at her? I imagined a letter I would send a client when a book was finished that went something like this:

To Whom It May Concern,

You thought you had used me, thanked me, paid me, and sent me on my way. Your work is done, you said. Now make like a ghost and disappear. You thought you had stopped me in my tracks, dissolved me, incinerated me, and laid me to rest, complete with a stake in my heart, never to be seen or heard from again.

You were wrong. Out of the ashes I rise, your dreaded ghostwriter, a powerful zombie to be reckoned with, a phantom with whom you will remain eternally entwined.

But really, what did I expect? Like a backup singer or the "other woman," I had agreed to be the ghost, hiding beneath my sheet of invisibility, my name usually appearing somewhere in the third or fourth paragraph of the author's acknowledgments, which show up at the end (it used to be the beginning) of a newly published work. I am familiar with being feebly thanked in a sentence or two, mostly in clichés and unremarkable ambiguous statements, badly worded because in most cases those are the only words in the book that I didn't write myself.

I was familiar with being sidelined, and I had to admit that I'd agreed to it. "I told you how it would be," the married man reminds his forlorn mistress when the holidays roll around. "I never lied to you."

No one ever lied to me about what ghostwriting entailed. A veritable Rumpelstiltskin of the book world, I had learned to spin the straw of others' lives into words of golden floss that mystically fit together on the page. I knew how it felt to go beneath the sheet and give up a piece of my soul to climb into foreign skin, to change my speech patterns on paper to reflect someone else's, and to restrict my vocabulary to words that they would use. I also knew the righteous anger that arose when the glory of being number one remained one sheet away.

When a book is about to be published, as a gesture of good faith, the author and her "With" (that would be me) are routinely sent advance copies of the cover the designer has created. Technically, the publishers own the book, and they can put any cover on it they please, but a satisfied client who likes her cover is apt to do a better job of advertising her memoir, which will boost sales, so they do their best to please the celebrity.

As the years have passed, I have been constantly impressed that publishers and their editors never seem to run out of creative ways to torment the ghost, to put me in my place. In 2007—I was accustomed to being a "With" by then—I finished a memoir for a rock star. The next step was for the on-staff graphic design artist of that particular publishing house to put together a compelling, eye-catching cover. Hers was a very important job; sales hinge upon how much a book cover catches a buyer's eye when it is displayed on the online list of Amazon books or the New Arrivals table in whichever bookstores are still around.

When I received my advance copy of the rock star's book cover with an accompanying letter suggesting I "enjoy the artwork," I was extremely disappointed. I didn't particularly like the photograph they had chosen of the star or the way they had arranged the graphics and artwork. I could live with that if she could, but I felt affronted that they had printed my name in gray and placed it over a black background. They had featured me and made me disappear all at the same time—one more slap in the face of the ghost, one more way to render me invisible. The value of a sense of humor in this phase of the work cannot be overstated.

Maybe the rock star could help me with this, I thought. She and I had forged a strong bond over the last six months, so I picked up the phone. She wasn't any happier than I was.

"The picture of me they chose is awful. I either had really bad PMS when they were taking it or I was smack in the middle of menopause. I look terrible, the colors are drab, and I'm going to call the artist and get it changed."

"While you're at it," I said, "can you please tell her that if she intends to keep my name in gray lettering, maybe she could use a light background so it actually shows up?"

She laughed and assured me that she would. I got a call back about fifteen minutes later.

"What did she say?" I asked.

"I told the artist I didn't like it," she said, "and she got defensive. She named a bunch of famous books she'd done covers for and said everyone had been satisfied. So I told her, 'Yeah, I did a lot of albums. Some of them were great, and some of them really sucked. You need to redo this.' She's also fixing your lettering."

The next version of the cover worked for both of us, thanks to the rock star's self-declared big mouth and her willingness to use it to help me as well as herself. So it makes sense with all these shenanigans that I feel relieved when a project is finished, when there are no more imminent surprises, the book is no longer my responsibility, and I have released all my expectations. That's when I fly out the window and turn to dust like a vampire of the twenty-first century. That's the way it's supposed to be; I'm meant to dissolve into nothingness so the celebrity can claim the book that she has "written" and promote it with enthusiasm and know-how. In fact, I've gotten so good at paving the way before I step back that there have been several occasions when the celebrity actually believed she had written the book without me and, therefore, was fully qualified to discuss the writing process with audiences all across the country.

To that end, some of the agreements in my contract look vaguely like this:

1. I agree to assist you, the celebrity, in writing the "Book."

2. I shall receive an acknowledgment on the acknowledgment page of the Book, but you shall otherwise have no obligation whatsoever to accord any reference or credit to me. (Unless we make a deal to make me a "With.")

3. I hereby acknowledge and agree that you are and will be the author, owner, and proprietor, exclusively, PERPETUALLY, and throughout the UNIVERSE, of all rights of every kind and character whatsoever. I will have NO RIGHT to use the Material for ANY PURPOSE OR REASON WHATSOEVER, in your sole discretion.

4. You will have the PERPETUAL right to use and to authorize others to use my name and likeness, including videotapes of me, for advertising and publicity purposes in connection with any use or proposed use of the Material. (They never act on this. They don't want anybody to know that I exist.)

5. You will have the right to terminate my engagement thereunder for any reason whatsoever in your sole discretion upon twenty-four hours' notice.

6. I acknowledge and agree that any disclosure of this Confidential Information to third parties will damage your ability to conduct your business successfully.

7. I agree not to divulge the terms or existence of this agreement to any party other than our representatives.

Not only does the boilerplate ghostwriting contract stipulate that I'm not free to discuss the celebrity's life, what she says, or what she was wearing to lunch that day, I'm not even free to admit that the contract exists. So it really wasn't that much of a stretch to see my existence taped over on national television. To be or not to be was never the question. Not to be was the predetermined agreement.

That agreement is highlighted when a fan of one of my clients, (this happens a lot) in an effort to make contact with the celebrity, sends me an email. It often starts with an introduction that seems like they want to be my new best friend. He or she compliments me on my work, asks a few personal questions, and finally gets to the point. Can I send the diva his latest book and get it autographed? Would the athlete be interested in doing an interview for her radio or TV show? Would I please send along the email address or phone number of the VIP in question since there is a rare opportunity that the celeb wouldn't want to miss? Why don't I just get the motivational speaker to give a call? Or the rock star? It'll be well worth it, he or she assures me.

I always do the same thing. I forward it to the celeb's publicist who can sort through it and figure out what to do with it.

So when does it stop? You might be wondering how and when I come out of hiding and start being myself.

It happens slowly, after a book is "put to bed" in literary terms and the celebrity has finished her rounds of publicity. When she's on to her next project, when sales are leveling, and no one is asking her to appear on their TV or radio shows, my sheet of invisibility begins to loosen and lift along the edges. I carefully remove it, trying not to tear off too much skin in the process. I toss the sheet into the washing machine, the real me is revealed, and I take stock of my gains, like the uptick in my bank account, and my losses, of which there are many.

It is undeniable that I am paid nicely and I gain nuggets of wisdom and experience from each project, making me more than I was before. But when a book is done, I have to wonder: What do I do with my treasure trove of secrets—precious, sought after, and juicy as hell—that can never be uttered aloud or written anywhere? Do I have my own opinions back or are someone else's lingering? If a bus hits me dead-on or my airplane crashes or if I'm diagnosed with a terminal illness, whatever fate has in store for me for my final exit, whose life will flash before me? Will

I be a black girl singer from Detroit, a self-serving spiritual guru, an ego-centric self-help motivational speaker, a rock star with a dirty mouth, an inspiring role model who lost her legs to frostbite and set speed records on prosthetics, or the long-standing executive producer for a legendary TV host? When it all comes to a stop and I have a moment to return to myself and reflect, am I closer to my heart than before or further away?

When I scan one of my many books that have graced the best-seller lists and bookshelves all across the country, I vaguely recall the words inside, which have often been tainted by someone else's final edit. Some of the sentences that I worked out fastidiously are inverted and devoid of rhythm, filled with extra words that are cacophonous to my ear. They seem to have something to do with me, but I'm not entirely sure what it is, and I have to muse: Was my brain robbed? Were the ideas in this book snatched from my mind while I was bound and gagged with a white sheet? Or did I give them up willingly? Are the statements in the book fabrications I was paid to create or truths I was paid to dig out and expose? Am I a liar or an archeologist? Am I a guide to enlightenment or a coconspirator in a plot to dupe the reading public? Am I clever enough to have found a profitable outlet for my love of writing, or am I colluding with a system devoted to cranking out mass quantities of below par commercial clones that magnetize the big bucks? If and when I sign on for the next one, will I be a glutton for punishment once again, or will I simply be unable to resist the challenge of digging into one more fascinating psyche and rooting out and bringing to light the treasures buried there so long ago?

When I think back to what feels like a past life, I recall that my average day as a ballet dancer was so opposite to that of a ghostwriter, I could never have imagined that I would leave center stage to hide beneath a sheet. For example, in 1965 I was in a select group of dancers who appeared in a command performance in the East Room of the White House for President Johnson and Lady Bird. The audience was star studded, the atmosphere regal, as I danced the lead in a specially choreographed ballet to the haunting music of Charles-Camille Saint-Saëns. At the time, I was sixteen, I traveled most of the time, lived in mediocre hotels, and was accustomed to being on stage, wearing golden tutus, sparkling rhinestone earrings glued to my ears, and tiaras pinned onto my head. Or I was tucked into a full-length white body suit that hugged my trim torso so perfectly, it was hard to know where my body ended and the costume began. Male ballet dancers lifted me high into the air, balanced me on their shoulders, and threw me across the stage into the arms of someone else.

During that time, I was high on the act of performing, on showing off what I had perfected over many years by the sweat of my brow. It was intoxicating to do things that for other people would be impossible, to know my muscles and tendons so intimately, I understood exactly how far to push myself. And then, to go farther. To feel light as air, as if I could float a few feet above the stage and still be grounded enough not to lose my balance or my footing.

On Stage

16

How could I predict that decades later my life would be so different, that I would prefer to nest rather than travel and that I'd be happy to live in jeans and T-shirts and go barefoot instead of pouring myself into tight costumes and pointe shoes that were like a second skin? It's a surprise that I chose to hide beneath a ghostly white sheet for a living rather than being front and center, and that I use words and sentences instead of music and my body to express myself.

Now my life is inverting once again as I move into a brand-new arena, telling my own story instead of someone else's, pondering my personal failures and triumphs instead of digging for another's, admitting to and citing my fears, failures, and courageous attempts to live my life authentically, and doing everything I can to put my truth on the page. It feels somewhat lonely as I move forward, because unlike my clients, I have no one like me on the outside to prompt me or goad me, no one to call late at night when I'm sure I'm writing garbage, no one to arrive with tape recorder in hand, computer waiting patiently for her to tap out the magical rhythms of my words. No one else will show up to breathe life into my story in much the same way that a sculptor breathes life into a lump of clay. This time, it's all on me.

While some of the people's lives about which I've written seem to move chronologically, one event naturally leading into the next one, the threads that make up the mosaic of my life have not been woven in a straight line. One thing does not flow gently into another, and in keeping with my life's trajectory, neither do the chapters of this book. There are stories within stories, quick exits from one time zone to another and back again with overlaps that are neither subtle nor predictable. While my life themes are clear, and the lessons are obvious, my path swoops, arcs, and shifts, often without warning, from one event to the next and back to the beginning again. This is the way my life has unfolded, with hairpin curves and U-turns that mess with my equilibrium, and to write it any other way would be doing myself and my life experiences an injustice.

It's time to tell my story now, but after this book is done, I can't help but wonder if I'll ever become a ghost again. Will I find myself one more time exerting the right amounts of pressure and compassion as I usher in a sudden recall of someone else's actions, feelings, and conversations that will inevitably open the way to the heart of the matter? Will I slide back under the white sheet, linger in the shadows, and do what I have learned to do so well and efficiently? Or will I remain standing in the light of my own life? It's impossible to know because I still hold the ghostly process in high regard, no matter the pitfalls, difficulties, and clashes along the way.

The truth is that I have some form of affection for almost everyone I've worked with. Writing a book is an intimate experience, and each time I'm grateful to be able to join forces to talk about other people's lives, as we go straight to the center of their cyclone and chisel out the full catastrophe, in the words of Zorba the Greek. I have respect for people's willingness to expose their stories from the inside out. And above all else, I am profoundly grateful for the handful of enduring friendships I have made with some of my clients, in which we have become peers, now that I know their innermost secrets that make up the book that I will never write.

Chapter Two

AUDITIONS

I had to stop going to auditions thinking, "Oh, I hope they like me."

I had to go in thinking I was the answer to their problem.

— George Clooney

I sat in a finely upholstered straight-backed chair in the lobby of an elegant hotel in New York City, waiting. It was the spring of 1998, I'd ghostwritten for a number of celebrities over the past few years, and I was about to meet a Monte Carlo royal who was looking for someone to help her write a book. It was my first time meeting with a royal, and I wondered what it would be like.

The princess had flown me to New York from Los Angeles the day before, and we were about to have our first discussion. She had heard about me from her agent, with whom I'd worked on several jobs over the last few years. His power of persuasion was considerable. Once he had given her my name, explained how I worked, and extolled my virtues, she was interested enough to fly me to New York. I knew she was seeing other writers, but I put that out of my mind. I was accustomed to competition; the first meeting with a potential client was always an audition of sorts.

I was no stranger to auditions. I had endured epic ones when I was climbing the ranks of the ballet world, and a meeting/audition preceded every writing job I'd ever done. But I still got a little bit jittery. The butterflies in my stomach were not so much about my performance. I trusted I knew how to handle myself. I'd been in this position many times before with celebrities who carried power and mystique. But there was so much to do and figure out in such a short period of time. I needed to make a good first impression. I needed to get a sense of my prospective client and how she viewed the world around her. And I needed to see if she could "play well with other children." In order to do that, I had to be able to grasp who she really was apart from the preconceived notions and the abounding rumors that always circled these kinds of men and women.

I had a good track record at not getting caught up in the illusion that a celebrity was better or more important than I was, but at times it was more difficult than others. I once had a meeting with a basketball star who was huge, both in the physical sense and the fact that he was famous and beloved all over the world. I had to talk myself down when I was waiting to meet him because he had such a sterling reputation. *He's just a person, like me or anyone else,* I coached myself—until he walked into the room. He towered over me, the hand he extended was twice the size of mine, he was wearing workout gear that made his legs look a mile long, and his smile was so big, I lost my bearings for a moment, imagining him running across a basketball court, making a slam dunk, and magically saving the team in overtime. I got myself back pretty quickly, but it took a lot of self-talk not to swoon and become stupid under his spell.

And then there was the legendary diva. I was fine when I first met her—I kept things in proportion in my mind—until she began to sing along with the radio one afternoon. They were playing one of her songs while we were working, and the moment she opened her mouth and I heard that voice, I began to swim in adoration of her talent and charisma. I reined it in, forcing myself to recognize her as a peer, because no matter how magical the persona, she was certain to do something along the way to remind me that she was human. The more I kept that in mind, the easier it would be to accept her frailties and insecurities, which would inevitably show up sooner or later. In fact, I'm grateful for the disillusionment that comes with getting to know someone whom people look up to and consider better or more than they are. When I walk away from the maelstrom of a famous person's day-to-day existence, I have a deeper gratitude for the quiet and simplicity in my life and the anonymity and ease with which I can move around in my world.

I checked my watch and looked around the lobby where I was waiting. If the princess and I decided to do a book together, she would have to tell me her secrets and work closely with me for at least six months. Did she expect to do any of the actual writing? While it might sound like that would make my job easier, it never did. When a nonwriter fancied herself an author, I needed the patience of a saint and the tact of an ambassador to bring the writing up to the necessary standard without angering her or making her feel insecure. I hoped that the princess would leave the writing to me and that she would feel comfortable enough to be herself around me. Would she "get" who I was, and would she believe that I could "get" her? The truth was that even if I decided I didn't want the job, I wanted her to want me—the way you might feel about a blind date.

It was tricky business getting a celebrity to trust me. After years of being battered, misrepresented, and misquoted by the press, celebrities are often gun-shy and tight-lipped when it comes to opening up about their lives. Would the princess have the courage to tell me the truth about herself? It always showed up in the writing if a subject pretended to be someone she wasn't. Would she be willing to take direction from me? Celebrities, royals in particular, are accustomed to giving orders, not taking them. And then, I had to wonder, did she have anything of value to say? One of my pet peeves was meeting with would-be authors who "wanted a book," but really, they had no idea what they wanted to say. "What do you think I should write about?" they would ask. They wanted me, the writer, not only to shape the book and get the information on the page but also to decide what they should talk about in the first place. That was a deal breaker for me. I had an hour or less to determine whether or not I could work with this woman and to figure out why she wasn't hiring the writer who had penned her memoir, which had become a best seller several years prior.

Like in any relationship, the first thing I did in an initial meeting was look for chemistry. The client and I basically had to like each other. There had to be a sense of mutual respect and a willingness on her part to listen to my direction when I felt it was necessary. And she had to have a sense of humor. She needed to be able to laugh at herself, especially when the material got challenging. It always did, and the client was usually shocked when it happened. Finally, I had to feel that I could pick up her speech patterns, determine the kinds of words she used, and, in a sense, jump into her skin to understand how she thought, what mattered to her, and how she expressed herself. If jumping into her skin was repulsive or seemed impossible, I would have to decline the project.

I had a pretty wide berth, though, when it came to my willingness to invade the psyche of someone else. Over the years, I knew vicariously what it was like to be in prison in Afghanistan, to perform for thousands of screaming fans, to lose my legs and become a medal-winning runner on prosthetics, to lose my children in a car accident, to have a split personality, to marry my childhood sweetheart, to bungee jump in Australia, and to have so much money, I couldn't give it away fast enough. In the end, the difficulty of a task didn't turn me away. It was about the attitide of the person who was hiring me to become a facsimile of who they were or who they wanted to be.

My reverie was interrupted when a man in a crisp white shirt and perfectly tailored gray wool pants approached me. "Mlle Cagan," he said with a delicious French accent. "Lovely to see you. Thank you for waiting. Please come with me. The princess is looking forward to meeting you."

I stood and gathered my purse, notebook, and bottle of water. This man had recognized me, which meant that I had been picked up on a closed-circuit surveillance camera right then or I had been vetted previously, complete with a photograph. And why not, since I was about to breathe the rarified air around a royal with a personal security detail and a host of servants, including the man who was collecting me, who catered to her every whim? Celebrities without entourages and royals without staffs of servants who say "yes" all the time are practically nonexistent.

I followed the gentleman into the elevator and we headed up, up, up to the forty-second floor. When the door opened, a plainclothes security guard met us, as if we were on a high-roller floor in a Las Vegas hotel. "Please follow me," Tony said (of course that was his name), as we walked down the hall, stopping at the corner suite. He entered an inner lobby without knocking. I followed, and he asked me to sit down as he disappeared into another room.

A moment later, in walked a young woman, probably in her midthirties, looking slightly nervous, her thin, dark hair pulled into a plain-looking bun at the back of her head. This was undoubtedly the princess's personal assistant or secretary. Whatever she was called in Monaco, I was always on the lookout for the woman in this coveted position, because she held the key to the celebrity's inner sanctum. She was usually a lot less attractive than her boss, an unspoken requirement in her job description, and sometimes she was the best functioning (or only functioning) part of her boss's brain.

She half smiled and said, "I'm Chantal. Lovely to meet you. Her Highness is ready to see you now." Smiling seemed uncomfortable for her, but I could see she was trying.

I smiled back. *Her Highness.* It was hard to wrap my mind around that one as we entered a large living room filled with light and bustling people, including the princess's attendants and several men with earphones talking into their wrist cuffs. A guard stood over in the corner with Lawrence, the princess's literary agent. He and I exchanged smiles. I had seen this man at his worst, disheveled and hungover from the night before (he really liked his Scotch), at his desk with his shirtsleeves folded up, juggling phone calls, barking at assistants, and I marveled at how well he cleaned up in his Armani suit, Brooks Brothers shirt and tie, and Bruno Magli shoes. The quintessential agent, he knew how to lie, cheat, and steal and somehow remain calm, likeable, and knowledgeable in the process.

And there she was, the princess, the slender, buff, radiant queen bee with her favorite drones buzzing around her. She sat in the center of a beige-colored couch, the auburn highlights in her shock of choppy light-brown hair glowing in the sunshine that was streaming in from the large picture windows, her skin looking like fine porcelain. Known for her athleticism and her fabulous fit body even after she'd had twins, a boy and a girl, she was wearing a Chanel jacket over black pants that fit her remarkably well. A pair of glasses hung on a jeweled chain around her neck. Lawrence took a seat beside her as I approached and stood in front of them.

Chantal, standing beside me, placed her right foot behind her left leg and lightly genuflected. The princess nodded, and a moment later, Chantal made an exit into the adjoining bedroom of the suite. The princess gestured for me to sit on a chair opposite the couch, which I did, as she called out, "Chantal!" The harried woman scurried back into the room and curtsied again. Did she expect me to curtsy too? Nothing would kill my ability to work with this woman faster. Lawrence glanced at me and raised his eyebrows conspiratorially.

"Oui?" Chantal said, waiting for orders.

"Call downstairs," the princess said, "and see if they can send up some proper mayonnaise for that artichoke sandwich. Americans have the worst mayonnaise I've ever tasted," she added, looking straight at me. "They don't put enough eggs in it." I nodded. There was no reason to let her know that I wasn't a fan of mayonnaise, with or without extra eggs, and I thought she was acting like, well, a spoiled royal.

Lawrence spoke up, cutting off the princess's tirade on American food to introduce us. She smiled at me and spoke in a self-assured, low-pitched voice about her quest to find deeper meaning in her life. She had done her memoir several years prior (a ghostwriter had penned it), and now she wanted to write about her spiritual leanings, she told me. She had a spiritual advisor who was guiding her through the current phase of her life, she had had an awakening of sorts, and she wanted to share that with her public. I'd heard worse reasons for writing a book. At least she wasn't doing it "for the money" or "because my agent says it would be great for my career."

We dropped into relaxed conversation, she listened to me when I spoke, and I appreciated her self-deprecating sense of humor. She seemed to be in harmony with me—until I told her I would be taping our interviews and would write the book from the transcriptions. She withdrew slightly, a look of fear clouding her face, until Lawrence, ever the diplomat, suggested that she could have a transcriber of her own at the ready. That way, no one else would ever hear the tapes, and she could review the material before she handed it over to me. She seemed satisfied with that, so apart from the mayonnaise rant, she was easy to be with, and she seemed sincere about her desire to write something interesting and inspirational.

About a half hour into the meeting, she said, "The question is, where shall we work?" I glanced at Lawrence. Did that mean she had decided to hire me? He remained poker-faced as she continued, "We can't work here. It costs me a bloody fortune to be here for a weekend. There's the price of the flight for my assistant and me, and my security detail sleeps in the next room. I have to bring too many people with me. But working *chez moi* is absolutely out of the question. I have no time, and there are too many distractions. I want to be able to give the book my undivided attention."

That was a hopeful sentiment, but where else could we work? I wondered. She mentioned a couple of homes at her disposal—one in London, the other in Argentina. "We could take a whole week and just write," she said, lighting up at the mention of it. "No staff around to interrupt." I wondered (silently of course) when she had last boiled an egg, made herself a cup of tea, or drawn her own bath. I expected it had been a long time, and I was *not* about to become her handmaiden, but the idea of getting her alone and seeing what came up was attractive to me. All in all, she seemed intelligent, I thought we could get along, and she sincerely wanted to do this book for the right reasons, it seemed. And then, I have to admit that hobnobbing with royalty sounded like a grand adventure. I decided if she offered me the job, I would take it. I couldn't see any reason not to.

I'd been there nearly an hour when she called the meeting to a close. She had a fashion magazine interview coming up, and she needed to get her hair and makeup touched up. We shook hands, and when I left and stepped out onto the street, a sense of relief washed over me. When a meeting is over, especially a highly anticipated one like I'd just had, I usually feel the release right away. It isn't in my nature to obsess over what I did or didn't say. It's too late to fix anything, anyway, I tell myself. What's done is done. And it's too early to feel anxiety because I never know when I'll find out if I got the job. In five minutes or five days? Or maybe five weeks?

I began to wander back to my own hotel a dozen blocks away, watching chicly dressed New Yorkers walking briskly down the street as I window-shopped and admired the latest fashions. I was thinking about a nap before dinner—I hadn't slept that well the night before—but when my cell phone rang and I answered it, I was surprised to hear Lawrence on the other end of the line.

"She loved you," he said. "She wants you to start in a couple of weeks." I was pretty excited about it when I flew home the next day—until a week later when I got another call from Lawrence telling me that the princess was sending me a first-class (I liked that part) round-trip plane ticket to the south of France. I knew the south of France and I loved it. I had lived in Monaco for a year when I was in the ballet. But as exotic as this seemed, it was not a good sign. She was flying me to the very place where she said she simply couldn't work. So much for avoiding distractions and making her own mayonnaise.

I thoroughly enjoyed my flight abroad. Air France treated me like a princess, which only seemed fitting. I was given a sweat suit to change into so my clothes wouldn't be wrinkled when I arrived. I was offered a massage or a manicure before a wonderful dinner. I opted for the massage. And when I was finished, my seat went flat like a bed, and I slept the whole way there. It felt like a good omen.

During my first few days at the sumptuous chalet where the princess lived, while my accommodations were something to write home about (I would have, if I hadn't signed a tome of confidentiality papers), I got to witness one of the princess's unsavory temper tantrums (apparently they happened at regular intervals) as she chewed out Chantal for breathing or something equally ridiculous. And I was amazed that before we even started, she complained bitterly about having to write a book to advance her career. Wait a minute. What about her spiritual awakening, her desire to inspire her fans? And then there was her spiritual advisor, a tall, unkempt American man in his early forties who was always present, skewing our meetings into therapy sessions during which he probed her about why she hated her *maman*. Or her *papa*.

"Talking about emotions is not my *forté*," she told me, "so he's going to speak for me. He really knows me." He began answering my questions as if he were she, and she nodded her head at his answers. It felt surreal, and I didn't get any usable material.

When our first interview was over, I told the princess privately that it wasn't working and maybe we could try doing an interview, just the two of us. She declined. Apparently this man's presence was mandatory. And then, to make matters worse, which I didn't think was possible, three days into the week that she supposedly had carved out for me, she decided to take Mr. Advisor with her to London for a few days, for God only knew what reason. I was left behind to wander the palatial home, listening to the clicking sound my shoes made on the hardwood floors, studying the artwork on the walls, and poring over private photo albums. Doing this for a few days might have been a welcome way to pass time under different circumstances, but I had a job to do. I was contemplating how I would get that job done on my way down a long, curving stairway when a butler appeared at the bottom of the steps. "Madamoiselle," he said.

I looked behind me to see whom he was calling "madamoiselle."

"You, madamoiselle," he said. He was referring to me. "There's a phone call for you." Embarrassed, I walked over to a phone on a wooden desk in the hallway. It was Lawrence calling from New York, wondering how things were going.

"Not too well," I said. "She isn't even here." As I continued the conversation, the butler walked away to give me some privacy, and I expected I had become fair game for the staff, who had to be whispering about me in the servants' quarters.

After getting a pep talk from Lawrence, I hung up the phone, wishing I were anywhere else as I went to sit on the edge of my bed, wondering how on earth I would ever extract any usable material from the absentee princess. Munching on a chocolate bar that a friend had given me—"in case she tries to starve you or the food is too rich"—I realized that the princess had done an Oscar-worthy performance during the initial audition, pretending to be who she wished she were instead of who she really was. She was far from ready to buckle down and share her experiences about her spiritual quest in order to inspire her readers. She had actually flown to London, a different country, to avoid it. Why hadn't I seen through it? Had I wanted it to work so much that I'd refused to acknowledge what was right in front of my face?

Forty-eight hours later, the princess returned, advisorless—she had left him in London—and she gave me two hours in a private room, doing an interview that might have worked if I'd had more time with her. I was scheduled to fly back home the day after tomorrow. Maybe she would dedicate the entire next day to the book. I tried to ratchet up some hope, making a list of questions I would ask her during the interviews that I really wanted to happen, until Chantal showed up at my bedroom door.

"Her Highness would like to see you in her sitting room," she said.

Maybe Her Highness wants to do a night session, I thought. But when I arrived at her room, she was popping the cork on a bottle of champagne "to celebrate finishing our work." She had faith in the book, she told me, a nonexistent manuscript of around 250 pages (in her dreams) that I was expected to produce out of nothing. I got a little tipsy as she spent some time cautioning me that the information she had given me was precious, her transcriber was typing up the pages right now, and I needed to guard the transcripts with my life. She believed that there were "certain people" who watched her all the time; they might even be on my plane in order to steal those pages from me. I simply couldn't be too careful, and I should take them with me everywhere, even "when I went to the *toilette*."

I scanned the passengers on my flight home, feeling pretty depressed. No one looked remotely interested in me or the paltry eight pages the transcriber had handed me, and I wondered how the princess had become so delusional. It didn't really matter, though, because however badly the week had gone, it was still my responsibility to write the story that my client wanted to tell. I just couldn't stop chiding myself for missing the point during the initial audition. Were there signs I had overlooked? Could I have handled things differently? Had Lawrence known who the princess was all along and hoped I could make it work anyway? It was just like him to ambush me and hope for the best. Now I knew why the previous writer hadn't gotten on board for this project. She had had enough, I supposed, and now it was on me to create a best seller out of a few bad therapy sessions and gossip from the princess's kitchen staff. When I took a good look at my situation, it seemed that even after a lifetime of dealing with one audition after another, I still hadn't mastered them.

I had a long international flight to ponder the importance of auditions. I had had my share. During my childhood, while other kids played with dolls, rolled their hair in curlers, painted their nails, and jumped rope in their driveways, I was already onto a thread that would weave all the way through my life: auditions—the laser-like scrutiny, the moment of judgment that would get me one step closer to or further away from fulfilling my dream. They had been an integral part of my life in the ballet, but dance auditions were straightforward. Similar to the emotional, make-and-break auditions for the talent shows that we see on TV, they weren't two-way streets. It was clear who was auditioning whom, and there had been no way to pull the wool or the leg warmers over anyone's eyes, like the princess had done with me. It didn't take long in a dance audition to see whether or not you measured up.

I'd always had my sights set on becoming a ballerina. When I was a kid, and my friends and I fantasized about what we wanted to be when we grew up, for them it was a passing fancy. For me it was a career choice.

A Child's Dream

I was six years old when I was riveted by a newspaper photograph of Margot Fonteyn, prima ballerina of the Royal Ballet of London, in costume as the young peasant girl in the classical ballet *Giselle,* who went mad from unrequited love. I studied her pointe shoes, the delicate pink ribbons that looked like they'd been crafted by the angels, her laced bodice and layers of diaphanous tulle that draped her body, her dramatic eye makeup, and the way she gracefully held her arms above her head. I always admired the gymnasts in the Olympics—they were powerful, fast, and precise—but I wanted to be a ballerina who flitted on the tips of her toes on pink fairy shoes wearing long tulle skirts, just like Margot Fonteyn.

At the time, I had no idea what this entailed. I just loved to dance, and I became a hazard to my family as I leapt and pirouetted my way around the house, randomly throwing a leg behind me in an arabesque, hitting whomever was unfortunate enough to be standing back there. I had no idea about the trials that were ahead of me: the unrelenting discipline, grueling auditions, endless rehearsals, aching muscles, bleeding blisters, sprained ankles, and scathing competitiveness. I never imagined that I would need to perfect the art of looking beautiful when I was in extreme physical pain. That I would go to bed hungry and exhausted, wondering how I could get up in the morning and start over. I just didn't see my chosen career as something that needed to be attained. No six-year-old thinks like that. It felt like the ballet was already in me; it was a part of me, and the rest would just happen as I danced around the house, dreaming of sequins, tutus, and sugarplum fairies.

When I was eight, my mother enrolled me in ballet class with a local ballet teacher whom I adored in Worcester, Massachusetts, my hometown. My sister, Jill, was already her student when I began. I quickly became so obsessed and enthusiastic that most afternoons I took the bus by myself for the fifteen-minute ride from school to downtown, munching on carrot sticks or a bag of State Line potato chips. I was the apple of my ballet teacher's eye. She was proud of me and responsive to my enthusiasm, and what she lacked in technical know-how, she made up for in emotional expression as she encouraged me to perform from my heart and interpret the music with my entire body.

When I was eleven, my mother found a ballet school in Boston run by a teacher who was knowledgeable in technique. She had placed a number of her dancers in New York ballet companies. She was a pro, the real thing. So I lengthened my bus rides to an hour and a half each way whenever my mother couldn't drive me, and I began to work harder and demand more of myself. The teacher was surprisingly overweight, she always wore black, and when she took her small foot out of her high-heeled shoe to demonstrate a step and show off her perfect arch, I studied her diligently, trying never to make the same mistake twice. "Don't eat that chocolate sundae like I do," she used to chide us. "And don't skip class. No ballet company will want you if you get fat or if you're lazy." I tried to eat well, and I showed up for class as often as I could, but not until I was fourteen did the reality of my chosen lifestyle hit me hard.

It was the summer of 1964 in New York City, and I was standing on the landing of a staircase at the world-famous School of American Ballet, looking down into a large studio filled with young ballet students. I was about to audition for the renowned choreographer George Balanchine, the artistic director of the New York City Ballet. His company was right up there with the Bolshoi and The Robert Joffrey Company, and auditioning for him was the big time, the dream of every ballet girl in every small town in the United States. It was like an actor from Hayes, Kansas, arriving in Hollywood for the first time and taking a screen test at Universal Studios. I was living the dream, and I felt equal parts excitement, anticipation, and terror as I watched the girls below me in their torn leotards, faded pink tights, thin wraparound sweaters with holes, and soiled pointe shoes.

These well-seasoned big-city dancers were stretching and fidgeting in the odd ways that dancers do, pulling at the rips in their leotards, rolling their necks from side to side to grind out layers of built-up lactic acid, some of them lying on the ground, their legs thrown over their heads like contortionists, their faces bobbing out the other end, some with one leg on the barre, bending forward from the waist until their flat chests kissed their shins.

It was a sweltering June day in Manhattan. Large corner fans in the massive studio blew the hot air around in anticipation of the start of ballet class. A piano was positioned at the right side of the room toward the front. The piano player, an effeminate-looking man in a white shirt with sweat circles under his arms and a ponytail, sat on the bench, perspiration on his brow, fanning himself with a piece of sheet music. A tall and painfully thin girl stood close to him, bending backward so far she looked like she might be able to rest her back against her rear end. Her tights had a long run in them, starting at her upper thigh and traveling down to the bottom of her calf. It all looked alien and unattainable to me. I was a small-town hick, and I looked like it—in my brand-new round-necked black leotard, clean pink tights, and pink ballet shoes. I might as well have been auditioning for a strip club in a pair of big white cotton underpants with an elastic waist while everyone else was wearing G-strings.

This is where it originated—the torn-clothing look, T-shirts falling off one shoulder and stretched out at the waist, tattered leotards coming apart at the seams, and ripped tights with flesh peeking through the holes. It was before *Flashdance*, way before Cirque de Soleil, before Madonna started wearing her underwear over her clothes, before it was fashionable to wear black stockings with unsightly runs, before there were websites teaching you how to make your clothing look aged, tattered, and ragged. Ballet dancers were the original ragamuffins, cutting off the sleeves of their leotards and letting them fray, rolling the sides up to make their legs look longer, cutting the necklines lower on their flat chests, letting their knitted leg warmers slouch so they formed pools of wool at the ankles, and squeezing their feet into filthy pink pointe shoes with frayed ribbons that they wore until they literally disintegrated because these coveted slippers were so expensive, and they were too poor to keep buying new ones.

The room was nearly full. I was on the late side since my mother and I had driven there from Massachusetts that morning, and we'd gotten lost several times along the way. When we finally arrived at the school, my mother parked the car while I rushed upstairs on my own and found the dressing room to change my clothes. All I had to do was follow my nose. The stuffy changing room reeked of sweat, Jean Nate eau de cologne, which dancers splashed on liberally, and mentholated Ben Gay, the greasy pain reliever that got slathered on aching thighs, calves, and shoulders. Several other girls were in there getting ready for class too. The tension in the dressing room was thick and unwelcoming, so I kept to myself, changing quickly and walking through the upper waiting room to find the door to the studio.

My mother was in the waiting room, and I glanced at her as she took a seat. No moms allowed in the studio. She had worked with my teacher from Boston to arrange this audition for me, an opportunity to prove myself, hopefully to become a small fish in the biggest pond there was, but she looked as rigid and uncomfortable as I felt. I swallowed hard, opened the door to the studio, and let it close behind me, shutting her out.

There I stood, alone, at the top of an open staircase without a railing, my shoulders taut, my fingers clenched as I fiddled with the waistband of my tights. I had a surge of anger at my mother for getting me there so late, ruining my chance to get into the studio before most of the other girls so I could be invisible. Now I would have to walk down the stairs in full view of everyone—not that anyone was looking.

The dancers below me were the cream of the crop who worked closely with George Balanchine, his name invoking an aura of success, perfection, and magic in an aspiring ballerina's mind. And here I was, seven steps above the main studio on Madison Avenue, about to take a dance class from none other than the famed Russian choreographer and ballet master. Balanchine was famous for his groundbreaking choreography, for working closely with Russian composer Igor Stravinsky, for training his girls to dance in and reflect his own specific style, and for taking up with six of his prima ballerinas and marrying four of them.

Among them was a delicate woman named Tanaquil LeClerq, who had begun dancing for Balanchine when she was fifteen, back in 1944. He was her greatest love, and in a charity event, the Russian choreographer had danced with her, playing a character named Polio while Tanaquil played the victim who was struck down. Eerily, some years later, Ms. LeClerq was stricken with polio for real when the ballet traveled to Copenhagen; the illness kept her in a wheelchair for the rest of her life. I remember seeing her wheelchair at the back of the theater when I went to watch the New York City Ballet perform.

Balanchine's current love object was a tall, brown-haired woman named Suzanne Farrell. He had trained her since she was a child (I spotted her immediately on the studio floor), and he would end up firing her the next year when she fell in love with one of the male ballet dancers in his company.

His dancers affectionately called him "Mr. B.," but how they drummed up affection for him, I couldn't say. It was common knowledge that his students starved themselves until they were skin and bones, eating low-fat cottage cheese and Jell-O, something I would end up doing too (cherry was my favorite) when I spent a summer studying with him. Balanchine's choreography was a far cry from the *Swan Lake, Sleeping Beauty* style associated with classical ballet companies. His style and choreography were innovative—there had never been anything like it—as he created modern-looking ballets like *Agon, La Sonnambula,* and *Serenade,* showing off not individual ballerinas but rather a set of moving geometric shapes and designs defined by human bodies in a process that removed all sense of femininity and personality. He listed his dancers in alphabetical order in the souvenir programs, shunning the star system, further depersonalizing and dehumanizing his female dancers, never hesitating to fire his favorites if they committed the mortal sin of finding love and getting married in an attempt to have a life outside the ballet.

And still, every young ballerina dreamed of working with him. It certainly had been a dream of mine, and there I was, ready to descend the open staircase to find out if the Grand Master of Anorexia, the King of Deprivation, the Mad Genius of Shape and Design, thought I had potential. There was no way I could fudge anything or make him see what wasn't there, like the French princess would do with me so many years into the future. A ballet audition was straightforward: Were my hips turned out enough? Was I tall enough? Were my toes the right length? Was I skinny enough? Did I have innate talent? Did I take direction without complaining? Was my pain threshold high enough? Did I understand tempo and rhythm? Was I willing to engage in hero worship? Was I bright and quick enough to remember the routines he would show the class only once?

The pressure was high, the competitive edge keen as I prepared to meet my fate. With my eyes straight ahead, trying to act casual and composed, I took the first step off the landing and slipped. I lost my footing, and, to my horror, I slid forward and began to fall loudly, step by step, down the staircase. Everyone stopped fidgeting, pulling, bending, and stretching for a brief moment and stared at me until I landed at the bottom. I had made my entrance into this parallel universe not neatly, quietly, and inconspicuously, but instead awkwardly with a roar and a bang, a red face, and a wounded body.

I had no idea if I was physically hurt at the time. I couldn't feel a thing except shame. I was on my feet as fast as a figure skater recovers from a nasty fall on the ice. No one came over to see if I was all right. They just returned to their endless wiggling and twitching as I stood up and walked into the room, searching for an empty space at the barre. It ran the length of three mirrored walls in the studio, but there didn't seem to be an opening anywhere. No one made room, and no one met my eyes, as if I wasn't there. Actually, at that moment, I was grateful no one was looking at me, and I wished I were anywhere else. Auditioning there was probably a big mistake, I thought, but it was too late to retreat, especially after that entrance. I walked across the room to the far corner, heading for the end of a long line of girls and a few boys, and I put my hand on the barre, trying to claim enough space for my body. The girl in front of me looked agitated and moved forward a miniscule amount, not attempting to make room for me but rather making sure she had ample room for herself.

I thanked God or the ballet angels, if there were any, that Mr. B. himself had not yet entered the room and so hadn't witnessed my humiliating entry into this alternate universe. If no one told him about it, he would never be the wiser, and chances were that no one would. Everyone was loath to bring attention to anyone but themselves. I exhaled hard and joined the other girls, stretching and bending my supple body into odd shapes like they did, while my knee throbbed where I had landed on it and a lump began to form on my left elbow. As long as Mr. B. didn't mistake it for a deformity, it didn't matter how I had entered the room, I reasoned. The thing was, I was there.

It was obvious the moment the Russian ballet master entered the room. A shot of electricity ran through each of us. I was filled with fear that he would think I wasn't good enough. The other girls were all about hope, that he would notice them today, look kindly on them, compliment them, single one of them out and see her as a potential member of his ballet company. A slim man of average height with keen eyes and an easy gait, Mr. B. seemed to leave energetic trails behind him as he walked the length of the room, meeting eyes with a lucky girl here or there, and giving me a nod. I was the new girl, and he would be watching me; I was pretty sure that was what his nod meant. I was beyond nervous. My reality had shrunk to my body and the small section of barre that I grasped with my hand as I listened to his directions. The piano music started, and we all began to do our pliés, the way ballet classes had started since the late 1800s, the days of some of the earliest ballet stars, Anna Pavlova and Vaslav Nijinsky.

I don't recall much about the rest of the class. I settled into the familiar exercises that I did every day, the requisite pliés, *tendus, battements, rond de jambes*, and *fondues* that warmed up my body and allowed me to forget where I was. The only moment that stood out was when we were still at the barre and Mr. B. walked over to me, took my left leg in his strong grip, and twisted it in my hip socket until it was almost facing backward, showing me that he wanted me to turn out my hips much more. I doubted I would be able to move at all like that, but I would try.

When the barre work was finished, he broke us up into four groups, each group in turn standing in the center of the room and performing the combinations of steps that he put together on the spot. At the front of the first group stood the regulars, the girls that he favored, and I watched them carefully to learn what he wanted us to do and how he wanted us to do it.

The class lasted an hour and a half. It felt much longer. At the end of it, Mr. B. exited the room quickly and left us all standing there. Deliberately not meeting anyone's eyes, I slowly walked back up the dreaded stairway and into the dressing room, changed into my street clothes, stuffed my sweaty practice clothes into my bag, and met my mother in the lobby. "How was it?" she wanted to know.

"OK" was all I said.

She didn't ask me any more questions, except whether I wanted to eat at the Automat across the street or wait until I got home. I opted to wait. I had no appetite, and I slept all the way home, exhausted and relieved that it was over. I kept my literal fall from grace a secret, thinking it had sealed my fate, so I was amazed when a phone call came from someone on the board of the School of American Ballet a few days later, offering me a Ford Foundation scholarship to study there for the remainder of the summer. I took the offer and became a regular that summer under the tutelage of Mr. B.'s gang of teachers, who were the finest in the country.

I spent two months living in Brooklyn with an aunt I'd just met who was morbidly obese. She kept the pockets of her muumuu filled with M&Ms as she huffed and gasped around the apartment, and I took the subway to the city every day, starving myself and perspiring through two daily classes at the School of American Ballet. It didn't take long for my leotard to tear in all the right places, for my tights to get the appropriate runs, for my pointe shoes to become filthy, and I soon found myself twitching and cracking, dressed like a veteran, looking like the rest of the girls in my class.

Twitching & Cracking

We had a variety of brilliant teachers, including a kind Danish gentleman, a British woman as tall and wide-backed as a man, and one of Balanchine's ex-lovers, a Russian grand dame who wore a variety of pastel colors with matching scarves that she constantly swept around her trim and agile body. I sweat buckets every day, and like the other dancers, I went to bed hungry, feeling noble about it, that I didn't even need to eat, and I worked my body strenuously, always vying for Mr. B.'s attention. During that summer, a few girls from cities across the United States joined my class once in a while to audition for him just like I had, but none of them made a grand entrance by falling down the stairs.

When the summer came to a close, I could have stayed on in New York and kept living with my aunt, attending Professional Children's

School in Manhattan and escalating my anorexia, hoping that Mr. B. the Great and Powerful would make me a bona fide member of the New York City Ballet. The school was willing to extend my scholarship, but I decided against it. I somehow understood that I would wilt in that place, that I wasn't tough enough, and the cutthroat atmosphere would eat me alive.

When I boldly walked away from the School of American Ballet and left New York, my mother, always supportive of my dream, understood. She had felt the raw energy there, the competitive edge that stung so hard, and she found a school in Washington, DC, that offered ballet and academic subjects under the same roof, the first of its kind in the United States. After we went there for a visit, I decided to relocate to that kinder, gentler atmosphere, where I stayed for two years, but that's another story.

In case you're wondering, I called a halt to the princess's book before it was finished—the first and last time I ever quit a project midstream and walked away. Three weeks after our noninterviews at her home, I met her in New York again and presented her with some material I had plucked out of thin air—a hundred and fifty pages' worth. I was proud that somehow I had worked our meager eight pages into the beginning of a viable book, and I expected she would be amazed and gratified. She wasn't. She took it from me, looked at me with contempt, smacked the manuscript on the table, and demanded, "Where's the rest of it?"

"This is as much as I've done," I told her. "It's only been three weeks, and we didn't do many interviews. I hope you like it."

"The other writer finished the whole thing in a month."

"Then maybe you should rehire her," I said quietly. And that was that. I was out of there. The princess's musings about the spirit would have to wait, at least until she found another writer. And then there was the battle that ensued because she didn't want to pay me for the work I'd done, but she wanted to keep the material anyway to use at her convenience. I ended up winning that one with the help of a good lawyer, and after I got my money, I went on to my next project, taking with me my hard-earned wisdom about the pitfalls of writing auditions, which would come in handy in the future.

I don't know if the princess ever tried to find another writer for that book. I don't think so because I never saw it on the bookstands. I ended up making a royal enemy, which didn't feel very good to me. But when a close girlfriend said, "I can't believe you know one of the royals well enough to be in a feud with her," I have to admit I felt a sudden and unexpected surge of pride.

Chapter Three

IMPERMANENCE

Some people, sweet and attractive, and strong and healthy,

happen to die young.

They are masters in disguise

teaching us about impermanence.

— The Dalai Lama

When I received a phone call from my literary agent telling me I was being considered to write a biography for a fifty-year-old East Indian guru, I was flooded with memories from the sixties. I'd been living with my first husband (a.k.a. "the maniac") in a rustic wooden cabin in Laurel Canyon. I was ingesting the popular mind-expanding drugs of the period and, like a good little hippy, crafting leather-fringed bags and practicing yoga, when I heard about a thirteen-year-old boy, a child guru from India, who had come to the West to offer his path to peace that he called "Knowledge." The sixties was the era of the guru; so many of them migrated to the West back then to fulfill the yearnings of the "counterculture," a youth movement that was hungry for spiritual growth, nuclear disarmament, world peace, and sexual liberation.

In 2005, close to thirty-five years later, I had an initial meeting with the guru's staff. It went well; I liked them and they liked me, and I was hired to write the book. I started my research with a broad Internet search on the influx of Indian gurus to the United States during the sixties, when the young boy had first arrived. The list was long, headed by Richard Alpert a.k.a. Baba Ram Das, who journeyed to India, brought back the teachings of his guru, Neem Karoli Baba, and wrote a seminal book on spirituality and enlightenment called *Remember: Be Here Now.* Included in the guru list of positive influences was Maharishi Mahesh Yogi, founder of Transcendental Mediation (TM), whom the Beatles had made famous. Sai Baba was a renowned sage with the apparent ability to materialize *vibhuti,* holy ash, by fluttering his fingers. And there was Paramahansa Yogananda, who introduced millions of Westerners to meditation and a practice he called kriya yoga, a system of breath work intended to accelerate spirituality and grace the practitioner with tranquility and a connection to the Divine.

During this research phase, I found an amusing article written by a reporter for Reuter's Daily News. A few minutes before noon on December 14, 1998, a trio of Buddhist monks were sighted in Houston, Texas, heading for the Golden Arches. Not the gates of heaven, as one logically might assume. The reporter was referring to the popular advertising symbol of McDonald's fast-food restaurants.

Fully robed and hungry, the monks were taking a break from performing *dul-tson-kyil-khor* at the Houston Museum of Fine Arts. This ancient Tibetan art form, translated as "mandala of colored powders," also called "Tibetan sand painting," had been preserved in the monasteries of Tibet and India for some two and a half thousand years. Originally practiced in seclusion, it went public during the last several decades, allowing international onlookers to witness the complex ritual in its phases of construction and subsequent deconstruction.

With half a day's work behind them, the trio casually strode through the swinging glass doors of the fast-food franchise that was less than a block away from the museum and placed their orders. There would be no sacred chants or meditations over steamed veggies and brown rice for this group. They paid their money, got their fast food on a tray, and sat in a booth, happily munching filets of fish and quarter-pounder extra-value meals with fries and Cokes, giggling in the face of impermanence.

Nowhere is the transient and impermanent nature of life more strikingly demonstrated than in the Tibetan Buddhist tradition of colored sand painting. The event spans about a week's time, as the robed lamas (Tibetan priests) open the ceremony and consecrate the site by chanting, declaring their intentions, playing music, visualizing elevated states of consciousness, and reciting sacred text, calling forth the forces of goodness. Next they don industrial-looking white aprons to map out a mystical design on a wooden platform using chalk, dust, string, and pencils. The ensuing composition suggests a mandala, a series of geometric designs, revelatory symbols of cosmic truth that represent the universe and serve as instructional charts of the spiritual aspect of the human experience.

When the foundational grid has been laid, the monks remove their aprons, sit cross-legged, and bend forward, literally putting their shaved heads together for days as they proceed to pour millions of grains of sand made from colored pigments, minerals, and crystals onto the platform. In one hand, they hold a funnel-shaped instrument called a *chak-pur* or a cornet as they blow small streams of brightly colored sand through the tip. With the other hand, they run a metal rod along the grated surface, making a perpetual scraping sound as the sand flows like liquid and the mandala begins to take form.

They start at the inside of the design and work outward, a sequence that symbolizes how the child, a mere drop of sperm and ovum at birth, steadily grows until he or she experiences the entire universe through the senses. Those present during the creation of these sacred mandalas are thought to be purified and uplifted by the powers of the holy energies that are invoked.

I had the good fortune to witness a part of one of these rituals in Santa Monica some years ago; I stood riveted amid the constant drone of scratching as brilliant forms and pictures took shape on the platform: flaming swords; lotus blossoms; mythical creatures commandeering chariots; human beings clothed in colorful robes; and images of the sacred Buddha sitting in meditation, watching over the world. The beauty of the finished product, mindfully created and protected all along the way, was unequalled and breathtaking, but the real spectacle occurred once the mandala was finished.

When the design was complete, after the local spirits were ceremonially thanked and the mandala was dedicated to the fulfillment of universal benefit, a stunning deconstruction began. Amid chanting, music, and prayer, the most senior monk placed his index finger on one side of the finished masterpiece, pressed downward, and swept it across the sand several times, upsetting the continuity of the mandala with crossing lines that extended the length and width of the design. Then the rest of the monks took pieces of ordinary cardboard and foam rubber, swept the entire sand design into a random pile, and poured the scrambled colored swirl into an urn, which they would later deposit into a nearby body of water. Nothing was left but the original platform, offering a stunning demonstration of impermanence, how all matter, regardless of its beauty or intrinsic value, comes out of nothingness and eventually returns to it.

This Eastern tradition was birthed in a culture whose response to the certainty of death is a commitment to fully embracing life, a reminder to appreciate beauty and existence here and now, to make the most of it before it's over. British-born philosopher Alan Watts, a popular interpreter of Eastern philosophy for Western audiences who came to prominence in the sixties, said, "The only way to make sense out of change is to plunge into it, move with it, and join the dance." According to Buddhist beliefs, as soon as children are old enough to grasp the concept that their time in a physical body is limited, their lessons in accepting what can't be changed and appreciating and celebrating life vigorously and wholeheartedly begin.

Here in the West, however, in direct opposition to Eastern ways, when a child asks about the meaning of death, the common answers are "You're too young to be thinking about such things" or "It won't happen for a long time." Then the subject is changed quite deliberately, as if the mere mention of dying summons it closer. Most Westerners are trained to view death as distant, separated from us, and we generally strive to keep it that way, as if we will be immune if we don't think or talk about it.

I was five when my great-aunt Ruth passed away. She was my mother's aunt, the woman who taught me about unconditional love and gave me my first experience of death and impermanence. I was unprepared, confused, and deeply disturbed when she died, the same way I felt during her bout with cancer that went on for years. It's no wonder, then, that thirty years later, during the AIDS epidemic that struck in the eighties, I volunteered at a hospice, immersing myself in the processes of suffering and of death and dying, hungry to understand and accept what I couldn't when I lost my aunt Ruth.

When I think of her now, I remember that she was so beautiful that I believed the two large moles on her soft, rounded face were special markings from God. As a child, I stared with envy at the brown, protruding blemishes that my mother called "beauty marks," one in the middle of Ruth's forehead, the other on the right side of her chin, with two stiff, dark hairs sticking right out of the center. I scanned my own face for signs of similar markings that might place me in her category of loveliness. All I came up with was a small cyst on the left side of my cheek near my eye that eventually had to be surgically removed.

Aunt Ruth owned a boarding house called the Tide Rock House in Old Orchard Beach, Maine, on Union Avenue, where Canadian blue-collar workers, many of them French-speaking from Quebec, returned summer after summer to vacation near the beach for their yearly two weeks off. When my aunt fell ill and needed help with the upkeep, my mother showed up, bringing my sister, Jill, and me to stay with her in Maine for extended periods of time in the summers (my father stayed home during the week to work), and the Tide Rock House became an antidote for my feeling like a misfit in my life, trying to fit in. I just felt so at home there.

What if I actually belonged to a different family, I often wondered, and they'd made a mistake at the hospital? Worse, what if I was a character in somebody else's dream, and when the dreamer woke up, I would dissolve like a fleeting memory? I pressed my feet hard onto the ground beneath me back then, making sure I was solid, that my life was more than a thought or somebody's dream or a well-kept secret. The Tide Rock House, with its comforting smells and soothing pastel colors, served as reassurance that my life was not a shadow world, and I was not a ghost. The house was my rainbow and my hope, its walls a mothering embrace that soothed my childish emotions and protected my vulnerability.

When nighttime blanketed Union Avenue, and massive numbers of fireflies twinkled in their bioluminescent glory, I lay quietly and listened to my sister's breath become rhythmical in a bed across from mine. I was not afraid of the dark—I was born with keen night eyes—and I nestled into my small bed in the corner, watching glittering spirit forms shape-shift outside the windows. I invited these evanescent sylphs and devas inside to play among the flowered paper on the walls, watching them lightly bounce from blossom to blossom, appearing and disappearing until my eyelids drooped. It was against this backdrop of mystical interplay that I melted into my dreams during those summer nights, secure with my playmates from the other world.

The two-story wooden cottage on Union Avenue, with its long front porch and whitewashed fence, had a soul. Houses often do, particularly old ones, and the soul of the Tide Rock House was ancient like the icy seawater that washed against the shoreline several hundred yards from the end of the street. I climbed the rocks and poked my small fingers into the sudsy tide pools, upsetting small fish, miniature crabs with transparent legs, shell chips, and seaweed strands, all scattered amid colorful pieces of broken plastic and the occasional used condom that I mistook for jellyfish body parts. I walked the beach every day all by myself—kids could do that safely back then—and I performed gymnastic stunts on the sand, counting out one hundred tumble-saults and then lying on my back, motionless, until the world stopped spinning. I rescued rare shell specimens, brought them home, washed off the sand, and placed them on top of my old wooden dresser with the drawers that stuck.

One time a tiny crab crawled out of one of the shells; I watched it scramble the length of the creaky old dresser, scale down the side, and imbed itself in a crack between two uneven drawers. Perhaps it was attracted to the darkness, out of sight, avoiding intrusion, reclaiming its destiny from the hands of someone it never even knew was there. I watched it for a while, willing it to come out, until something distracted me, and I forgot about it until the next day. When I went back to search for it, it was gone. Maybe it fell to the ground and got stepped on. I preferred to think the house protected it until no one was around and then somehow helped it crawl away and find its way back to the ocean. It could have happened; the Tide Rock House was magical like that.

The old house where I spent so many summers of my youth was weathered like beach houses get, wallpaper peeling from the humidity and lumpy mattresses sitting atop creaky metal box springs. The sound of rusted, whining bed rollers was not uncommon; they didn't fasten tightly enough to the floor, jerking and moaning beneath a fitful sleeper or someone who tried to rearrange the furniture in one of the rooms.

The kitchen had a black potbelly stove that heated the room and spit out smoldering smoke from its bowels. It broke regularly, and my mother threatened to get rid of "the outdated monstrosity" and replace it with one of those dreamy new electric ranges people won on game shows like *The Price Is Right* or *Beat the Clock*.

As an offside, my parents were contestants on *Beat the Clock* when I was about seven, performing stunts and answering questions for several days before they were eliminated. Gifts galore arrived at our home several weeks later, including a useless set of china and a vibrating leather chair that Jill and I fought over whenever one of us was sitting in it.

Back to the Tide Rock House. When my mother complained about the stove, I protested. The stove belonged right where it was. I crouched beside it on cold, stormy nights, and I lay my nightgown on it after supper, taking its warmth and smell to bed with me. One evening, after the black dinosaur sputtered its insides all over the black-and-white checkered linoleum floor right before a lobster and steamed-clam feast, I cried because I knew it was about to be replaced. The heart of the house beat inside that potbelly stove, and when we finally had it hauled away and got something new in its place, even if my mother didn't want to admit it, we all felt bereft.

The Tide Rock House had two owners' rooms for us, fourteen guest rooms, and an unmatched pair of one-bedroom apartments on the lower floor that opened out into a long, narrow dining hall for the guests. A staircase at the front of the house led upstairs to ten rooms and two bathrooms—one large, one small—that the guests shared. A second stairway led up to an annex at the back of the house, which had four additional guest rooms, two on either side of the tapered hallway. These rooms were undersized, dollhouse-like, with slanted ceilings, and my father showed me how a tennis ball placed on one of their windowsills would roll to the other side, bouncing onto the slanted, scuffed wooden floors. To my delight, the annex was all atilt, and when it was vacant, my mother let me play up there, one of my favorite places for hide-and-seek. Not only were there inviting corners and angles, it was also the apex of the house, which satisfied my love of high places.

A third stairway, winding, dusty, and dark, began upstairs next to the smaller bathroom and ended in our kitchen down below. Hardly anyone used those stairs, and I climbed halfway up and sat there every now and then, just to think and listen. Sometimes I sat beside the big white icebox on our back porch. Long-legged spiders hung from intricate networks of cobwebs in this dark, dank place, and since most of the other kids hated it there, that area belonged to me and the ice man.

On Tuesday, Thursday, and Saturday mornings, a real live ice man in a brown uniform and thick brown canvas gloves delivered two huge, steaming blocks of ice. He carried them between industrial-strength metal tongs, a tough job for a strong man. The driveway had to be clear on those mornings so he could pull his truck as close to the porch as possible. My father, who spent weekends with us, would arrive late Friday night and inevitably pull his car into the driveway, blocking access to the back porch. He either forgot about the ice man or maybe parking anywhere else made him feel unwelcome or maybe it was too much trouble. When I woke up on Saturday mornings to the sound of my mother in the next room, badgering him to move his car, I rushed out of bed to wait for the delivery.

After the Ice Man parked his squealing truck, he pulled a gigantic, square ice block from the back, expertly balancing it between the huge tongs. After transporting it swiftly to the icebox, he placed it inside with impressive skill, closed the heavy door, and returned to his truck to do it one more time. When he saw me lingering on the back porch, he smiled and winked. I shyly looked away, in awe of the ice man's strength and the importance of his job.

The wooden decking on the back porch that ran adjacent to the kitchen narrowed into a dark recess that housed the utility closet. A tattered floral drape covered the shelving, its red, yellow, and blue painted begonias blowing sideways in the wind to expose yet another hangout for spiders and their cousins, the roaches. My mother was unaffected by the insects that loitered along the darkened shelves. She reached right over them, brave as can be, grabbing cans of Ajax, Ammonia, or Lime-A-way, upsetting the complex circuitry of the sticky flytraps. She doggedly set about the business of cleaning, oblivious that an entire arachnid community had been rendered homeless with a sweep of her determined arm.

Pinpoints of light entered this area in the daytime, but it was pitch black at night, the perfect spot for telling ghost stories. I gathered the children of the house there after dinner and scared them with my dark tales, feeling graced with good luck when a spider crawled into our midst in the middle of a hair-raising climax. In retrospect, it was not the stories themselves that produced their fear. It was my use of eerie sounds that echoed so deliciously in that close space. My audience was breathless with anticipation as I told them the one about the man with the golden leg or the woman who rose from the dead. I shifted the story line from time to time, but I always knocked on the wooden decking with my knuckles, louder and louder as the predator got nearer. When I decided my listeners were adequately on edge, I screamed out loud, scaring them all silly. I inspired more than one nightmare for my captive audience. I knew that, but I continued in my evil ways, finding it an irresistible source of power. And the kids always came back for more.

The Tide Rock House had a rolltop desk in the living room, where my aunt kept up her correspondence. She stored fine things in the slender pine drawers: embossed stationery, envelopes with the return address printed on the back, a variety of fountain pens with sharply pointed tips, pots of blue and black ink, a felt blotter, stamps, and a brown leather-bound guest book. My aunt's handwriting was perfect, and so was my mother's, as they worked on business correspondence and sent notes to various friends and relatives.

Catty-corner to the desk stood an antique Steinway piano, its mahogany visibly chipped in several places. A trio of foot pedals, most of their red velvet worn away, were located beneath the piano. There were two yellowed ivory keys at the bass end of the keyboard and a broken one at the treble, giving the piano its singular character. It had stood right there on its curvy wooden legs since the late forties, when my aunt Ruth had bought the place, and I was delighted when once in a great while, a piano man came by to tune the instrument. I banged on the keys whenever I could get away with it, but I was under no illusions. I had no talent for music. I just liked making noise, and Aunt Ruth usually let me do it. For all of these reasons and so many more, in my eyes, Ruth could do no wrong. She smelled of violets, and her deep-brown eyes filled my heart to overflowing. We were two lonely people, one at the beginning of her life, the other at the end, comforting each other and making each other feel safe.

During the last autumn of Aunt Ruth's life, she lived with us in Massachusetts, and three days a week after breakfast, while my mother did the housework, Aunt Ruth and I would walk several blocks to the corner market to pick up groceries. I'd jump up onto the raised cement curbstone along the way and walk carefully, placing one foot in front of the other as if I was a gymnast on a balance beam. Ruth held my hand, her soft skin a caress on my own (she used Jergens lotion every day) as she walked beside me, energized by my presence.

When we arrived at the market, I jumped off the curb, threw my arms high in the air in a champion-style stance that I had seen during the Olympics, and ran in to greet Mr. Humphrey, the shopkeeper. His bald head shone—I figured he waxed it at night before he went to bed— and once he let me stroke it. It didn't feel waxy; it felt more like a layer of stretched-out Bazooka bubble gum when you blew into it to make a large bubble. He and Ruth chatted while I looked through the glass at the candy. I was partial to the multicolored sugar dots stuck on pieces of white paper, four across in long rows of twelve. I also liked Lik-M-Aids, colored powdered sugar that I sprinkled on my tongue, and Nik-L-Nips, miniature wax bottles filled with colored sugar water. When I chose what I wanted that day, Ruth kept it for me until after lunch, a more appropriate time for sweets, according to my mother. If I wanted something right away, I could get the black wax moustache or the thick, red wax lips that weren't candy so you didn't eat them. When I bit part-way into the lips and held them over my own and tried to talk, I felt like Betty Boop.

Aunt Ruth would pick up a loaf of bread, some Ivory liquid soap, or a *Reader's Digest*, and one day, before we headed home, she handed me a dime. "Andrea, put it in there," she said, pointing to a cardboard square with the words "March of Dimes" printed across the top. It had a bunch of empty slots waiting to be filled with coins with a smiling picture of the poster girl just below the printing. She looked no older than I was, sitting in a wheelchair with braces on her legs and a big smile on her face. I wanted to give her the dime, but I hesitated.

"What's wrong?" Aunt Ruth asked.

"Are you sure this is OK? Mom doesn't like me throwing money away."

"This isn't throwing it away. I don't think she'll mind," Ruth said. "That little girl may be able to walk again, all because of you. Don't you want to help her?"

I did. I decided not to tell my mother as I pressed my dime into the cardboard slot, and the poster girl smiled directly at me. On the walk back home, I marveled that Ruth cared so much about people she'd never met that she actually gave them money. I figured her heart was so full, if she didn't give some of it away, she would have drowned in a flood of her own love.

From then on, my ten-cent offerings became as important a part of our ritual as the candy, maybe even more important. I named the March of Dimes girl Nan after one of the Bobbsey twins, Jill's favorite mystery-book heroine, and I looked forward to filling up that card, saving every dime I could find for Nan.

Aunt Ruth was an avid moviegoer; she took me to all the latest Disney films and any other musicals that had a matinee showing at our local movie theater. She bought a small buttered popcorn for herself and a Fudgsicle or a Creamsicle for me, and we took two seats at the end of a row. When the music started, I jumped up, walked over Aunt Ruth's lap, and danced up and down the aisles, swaying, twirling, and jumping. When the song ended, I sat back down and waited for the next one. One day Jill came to the movies with us to see *West Side Story*. When I heard the overture music, I stood up to begin my routine.

"What's she doing?" Jill whispered to Ruth as she watched me cavorting up and down the aisle.

"She's dancing," Ruth said.

"Right here?"

"Right here."

"Why?"

"She always does it," Ruth said.

"But why?"

"She likes it."

"But we're in public. This is so embarrassing. Can't you stop her? People might see me with her."

"She's a little girl. Nobody cares. Just watch the movie."

Jill got up in a huff, made her way across Ruth's legs and into the aisle, found an empty seat on the other side of the theater, and sat there for the rest of the movie. I didn't think much about it. You could never tell what my older sister would do next or why, and I didn't put two and two together when she declined the invitation to see *South Pacific* with Ruth and me the very next week.

One afternoon, after Ruth and I returned from seeing *Westward Ho the Wagons*, I ran to find my mother. She was in the basement, sitting at the mangler, an electrical contraption my father had bought her for an anniversary present. This bulky machine for ironing sheets had a thick, soft wheel covered with several layers of white cotton that heated up when you pushed the On button. Sometimes my mother let me push it, but only when she was watching. The large, dangerous wheel could burn my hands badly, she warned me, so I was never allowed to plug it in or turn it on unless she was there.

When it heated up and steam rose from the hot wheel, my mother fed a sheet into one side, expertly angling it as it rolled, catching it perfectly with her other hand as it dropped, wrinkle-free, on the other side. I stood in front of her that afternoon as she fed a pillowcase into the machine, both of us mesmerized by the material rolling through and dropping smack out the other side into her waiting hand. My breathing was loud, since I had just danced all the way home from the movie theater.

"What is it, honey?" my mother asked, keeping her eyes glued to the hot wheel. "You're out of breath."

"No, I'm not," I said. "I have to ask you something."

"Go ahead."

I paused. "Well, I don't know if I should."

"You can ask me anything," she said. "I'm your mother."

I inhaled. "If I told you I liked Aunt Ruth better than you, would you be mad?"

She looked up at me, her hazel eyes suddenly veiled. "No, that's fine."

I stared at my feet. "I'm not saying it's true. I just wondered if it would be OK."

"You love your great-aunt, don't you?"

"Yes."

My mother smiled. "It's OK. I love her too." She turned her attention back to her work, and I ran upstairs to my room, feeling slightly guilty but a little lighter from having confessed. I was sure Aunt Ruth should have been my real mother.

Ruth had only one breast. You couldn't tell when she was dressed, but I saw her take off her bra once and pull a spongy-looking white mound out from the right cup. I asked her if I could hold it. It was a pretty heavy thing to be carting around in her bra all day. When Ruth was naked, her right breast flopped to her waist, while the left side of her chest was completely flat except for a long scar and a strange piece of knotted-up, dark skin. She let me look at it and touch it when I climbed into bed to take a nap with her. It was hard and knobby, but it didn't scare me. I loved her too much.

"What happened?" I asked her. "Mom has two breasts. Where did it go?"

"The doctor took it off. It got sick, and they thought I'd feel better without it."

"Do you?"

"Yes, honey."

I vowed never to grow breasts. If they could get sick and have to be removed, what good were they?

One afternoon I stood in Ruth's room, watching her packing some clothes into her rectangular red suitcase with the gold clasps. She stopped a moment and knelt down to hug me really hard. Then she held me gently away from her and looked straight into my eyes. "I have to go away for a rest," she said. A faint smell of violets lingered around her neck.

"Why can't you rest here?" I placed my arms tightly around her soft middle. "You don't have to go. I can be very quiet."

She smiled, but she didn't look happy. "I have to go to the hospital for a little while so they can take care of me."

"I'll take care of you. You can sleep in my bed with me, and I'll do everything for you. You can wake me up in the middle of the night, and I won't even cry."

"I wish I could do that. It sounds so good, but I have to go. Don't worry, honey. I'll be back soon."

"Can I come with you? I'll be very good while you're resting. I promise. I'll read to you—as soon as I learn how."

"I'd love that, but they don't allow children in the hospital."

"Even if they're sick?"

"Maybe if they're sick. But I'll be back before you know it. I promise. You won't even know I'm gone."

Aunt Ruth was usually right, but I knew she was wrong about that. I would miss her every minute. I already missed her, and she hadn't even left. She kissed me on the cheek, the hairs from her beauty mark poking into my skin. I stayed close to her, watching her pack two white towels, a hand-embroidered white handkerchief, several pairs of white cotton underpants, her hairbrush, her toothbrush, a travel-size tube of Colgate toothpaste, and Listerine mouthwash. She put her favorite pink nightgown in a special compartment in the front flap of the suitcase, pulled the two ends of pink satin ribbon across it, and tied them into a bow. She put a book on top, patted it all down, closed it up, and fastened the clasps. Then she placed her eyeglasses in a case in her purse, and we both went downstairs. About a half hour later, my father carried her suitcase into the car. When Ruth got into the passenger seat and closed the door, I sobbed, begging to go with them, but they wouldn't let me. She threw me a kiss good-bye, and I cried for a long time after they left.

I missed Aunt Ruth most in the mornings after breakfast. I was deeply concerned about Nan, our poster girl. If I stopped putting dimes in the slots, she'd never learn to walk. I considered asking my mother to take me to the store, but I doubted she'd let me give away the dime. I'd just have to wait until Ruth came back. Then, one afternoon, when I got home from playing with a girlfriend down the street, my mother told me Ruth was back. I started to race toward her room, but my mother stopped me. "She's sleeping, honey. Let her rest."

"She won't mind waking up to hug me," I said.

"She took a pill, and you won't be able to wake her up. You can see her when she gets up."

When I sat down to supper with Jill and my parents, Aunt Ruth was still asleep. "If she went away to rest, why is she so tired?" I asked.

"Because it's tiring being in the hospital."

"They didn't do a very good job there, did they?" I said. "She should have stayed here. I told her I'd take care of her. I bet she'd be feeling a lot better now."

"Honey, she's tired because she's sick. You have to let her sleep," my mother said.

"When's she gonna get better?" I'd had the flu a few weeks earlier and it had taken me three days to feel better. Ruth had been gone a lot longer than that.

"I don't know. We'll have to wait and see."

"Will she feel better when she wakes up?"

"I said I don't know."

"When can she take me to the store?"

"Not for a while." My mother glanced at my father for support. He placed a forkful of food in his mouth without looking up.

"Well, I hope it's not too long," I said. "We have to go to the store, you know. It's really important. Do you think we can go tomorrow?"

"You let your aunt rest," my father scolded me. "She doesn't need you pestering her to go to the store. What do you need, anyway? You're a little girl."

I scowled, pushing the food around my plate until I asked to be excused. They let me go, and I tiptoed to the door of Ruth's bedroom. It was partially open, and I peered in. She lay there, breathing slowly, her milky eyes staring at the ceiling. I exhaled loudly. When she turned her head and saw me, a big smile spread across her face, and she motioned for me to come in. I stood by the edge of her bed.

"How are you, honey?" she asked. "Did you have fun while I was gone?" Her smooth, white skin was spotted in places, red and slightly rough.

"It was OK. How do you think Nan is doing? You know, our poster girl."

"I think you helped her so much, she's better already. You'll probably see her walking down the street some day."

I smiled and nodded, relieved.

"Come here. Come closer to me," Ruth said, pulling back the covers. I crawled in, and she pulled the covers over the two of us as I nestled into her side. She encircled me with her arms. "I'm sick," she whispered into my ear.

"That's OK," I assured her. "You'll get better. I'll make sure of that."

"I may have to go away for a long time, but don't ever forget that I love you."

I cried into her scar, and she held me until I dropped off to sleep. When I woke up, I was in my own bed, and I knew Ruth wasn't going to get better. I visited her several times each day, and I napped with her in the afternoons when she let me. We hardly spoke; there was nothing to say. We just breathed together, the two lonely ones, silent and waiting. I understood that something bad was happening to her. I didn't know what it was, but I knew it was important for us to be close.

One day an ambulance arrived, and two men carried Ruth out on a stretcher, my mother following close behind, clutching a handkerchief. My aunt looked at me. She was scared, and so was I, especially when my mother said she was going to have an operation on her head.

"Why don't they just take her other breast? She doesn't need it. Does she?"

"I really can't explain it to you."

"When's she coming back?"

"I don't know," my mother told me. "Not for a while. After the surgery, they're going to send her to a rest home where they can take really good care of her."

I was doubtful. I'd seen the shape she'd been in the last time someone was supposed to take care of her. I asked about her every day, and I got the same shrugging response. "She's doing OK," my mother said. "They're taking good care of her."

One afternoon my mother told Jill and me that we were going to visit Aunt Ruth. I was ecstatic. I rushed to put on my black patent leather shoes and the red dress with the white lace trim that Ruth had bought me for my fifth birthday. Red was my favorite color.

"Is she coming back home with us?" Jill asked when we were in the car.

"No," my mother answered.

"Why not? Don't you want her anymore?"

"Don't talk foolishness, Jill. Of course I want her. She's my aunt. What kind of a person do you think I am? It's just that she's very sick, and she needs constant attention."

"We haven't seen her for a while, so how do you know she's still sick?" I asked. "Maybe she's better."

"I visit her a lot, and the nurses told me."

"I keep telling you I'll take care of her," I reminded my mother. "I'm just a kid, and I really don't have anything else to do."

"Honey, I know how much you love her, but Ruth needs a special kind of care she can only get from doctors and nurses."

"I'll learn, please," I whined. "I know I can do it. I just turned six."

My mother sighed. "Please, Andrea. I'm very tired. Let's just pay Ruth a nice visit. She'll be very happy to see you girls."

We pulled up in front of a two-story brick house, layers of ivy climbing the walls, peacock-blue paint peeking out, making a loud, cheery statement that I didn't believe for a second. A nurse met us at the door. "Hello, Charlotte," she said. "How are you today?" Without waiting for an answer, she turned to Jill and me. "So, you've come to see your aunt. I told her you were coming, and she's very excited. She really misses you."

"Did she tell you that?" I asked.

"Oh, yes." The nurse's fat rubber shoes squeaked along the linoleum, the laces tied in square knots, as she led us down a narrow hallway. Everything smelled like the alcohol that my mother rubbed on my chest when I had a fever. We stopped in front of a room, and the nurse opened the door without knocking and motioned for us to follow her in.

"Why is it so dark in here?" I whispered to my mother.

"The light hurts Ruth's eyes," she said.

Jill walked in behind my mother, and I followed them, stepping up to a single bed with bars on four sides. A woman in a faded gray nightgown with frayed edges lay in the bed. "I think we're in the wrong room," I told the nurse. "We're here to see Aunt Ruth."

No one said anything. My mother just stood there, silent as a stone, and as my eyes got used to the low light, I examined the woman in the bed. Layers of thin, transparent skin hung from her bony arms in folds, the top of her bald head was bandaged and a little bit of yellow liquid seeped out one side. I grabbed onto the metal bars and looked into the cage disguised as a bed.

"Hello, Ruth," Miss Squeaky Shoes said loudly, her voice rising unnaturally. "We have some special visitors. Look who's here."

The woman in the bed reached a bony arm toward me. I saw the edge of a diaper peeking out from under her gray nightgown. That wasn't Ruth. She didn't wear diapers, and where was her pink nightgown, the one she had packed in the red suitcase when she left for the hospital the first time? When I spotted the beauty mark on her chin, our eyes met, and she opened her mouth in a jerky motion, a horrific moan issuing from her throat like an animal baying at the moon, screaming to be set free. Her hand, the fingers arthritically twisted, reached toward my chest.

The terrible imploring guttural sounds continued. She wanted something. I think it was me. I tried to speak, but nothing would come out as the arm kept reaching, a spiny tentacle flailing in the emptiness. I made no attempt to touch it. I looked miserably at my mother, who refused to look back at me.

"Where's Aunt Ruth?" I whispered to her harshly.

She met my rage with her own. "What are you talking about? She's right here. You're looking at her."

I looked back toward the bed at a woman I once loved. They'd ruined her. How could my mother have let them do this? How could she not have told me? How could we possibly bring Aunt Ruth back home when she couldn't even talk?

"Well then," my mother said. "Let's say good-bye, girls. We need to let your aunt Ruth rest." She turned toward the nurse. "Sorry, I guess they were a little young for this. I'll be back on my own day after tomorrow. Usual time."

"Good! I'll tell Ruth," the nurse spoke loudly, as if she were calling over from the next room. "Good-bye, girls. You really made your aunt's day. Did you see how happy she was?"

"What did they do to her?" Jill spoke through the depressed silence once we were back in the car.

"They didn't do anything to her," my mother insisted. "She had a brain tumor, and they had to give her an operation. They're trying to help her."

"Well," I said, "she looked OK when she left the house, and now she looks terrible. She doesn't look human."

"Andrea, that's not a very nice thing to say. If you can't say something nice, don't say anything."

I looked at Jill, who leaned back and disappeared.

"When's her hair gonna grow back?" I demanded. "When can she come home?"

"She can't come home. Your father and I thought she'd like to see you girls."

My mother went silent and withdrew, a tortoise retreating into her shell. When we got home, she walked straight upstairs and hid in her bedroom. I went into Aunt Ruth's room, pulled back the covers, climbed in bed, and laid my head on the embroidered pillowcase. The scent of violets was in the air, distant but somehow still there. I wanted to pretend Ruth was away or on vacation, but I couldn't. I'd looked into her eyes, and I'd recognized her beauty mark. The bald-headed skeleton in the cage wearing the gray nightgown and the diaper was Ruth. She was not an imposter who had stolen my aunt's beauty marks. I dozed in her bed and dreamed about her being healthy, dressed in a pink nightgown, holding my hand with one of hers, her red suitcase in the other as she led me down a tunnel. Nan, the poster girl, walked beside us, taking long strides on her healthy legs, triumphant and smiling.

I never asked to see my aunt again, and my mother didn't offer. I avoided the local market, although I missed Mr. Humphrey. I had no idea how much time had passed when my mother arrived home one afternoon (Jill was at a friend's house) and motioned for me to follow her into the empty living room. Her step was heavy and flat, her arms limp as she dropped onto a large green velvet chair. "Aunt Ruth died today," she said.

She opened out her arms with resignation, a deep exhalation escaping her lips, reluctantly inviting me to climb into her lap. I did it—I didn't want to hurt her feelings—and I lay my head stiffly on her chest and cried softly. She rested one hand on my back, mechanically stroking my forehead with the other, barely tolerating my sorrow. When I stopped crying to take a breather, she rose up from under me like I was a small lap cat, went to her room upstairs, and closed the door. I lay my head back down on the empty chair and continued to cry.

Jill and I stayed home when my parents went to lay my aunt's body to rest the next day. I strained to meet my mother's gaze as she left the house, but she was wearing a black hat with a veil that covered her eyes. I would have gone with her, but I wasn't invited. My mother must have thought I was too young for a funeral, or maybe she didn't want to be responsible for watching over me.

When she stripped the bed and cleared out Aunt Ruth's room a week later, my mother couldn't find the red suitcase with the gold clasps. She couldn't imagine where it was; maybe it got left in the hospital or in the nursing home. She searched the house for it and made some phone calls, but no one had seen it. Except me. It was hidden in the back of my closet beside my black patent leather shoes, underneath the red dress with the white lace that Aunt Ruth had bought me, still filled with her things.

Chapter Four

INTREPID

Life shrinks or expands in proportion to one's courage.

— Anaïs Nin

It was 1967. I was in Brussels on tour with my ballet company, perhaps risking my life by eating frogs' legs steeped in garlic, when I put myself in harm's way for real. After dinner and a sexy flirt with a young, handsome Belgian man at the restaurant, my girlfriends went back to our hotel, and I followed the stranger to a private club to go dancing. I felt like I was in control because I was reasonably fluent in French, but how stupid could I be? We arrived and were cleared to pass through the locked entryway. Not surprisingly, a short time later, this man put the moves on me in an upstairs room. I had really thought we were going dancing. When I refused to have sex with him, he grabbed my shoulder, pulled me down the stairs behind him, shoved me outside the club, and shut the door. I had been summarily dumped. At least I'd avoided the more obvious nightmare, but the evening wasn't over.

On my own in a foreign country in the middle of the night, I was walking aimlessly down the darkened streets, scared to death, chastising myself for being so careless, when I noticed a light coming from one of the buildings. I knocked. A night watchman answered and leered at me for a moment or two, and then he let me come in and call a cab. He kept his gaze fixed on me while I waited for the taxi. I felt like he was undressing me, so it was a miracle I got back to the hotel safe and sound. I lay in my bed that night, feeling lucky and pretty stupid, aware that it all could have ended differently.

I had managed to beat the odds in Brussels, and I got lucky once again in Italy a few weeks later when I was walking through a pitch-black tunnel with a girlfriend just in front of me.

The normally sleepy town of Spoleto, located seventy-eight miles north of Rome, comes alive for three weeks during the *Festival dei Due Mondi* (Festival of Two Worlds). We were performing there, and my girlfriend and I decided to head back to our hotel that afternoon to take a rest before our performance that night. We knew we'd have to pass through a long tunnel to get there, but we felt like a walk. Yes, we should have turned around when we realized the dark tunnel only lit up when a car passed through, but we just kept walking in the dark, one hand glued to the wall beside us, brailling our way along, praying we wouldn't trip into the way of a speeding vehicle. Sometimes there's a fine line between naïveté and stupidity, and I was walking a thin edge.

We were about halfway through the tunnel, and I was vowing never to do this again, when the eerie sounds began. A couple of guys had been following us before we entered the tunnel, but that wasn't unusual. Italian men, mostly good-natured, had made a point of stalking the ballet dancers everywhere we went in Italy, hoping to pinch an ass or strike up a conversation. When we told the two guys to get lost with our exaggerated hand gestures, they had smiled and pretended to understand, and then they had disappeared.

But they hadn't gone far. They had quietly followed us into the tunnel, and now they were moaning and screeching, trying to scare us, doing a good job of it, as we picked up our pace. When I heard footsteps close behind me, I called out to my girlfriend, "Run!"

The guys were chasing us, close on my heels, and we ran as fast as our legs could carry us. But they were faster. They were almost upon me—a hand grazed my back—when I felt my shoe slip off my foot in the dark. How or why I did what came next is beyond my understanding, but when I realized I had lost my shoe, I stopped dead. The stalkers banged into me, and I turned toward them, screamed loudly into the darkness where their faces would have been, and bent down to pick up my shoe. They took off in the opposite direction, obviously more scared than I was.

My girlfriend and I kept on running as fast as we could until we saw the light at the other end. We rushed out of the tunnel and into civilization, panting, crying, and holding onto each other. It was another close call. I seemed to be pushing the fear envelope at the time, but I'm not sure why. I had rarely let fear stop me when I wanted to do something, and I can thank my father for that.

When I was small, he loved to toss me up in the air, reveling in my shrieks, slinging me upside down and running across our front lawn, my legs banging against his chest. He was teaching me about courage, showing me that I was safe even if I was scared or upended, encouraging me to cultivate playfulness, curiosity, and wonder, eliding fear of the unknown by skipping straight to the excitement part.

When I was eight, he reached into a drawer of his desk in his home office in our den and showed me a rectangular card with blue and silver graphics of two astronauts in spacesuits and helmets. They were holding oxygen tanks, walking on a white surface in boxy-looking yellow boots. "Guess what this is," he whispered.

"Why are we whispering?"

"Because it's a secret. If you promise not to tell, I'll let you in on it."

"I promise," I said quietly.

My father gestured for me to take a closer look at the card, which had a serial number and a signature in green ink.

Ticket to the Moon

"It's a ticket from Pan Am for the first space shuttle to the moon," he told me.

"You're going to the moon?" I whispered.

He nodded.

"When?"

"As soon as I can."

"What about me? Can I come too?" I raised my voice, pleading loudly, forgetting it was a secret. "You can't go without me!"

"Sh-h-h. I have four tickets—one for each of us. We're all going. But don't tell your mother. She'll think I'm nuts."

In the Sunday newspaper, Pan American World Airways were advertising places on their first commercial flight to the moon, which civilians could reserve, first come, first serve. Those were comparatively carefree days when flying was still an adventure, and your body, whatever shape it was, was sure to fit into the seat. It was before a terrorist explosion in 1988 on Pan Am Flight 103 claimed the lives of all 270 passengers. In the aftermath of crippling grief and fear and getting slammed with 300 million dollars in lawsuits (an unimaginable amount of money in the late eighties), the last victim was Pan Am itself. The airline folded under the pressure and went defunct in 1991, but more than twenty years prior, my father wrote them the following note in response to their newspaper ad:

Attention: Reservations

Gentlemen: I wish to reserve four (4) seats, first-class, for your first trip to the moon. Please advise when we can plan to make this trip and how much luggage we would be permitted to carry.

Thank you for confirmation.

Very truly yours,

Samuel M. Cagan

In two weeks, he received a signed confirmation letter with four tickets enclosed, declaring Sam Cagan's family to be members of the First Moon Flights Club. I was a member of a club I didn't even know about. It was all very official and exciting, and I was relieved he'd included the whole family, although I was pretty sure my mother would be a hard sell. I wasn't too sure about my sister, either.

The Pan Am confirmation letter read:

Dear Moon First Flighter,

Thank you for your confidence that Pan Am will pioneer commercial space travel, as it so often has here on Earth. We have every intention of living up to this confidence.

The enclosed cards confirm this intent, and formally recognize your INTREPID *spirit. It also reflects by serial number your family's position of record on our Waitlist for First Moon Flights. (All requests are handled in order of date received.)*

Starting date of service is not yet known. Equipment and route will, probably, be subjected to government approvals. Fares are not fully resolved, and may be out of this world. We ask you to be patient while these essentials are worked out. They are necessary requirements before we may accept deposits or make confirmed reservations.

Meanwhile, we plan to keep you informed of all important developments.

Again, thank you for coming to Pan Am first. That's exactly what we intend to be. On earth. To the moon. Any place else.

Sincerely, James Montgomery
Vice President, Sales

I didn't know what "intrepid" meant, but I was sure it described my father, who loved showing me mysterious worlds that I never imagined existed. Early one morning, I was asleep, and it was still dark outside, when he whispered in my ear, "Andrea, wake up." He touched my cheek lightly. "Get up and dress warm. I have a surprise for you."

My eyes flew open, and I caught sight of my father's back as he stole out of my bedroom and disappeared down the hall. Pushing back the warmth of the covers, I stood up in the chilly air, dropped my flannel nightgown on the floor, and stepped into a pair of light brown corduroy pants. I pulled a T-shirt and a sweatshirt over my head, put on yesterday's socks and a pair of Keds, and walked out into the hallway, rubbing tiny balls of sleep from the corners of my eyes. I made a quick stop at the bathroom and then silently headed downstairs.

It was 1957, the last Saturday in March, so early the stars were still sprinkled across the edge of the horizon as I stood beside my father in the kitchen next to our electric stove. Dressed in slacks and a thick tennis sweater with red, white, and-blue-stripes, my father chugged down a cup of instant Maxwell House coffee that was so hot, tears squeezed out of the corners of his eyes and rolled down his cheeks. He flashed me a wet wink and swiped at his face with a paper napkin. Then he poured some orange juice into a glass and handed it to me. When I finished it, he tossed me a jacket. I caught it and giggled.

"Sh-h-h! Don't wake up the sleepyheads," he whispered, gesturing toward the stairway that led to the upstairs bedrooms where my sister and mother were sleeping. I put on my jacket and buttoned it up as I watched my father flip the car keys into the air, pretending to drop them, making the catch just before they clattered onto the floor. I suppressed another giggle as he motioned for me to follow him out the door that led to the basement. He closed the door noiselessly behind us. We went down a flight of stairs, passed the furnace, went out the basement door, and ended up in the garage.

I had no idea where we were heading, but it was already a fine adventure, a private outing for my father and me. I climbed into the passenger seat of his car. He softly closed my door and walked around, got into the driver's side, and fit the key into the ignition. "We're going to the airport," he said as he slowly backed the car out of the driveway. "It's about twenty minutes from here."

"Why? Are we going on a plane?" I had never flown before.

"No, something is coming to us."

"A person?"

"Better. A solar eclipse. At six fourteen. When the sun starts to come up, the moon's going to cover it."

"Why?"

"The moon is jealous. It has to disappear every morning when the sun comes out. But today the moon wants extra attention. It'll start to get light, and then all of a sudden, it'll get dark again."

"Forever?"

"No, just for a little while. It's an eclipse. The moon is going to pass over the sun. We're going to the open field beside the runway to watch it. Remember when we saw the eclipse on the ceiling at the planetarium?"

I nodded, proud that I remembered what he was talking about. My father had a lifelong fascination with astronomy, and as soon as he thought I was old enough to sit still for half an hour, he took me to the planetarium to see the show—presumably to start my education for our upcoming moon flight. My father and I leaned back against the headrests of the gray upholstered steel chairs in the darkened dome-shaped room. "Look up at the ceiling," he whispered to me when the show was beginning. "Follow the white arrow with your eyes. It'll float right across the sky above you."

When the music started, I turned my gaze upward as thousands of stars were projected across the imaginary skies. I tried to follow the lackluster explanations from the droning voice that described the phases of the moon and named the constellations. I silently mouthed the strange words, trying to commit them to memory so my father and I could have our own special language: Orion, the Southern Cross, Capricorn, the Big Dipper, the Pleiades. When the show ended and the starry heavens vanished and became a domed ceiling once again, we filed out of the room and bounded up several long flights of stairs, two at a time, moving faster and making more noise than we should have. Delicious. Once we were outside on the roof, we peered into a massive telescope that allowed us to view the planets and stars up close, perusing star systems that were hundreds of light-years away. I had no idea what light-years were, but I liked the sound of the words.

On the way home, I voiced a concern. "Those stars we saw through the telescope," I said, "some of them aren't really there anymore, right?"

"That's right, honey. They exploded thousands, maybe millions of years ago. It takes the light so long to travel, we can still see them, but they're gone."

"The thing is," I said, "how can you be sure the moon is still there? What if we get Mom and Jill on the shuttle and get all the way to the moon and it's gone? They might get very disappointed."

"Good point." He didn't have a ready solution, but that was OK. I trusted he'd have it all worked out by the time we left.

On our way to the airport, I relaxed back into the seat of my father's Buick, inhaling the scent of coffee that hung in the air between us. Incandescent street lamps lit up the brick-and-wood houses that seemed to hover several feet in the air above the lawns that surrounded them like shiny grass skirts.

"How many light-years away is the eclipse?" I asked, using my new words, as we drove toward the airport before dawn that morning.

My father grinned. "I don't know, honey, a lot. And you know what? It won't happen again for seventy years."

"You'll be pretty old by then," I said.

"I will," he agreed. "Close to a hundred."

"Will you still have hair?"

"Yes. But it'll be white."

"How about your eyes? Will you be able to see?"

"My glasses might be a little thicker."

"Well, don't worry. I'll drive."

"Deal!"

I loved being privy to my father's secret passions. He had a world of interests that he kept to himself that I wanted in on. I used to sit quietly under his desk at night with my Venus Paradise colored pencils and a color-by-number sketchbook while he wrote stories that no one ever read. He was a stand-up comedian and emcee for special events. He always had four-by-five cards in his pocket so when he heard "a good one," he could jot it down. At the end of the day, he took his hand-written cards and filed them by subject. He taught himself a second language with a phonograph record that prompted him to repeat rudimentary Spanish phrases and their translations. He listened to opera when he was alone, and he went to the Boston Opera House by himself to see *Aida* and *Madame Butterfly*. My mother didn't care much for music. "It's not my cup of tea," she declared.

My father kept his secret world mostly to himself, so when he shared any of it with me, it was a wonderment. He was a man of many secrets, and he even had a secret about his last name, which had been changed from Cohen to Cagan before I was born. I didn't find this out until I ran across an essay my father had written in high school with the name Samuel Cohen written across the top. And then there was his "thing" about his shoes.

He refused to take them off in front of anyone other than his wife or his daughters, and he wouldn't tell us why. His feet looked fine. I checked, and he was not missing a digit, and he didn't have twisted toes, bad toenails, or even a hint of athlete's foot. And yet, if one of my mother's siblings or his own brother were coming over, he made sure to put on fresh socks and slip his feet snugly into his shoes before he answered the door. Diametrically opposed to the Buddhist ritual of removing one's shoes at home, my father stood firm in his commitment to having his feet covered, which reminds me of a famous family story. Although the details remain vague, his stubborn dedication to never removing his shoes, whether or not it reflected sound thinking, clearly describes my father at his secretive best.

A successful corporate salesman, Samuel Cagan had the rare privilege of being chosen by his company, Pratt & Whitney, to travel to Russia in the early seventies to explore the possibility of an international exchange of factory machinery. At the time, we still called the Russians "Reds," and the word "communist" filled an American's heart with fear and loathing. So when my father flew to Moscow to meet with a group of Russian businessmen and discuss an alliance over vodka and caviar, we all considered him to be courageous and forward thinking.

The story goes that his Russian hosts took him on a long, overnight train ride, offered him numerous shots of vodka, which he felt obliged to accept, and when they arrived in a town well outside of Moscow, they took him on a tour of a treasured museum. When they got to the entrance of the ancient site, his hosts removed their shoes, as had been the tradition for hundreds of years, and my father was asked to do the same. When he refused, the translator tried to coerce him, explaining that not only was it a sign of respect, it was also important to preserve the carpeting, which was as old as the building. He wouldn't budge. The upshot was that for the first time since Ivan the Terrible had ruled Russia, a man, an American no less, walked through this museum with his shoes still on his feet. I wondered if my father had holes in his socks or if he felt too vulnerable to the Reds without his shoes on, in case he suddenly needed to flee. I figured he must have had a reason for telling me the story, but when I asked him why he was so adamant about keeping on his shoes, he glibly answered, "I didn't want to leave them lying around."

In my father's never-ending quest to explore new things, he taught himself to do mathematics on a Chinese abacus board, adding and subtracting long lists of numbers. Sometimes he enrolled Jill to test his prowess. She'd add the numbers the regular way on a sheet of paper while he raced her with the abacus board. I was too young to take part in the race, so I got to shout out the name of the winner. Although Jill was fast, my father usually won the prize for accuracy. "Those Chinese," he'd say, shaking his head, "they really know their stuff."

It was still dark when my father and I arrived at the airport to view the eclipse that morning. He parked on an adjacent street, and we walked into the open field beside the runway, which he lit up with a flashlight. A few other adventurous souls milled around in the darkness. I resented their presence. This time belonged to my father and me, so I pretended we were alone. I held his hand tightly, pressing into his spongy thumb pad, allowing it to fill back out, and pressing it down again.

When we got to the middle of the field, we stopped. My sneakers were wet from the dew, and I looked up at my father while we waited, thrilled by his long, straight back and all the things he knew. The sun was starting to rise as a faint glow appeared along the horizon, lighting up the edges of the world. My father's upturned face became a dark silhouette against the glowing heavens. I reached my arms up toward him and the sky, stretching out my fingers as the oncoming light intensified—and then it began to reverse itself, just like my father had promised. My breath quickened as he and I smiled at each other. We looked back up and watched the light become dim as time stood still for a few moments—until the tentative darkness began slipping away, making room for the sun to swell and dominate the sky. I felt deeply connected to the world around me that was beginning to light up as the dawn became steady, illuminating the people who stood beside us. I didn't want the adventure to end, and I felt sad as the world became itself again, and my father and I began our slow walk back to the car.

Dad

A strikingly handsome man, my father always looked like he was ready to break out into a smile. He had a full head of smoky-brown hair, perfectly defined calves beneath muscular thighs, and an infectious sense of humor. I loved cavorting down the sidewalk beside him, matching his spirited gait as best I could, basking in what felt like his bottomless well of energy. He would toss me in the air, and when he put me back down, I ran beside him, and together we kissed the wind. I loved his zest for life, his sparkly eyes, his beautiful arms, and his wide back. He was a vital man, built for action, and it seemed like he was never afraid of anything.

Except death. When an uncle, one of my mother's brothers, was dying after fighting cancer for many months, family members gathered in the waiting room of the hospital in the little Massachusetts town called Framingham where my mother's family lived. One by one, the adults went into my uncle's room to say good-bye. They came out quietly, wiping away a tear and sitting down in the silence, turning inward. When my father took his turn, he went into the room like everyone else had done, but when he came back out, he announced in a loud voice, "He doesn't look too bad. I think he's gonna make it." No one looked up at him. My uncle died several hours later, and my father was the only one who was surprised.

His no-nonsense, death-denying, head-on approach to life was apparent in the way he spoke, moved, and even in the way he slept. He never admitted to being tired, as if sleep itself represented some sort of defeat. When he returned home on Saturday and Sunday afternoons after a tennis game (he was an avid tennis player, and he preferred singles so he didn't have to wait around between shots), he would eat a light lunch and announce he was going into the bedroom to read the newspaper. Two minutes later, the paper was on the floor and he was snoring.

My father refused to wait around for anything. He ate his meals in a straight line, hardly talking, one mouthful after the other, enamel meeting metal as he efficiently cleaned his fork, readying the next bite while he was still chewing the last one. No time wasted. My mother, Jill, and I were familiar with the sound of his chair pushing away from the table while our dinner plates were still half full. My mother ate slowly and methodically, nudging her food into small piles and patting them down with her fork before she put them into her mouth. She would have preferred for my father to stay at the table longer—she liked having the family all in one place—but she never said anything to him. She may have been holding tightly onto the purse strings, but my father was the undisputed master of his home and family, not required to answer to anyone concerning his words or his actions, the only one of us ever allowed to express anger about anything. According to him, life was for living, hard and fast, for gathering experiences, until one day destiny cruelly stopped you in your tracks—the final defeat at the end of a long, glorious, uphill battle.

Each evening when my father got home from work, he frowned at the obituaries in the newspaper that read someone had "succumbed to cancer" or "lost the battle with diabetes." He refused to succumb to anything, and he didn't think anyone else should either. He hated the idea of losing. He just pressed onward through his life, sidestepping as fast as he could to avoid getting the rug pulled out from under him. I think he believed that with enough know-how, speed, and perseverance, the grim reaper himself would tire of trying to catch up with Sam Cagan. I'm not sure if it was fear or denial that fueled his unwillingness to relax and slow down. It must have been a combination of both that made him always eager to go and do whatever needed to be done. He stayed on the move, he refused to let fear stand in his way of anything, and for as long as I can remember, he did what he could to pass that fearlessness on to my sister and me.

Maybe it's because of him that I've always been fascinated by people with the courage to attempt impossible physical feats like climbing Mount Everest or soaring high above the ground on a flying trapeze. In 2012 I stared at the TV, riveted, when circus performer Nick Wallenda defied high wind gales and blinding mists as he crossed Niagara Falls on a tightrope without a net, where one false step meant certain death. He just kept placing one foot in front of the other, sometimes kneeling down when the wind gusted too high, continually praising Jesus all the way. He walked a distance of six football fields and made it to the other side in one piece, where his family stood, ready to greet him.

While I never walked a tightrope or climbed a snow-covered mountain in the Himalayas (I did swing on a flying trapeze once, but it was in a controlled environment, and I had on a safety harness), the need for courage has shown up in my life much more subtly. Like one morning in 1988, when I stopped dead at the threshold of an AIDS hospice. I'd made an appointment to meet the volunteer coordinator several days earlier, but now that I was there, I was afraid to go inside. The hospice had twenty-six beds, and twenty-six dying people lay in them, most of them under thirty. There was no cure for AIDS in sight and no way to slow it down as yet. At the time, the hospice residents were all young, gay, and male, statistics that would change to include straight men and women of all ages in the not-too-distant future. AIDS would become an equal-opportunity invader, but right then, still in its infancy, it hadn't shown all of its faces yet. It was known only as the gay man's virus, and it was wreaking havoc in the gay community.

I had lost Michael, one of my closest friends, about two weeks earlier. He was thirty-two, a man I had known and loved for years. In a way, it was because of him that I was standing there. As courageous as they come, Michael wrote and directed a play featuring teenagers to teach schoolkids about AIDS and to encourage safe sex. Then he was ambushed with his own HIV diagnosis. He called me one night in terror, right after a rehearsal. He was sniffling, blowing his nose, and running a fever. "I'm sick," he said.

"It's just a cold or the flu, Mikey," I reassured him naively. "Everyone gets a cold now and then."

But it was much more than that. Two days later he was in the hospital, diagnosed with pneumocystis, an AIDS-related pneumonia. Over the following eight months, he struggled against a battery of devastating illnesses, swallowing a cornucopia of drugs that hardly helped at all. In fact, one of them, a powerful antibiotic, nearly killed him before they finally realized he was allergic. It was all so new and confusing back then.

I visited Michael daily when his illness first took hold. I was by his side during the three weeks he spent in the hospital and also when he got back home. He was relieved to have me there—he could talk about anything with me, and I seemed to have an endless capacity to listen and commiserate. But as the months wore on, I lost my footing, and I didn't remain stoic or steady. I started falling apart emotionally when it became clear that Michael's days and his disappearing T cells were numbered. I had lost hope, and I was losing my ability to pull off the normal day-to-day tasks that kept my own life together. As a result, he shut me out; he couldn't handle my inability to cope with his pain. During his last weeks,

I felt like I had seriously blown it, that I'd done everything wrong, from crowding him to becoming needier than *he* was, and finally, refusing to accept the inevitability of his death. I saw Michael for a few minutes right before he died, and we made peace, but I judged myself harshly, a bad habit of mine that I'm still trying to tame. It was clear to me that while I had helped my friend a lot in the beginning, I had also made some mistakes, and I had a lot to learn.

Determined to do whatever it took to learn it, I attended a weekend death and dying seminar, where I made friends with a young man named Ken sitting on the floor in front of me. He was about thirty, visibly ill with vulnerable eyes and purple spots on his skin, the signs of Kaposi's sarcoma, a cancerous skin disease associated with AIDS. When he asked me to come visit him at the AIDS hospice where he was staying, I agreed. But as I stood at the threshold of the front door that morning, determined to keep my word, I was paralyzed with fear.

For starters, I was afraid I had nothing to offer. What did I know, and what did AIDS patients need? I had no idea. And then, I had to admit that I feared the illness itself. It would have been stupid not to, when it was still so young and filled with bravado, eating everything and everyone in its path. It had been established recently in the medical community that you could acquire AIDS only by sharing bodily fluids like blood or semen with someone who was infected, but how could I be sure that was true? The illness was largely misunderstood. Very few studies had been conducted as yet, and researchers were only just discovering its various strains and potencies. What if there were unknown varieties lurking around that were airborne? What if they suddenly discovered that the virus attacked through the pores, infecting by touch or by extended exposure? These burning questions were in everyone's minds, and I was doing my best to accept the consensus that breathing, touching, and hugging could not cause transmission of the disease. I thought I had it down—until I stood in front of the hospice that morning and couldn't find the courage to walk in.

I might have stood there all day if a nurse hadn't parked his car in the lot and stepped in front of me to open the door. He and I walked in together, and he smiled at me and directed me down a hallway toward a sign with a red arrow that read "Volunteers." Clearly the powers that be had sent me a personal usher, and once I was inside and in motion, my fears began to dissipate, and I replaced them with curiosity and wonder, the things my father had taught me.

There had been no orientation class for volunteers—that would come in a year or two when enough people were volunteering at AIDS hospices to warrant a class—so I entered the small room designated for volunteers with about half a dozen empty chairs. I sat down. A man with graying hair and an easy smile, probably in his forties, soon came walking over to me. "I'm Brent," he said. "You must be Andrea."

I put out my hand to take his. I had spoken to him on the phone a few days earlier and told him my friend Ken was a resident there. Brent had encouraged me to stop by. I stood up. The chair beneath me was on its last legs, literally, and Brent stared at it. "We need to get a lesbian in here with a tool belt to fix that," he said. "God knows none of us guys have a clue what to do."

"Sorry," I said, smiling, "I'm no good with carpentry, but I'm happy to meet you. I'm here to see Ken, but I'd also like to volunteer one day a week. I just hope there's something for me to do."

"Oh, there's plenty for you to do," he said. "No problem there. It's almost time to deliver lunch trays, but I just came from Gary's room. He's one of our new residents. He's a recovering Catholic, just like me. Room two-twenty. He'd be a great place for you to start. He really needs to talk. After you visit Ken in one-eighteen, why don't you go upstairs and pay Gary a visit?"

Ken was happy to see me, but he seemed sicker than the weekend before when we had met, and we chatted for a few minutes until he began to doze. I promised to come back, squeezed his hand, and then headed upstairs and stopped at the threshold of Gary's room. I looked in cautiously, wondering how to approach him, but he invited me in the moment he saw me. I sat on the chair beside the bed, he thanked me for coming and started to talk, and I had begun my hospice work.

I listened for a while—he seemed happy to be talking with anyone—and then I carried lunch trays back and forth, inquiring along the way if anyone needed anything. I quickly learned that all I had to do was ask permission to enter a room, walk in, and sit down, and the resident took it from there. Ken had needed to sleep and had told me as much, and Gary needed to talk about religion. Down the hall, Brian told me about his mother, who refused to believe he was gay, but at least she hadn't cut him off. Grant, whose mother *had* cut him off, needed to hold someone's hand; he was terrified of dying alone. Larry liked to tell stupid jokes, and Chris kept getting up by himself, obsessed with the need to take a shower, and he kept falling down. Jim wanted me to steal chocolate for him from the kitchen, and Greg asked me to light his cigarette. I didn't hesitate. He had AIDS and cancer, a painful and deadly combo, so I figured he might as well smoke if it gave him pleasure.

Meeting and talking with these men who knew they were not long for this world was an immediate experience—we got right to the heart of the matter, whatever it was. There was no time for anything else. When I met Rick from Austria, I felt an instant kinship. He was Swiss, he had a slight German accent, and we shared a love of the arts. He had seen a lot of ballet, he was an aficionado, and he relished my stories about my past, like seeing Rudolph Nureyev in Monte Carlo, strutting across the beach in a purple bikini with purple suspenders. Rick used to frequent the opera, and when he talked about it, it made me wish I had gone there with my father, since he'd loved it so much. I guess I was too young back then to appreciate it, but Rick told me how much he loved the set designs, the costumes, and the drama of it all. We talked about our favorite movies and our favorite musicians.

"What's your favorite food?" I asked him, holding his hand as we spoke.

A grin came over his face.

"What's funny?" I asked him.

"Peanuts," he said.

I looked at him questioningly.

"My favorite food is peanuts. I bet you thought I was going to say caviar or squab or *crème chocolat*. The truth is that nothing tastes better to me than peanuts."

"That's so American," I said. "Salted or unsalted?"

"Salted."

"Loose or in the shell?"

"In the shell. The kind you get at a ball game. I guess it doesn't get much more American than that."

On my way to the hospice the very next Tuesday, I picked up a large bag of peanuts, salted and in the shell. I rushed in the front door of the hospice and bounded up the stairs to surprise Rick with his heart's desire, a far cry from how I had felt when I first entered the premises. I headed for his room all the way at the end of the hall and checked my energy for a moment before I got there. He might be asleep or feeling poorly, I reminded myself. I couldn't go barging into his room with my gift. I slowed down my breath, and, with a big smile on my face, I stopped at the doorway and looked in. Rick wasn't there; his bed was stripped, and his things were gone from the nightstand.

My eyes clouded with tears. Rick was gone. Really gone. And someone new was about to take his place as soon as they got the bed ready. The waiting list for new patients was getting longer every day, and they couldn't even afford twenty-four hours for turnaround. I walked quickly to the volunteer room and looked his name up in the printouts to be sure. "Deceased" was written next to his name. I holed up in a bathroom stall, trying to catch my breath. I had been unprepared, but this was not a hospital, I reminded myself. It was a hospice, and everyone here was dying. What did I expect?

I left the stall, splashed some cold water on my face, and exited the bathroom, dropping the bag of peanuts on a table in the common room where the residents gathered to watch TV. Having expectations around there was deadly, literally. I remembered a spiritual teacher, Stephen

Levine, telling his audience, "No appointments. No disappointments." I needed to remember that what happened to Rick could and would happen to everyone who checked in there. That was what the place was for, and the odds of having my heart broken over and over were pretty high. Did that mean I should guard my heart more, not get involved with people's lives, or should I let it break open? Was I strong enough to deal with this? I didn't know, but I realized that the twenty-six beds here were filled with twenty-six teachers, and I needed to stay present, help make each of them as comfortable as possible, and, above all else, I needed to be quiet and listen. Hopefully I'd learn something.

I once attended a three-day silent retreat facilitated by a Sufi master who told us that when he was a young man, he'd climbed the snow-covered Himalayas for three days and nights, searching for a spiritual teacher. He was looking for a *rishi*, an enlightened sacred poet reported to live up there. When he got to the top, he followed large footprints in the snow to a cave entrance. The *rishi* came to the opening, stared at the young man who was exhausted and shivering from the cold and lack of sleep, and said, "I can't believe you climbed that mountain when all you needed to do was look in the mirror. If you're not looking for a teacher and you don't talk too much, you can come in."

The young man spent several weeks with the *rishi*, not reciting lessons or reading esoteric books, but rather doing the mundane chores it took to survive in that grueling atmosphere. The Sufi master told us, "If you're looking for an enlightened teacher, don't ask any questions. Just listen, and when you find someone with great wit and compassion, you've found what you're looking for."

The hospice was filled with people who fit that description, so I made a point of listening more than talking, checking any judgments I might have, and doing whatever was needed in the moment. Carrying lunch trays. Cleaning up spills on night tables. Reading out loud. Holding hands.

A friend once told me that my hospice work had to be depressing and she couldn't imagine why on earth I chose it. The truth was that I found it exhausting but never depressing. It was a multifaceted opportunity: to leave my personal drama at the door (it was always waiting right there for me when I returned), to be mindful and present, and to meet a group of courageous young men who were beyond caring about political correctness or being right about anything. As they faced their imminent demise, they were unedited, brought to their knees by the fact that they would most certainly die in the very near future. And that same realization brought me to mine.

There was nothing complicated about my work there. I just made the rounds and absorbed the lessons each of them were offering, like how to be present with a person who was dying, what to say and what not to say, the power of quietly holding someone's hand, that we were all in this together, and that they had committed no crimes or done anything different or twisted that had made them ill. It could easily have been me in that bed, because all they had done was have sex, the same thing I was doing and so was everyone else.

During my volunteer Tuesdays, I saw a mother sitting with her son who had just died, talking quietly to him, smoothing his covers while she waited for the mortuary workers to arrive. I met a man who was grieving his boyfriend who in turn was grieving the end of his soon-to-be interrupted life. I was blessed to walk the halls of a place where race, age, and belief systems were irrelevant, where being alive was all that mattered, a gift that was never taken for granted. Most poignant of all, I met an elderly couple who, until a few days earlier, had had no idea their son was gay or that he had AIDS and was dying. They hadn't spoken to him for years. They had flown to Los Angeles that day, and they were in deep shock, trying to find a way to forgive themselves for turning their backs on their progeny, struggling to make a connection with a previously exiled son who had a few days left to live.

And then there was Willy. Nobody had been able to make any inroads with Willy, a wheelchair-bound African American man who never spoke and appeared withdrawn and depressed—until I entered the scene. No one knew his past. A woman had checked him in, but she had left abruptly and had never come back to see him. When I met him, Willy had been in the hospice for several months. He had apparently lost his looks and his musculature, and he hadn't spoken at all during that time. He hadn't warmed up to anyone, and they didn't think he ever would, but they kept trying. They asked me if I would be willing to take a stab at it.

Willy was watching television in the common room when I approached him cautiously and asked if I could sit next to him, a simple request. And lo and behold, the miracle happened. He took one look at me and smiled for the first time since he had arrived. Nobody knew why, least of all me, but Willy took to me the moment he saw me, and over the next two months, each Tuesday when I got there, Willy was waiting for me. We played cards and watched TV together, and sometimes I wheeled him into the backyard where he ate his lunch while I looked on. I spoke slowly to him, as if he could barely understand me, and I could see that he was listening. He had a childlike aura of innocence, and I wondered about his past. Where had he been, and what had he done? When he nodded at me or when we played cards, he seemed gentle and easy to get along with. But where were his friends? Had they all died? He appeared to have good manners as he ate slowly and he always acknowledged my good-byes when I left at the end of the day. Maybe it was the fact that I was younger than the other volunteers, or maybe I looked like an old friend or his mother. Whatever it was, Willy was always happy to see me, and I was happy to see him, even though he never said a word to me or to anyone else.

The inevitable Tuesday arrived, however, when Willy wasn't sitting in the common room when I got there. I went to find him and discovered that he couldn't get out of bed. The illness was taking over. I spent some time with him. He refused to eat, and he died in his sleep a few days afterward, gently, quietly, the same way he had lived in the hospice.

Brent called me at home to tell me that my friend had died. "You gave him a lot of love. You really made a difference with Willy." He invited me to the monthly memorial service for all the men who had died during the last thirty days, and I decided to go and represent Willy. There was a pretty good chance no one else would.

Each person who died had someone or a few people there to say something on his behalf and tell him good-bye. When they got to Willy, I was about to take the podium to wish him well—until a woman stood up. She was African American, wearing a low-cut tie-dyed T-shirt with a bare midriff, a very short skirt, very high heels, and lots of makeup, and she had dozens of piercings in her ears. Drooping slightly off to the right as she walked, she made her way up to the podium, leaned forward to the mike, showing plenty of cleavage, and said in somewhat of a slur, "Willy may have been a pimp and a thief, he may have been a gambler and a liar, but I loved him."

I had learned a few things about silence before I ever met Willy. During my silent Sufi retreat with about a hundred other people, I had thought it would get tougher each day, that the desire to speak would increase as time went by. But the opposite happened. The more time passed, the more all of our minds slowed down and quieted, and the more kindness and patience we showed each other—until lunch on the third day, when the silence directive was lifted so we could meet our fellow retreat attendees and exchange phone numbers. It felt strange to speak at first. We mostly smiled at each other, tested our voices, and exchanged some contact information. But in no time at all, someone pushed ahead of me in the lunch line. I felt resentful, as did a few other people. Someone got rude, someone took offense and spoke harshly, and it was all back. Still, my quiet time had made an impression on me.

Whatever Willy had done during his life, wherever he'd gone and whoever he'd been, he had dropped into deep silence for his last few months. He had lived simply, somebody had loved him, and he had died like an innocent child, just like we all do. Did the rest of it make any difference? I've heard it said that a spiritual awakening can happen in an instant. If that's true, Willy's courage to drop into silence and stay there made him my unexpected master. He may have been a pimp, a thief, a gambler, and a liar, but when it's my time to drop my body and move on, I only hope that I'll do it with as much grace as Willy did.

Chapter Five

BROKEN

No one saves us but ourselves.

No one can and no one may.

We ourselves must walk the path.

— Gautama Buddha, *Sayings of Buddha*

In the archaeological expedition of my life so far, my creative pursuits stand out like streaks of golden light, from the beauty of the ballet to the accomplished Philippine faith healers, from crafting fringed deer-skin bags to knitting cashmere and silk sweaters and scarves, from collecting quartz crystals to the interplay of words and phrases that I've set on the page and watched as they burst forth into living stories and pictures. When I'm lost and discouraged, these are the things that save me and fill me with gratitude.

In stark contrast, too many of the men I have known and loved, or at least tried to love, stand out like dark veins tainting the gold, eating up the light, weighing me down with saturnine lessons, the results of my own regrettable and self-punishing choices. If I'd known better, I'd have chosen differently, but I didn't. And so I got what I got.

If reincarnation is real, I can only imagine that I was a misogynist in a past life, and my bad fortune with men in this life is my comeuppance. I know that sounds dramatic, but as wonderful as my women and platonic male friends always have been and still are, I have known a great deal of loss, betrayal, and disappointment around the men I've invited into my bed. I could blame it all on them, but I can't really overlook the fact that I am the only constant in the equation. Unlike my parents, who modeled long-term devotion in a union that seemed devoid of passion but rich in respect, commitment, and steadiness, my relationships have burned very hot and then quickly burned out, the highs and lows leaving a lot of refuse, sorrow, and regrets in their wake. Recalling some of them causes me shame and regret; I just didn't make good choices or get it right in that arena, but I know I'm not alone.

I once wrote a book with a woman who was the first female police chief in a major American city. She had fought the boys' club at every turn, successfully infiltrating their ranks, bearing the brunt of their slander and cruel jokes, rising to the top, creating better positions for women in the force, and, most notably, pioneering the adaptation of bulletproof Kevlar vests to fit women's chests and keep them safe from gunshots. She was eventually removed; the men couldn't abide taking directions from a woman, and an enemy of hers in the force took her down with trumped-up drug charges against her husband.

Her reign came to a painful end, as did her marriage, but the strange truth is that as tough and powerful as she used to be, when we met, her current boyfriend was broke, he refused to get a job, and she allowed him to hole up in her house and in her bed while she tried to encourage and support him. He said he wanted to write, so, thinking I might be a source of inspiration for him, she introduced him to me. Later, he called me behind her back and asked me for a date. I turned him down and told him what I thought of him. When I called to tell her what he'd done, she shook her head and said, "It's sad, isn't it? What I'm willing to put up with? The woman in my force who used to teach women self-defense was being battered by her husband."

I was watching TV some years back when an African American healer, a spirited woman with a great sense of humor, was sitting beside Oprah. Women in the audience were telling her about the abusive ways a husband or a boyfriend had treated them, and she could relate, having her own history of abuse. After each audience member spoke, this woman put one hand on her brow, the other on the nape of her neck, and, with a big smile on her face, she said, "Save yourself. Nobody else will."

While some women meet great men and find fulfilling relationships and marriages, like my mother and, now, my sister in her second marriage, some of us have been blind, self-abusive, and in denial when it comes to men. Clearly, in people like me, something is broken, and I'm sorry to say that I've allowed a number of men to betray and take advantage of me, men whom I thought I loved and now would prefer to forget. But all's fair, it seems, in love and literature.

A short time back, when I sat down to work on this memoir and placed my fingers on the keyboard as usual to see what was there, I tapped out a few false starts. A phrase here, a memory there that I deleted and started over—when in a sudden blast of energy, my fingers took off and flew on their own as if I were holding the planchette of a Ouija board. I surrendered, allowing the trajectory to define itself without my will or direction. When I sat back to see what I had written, I was so horrified, I scatted the cat off my lap, pushed away from the computer, grabbed the sweater I was knitting, and rushed to my car. I drove over to La Knitterie Parisienne, my local knitting store, where I spent the next three hours in anonymity and avoidance, sitting at the large round table, working the threads of my latest project.

I've been knitting since I was six. I have a magnificent collection of sweaters, shrugs, jackets, a few hats, and some scarves in silk, cashmere, and mink yarns.

Knitted Treasure

For the rest of that afternoon, I lost myself in my favorite craft as my fingers flew and the strands easily intertwined. I was in the knit zone, lulled by the safe, idle gossip of a woman's circle (and a few gay men), delighting in the feel of the yarn and the mellifluent French accent of Edith, the elegant shop owner as she rolled her *r*'s, instructing, laughing, listening to stories, playfully chiding, and taking care of her patrons.

It was the name I had typed onto the page that had made me run, a simple quintet of letters, JERRY, configured with several other words: "I met Jerry in an era…" It was enough to make me double over, as it described a permanent stain on my psyche. *Oh, no, you don't. I'm not writing about that,* were the words that echoed in my mind as I catapulted, midsentence, from my ergonomic chair and into the car. But who was I kidding? I could almost hear folk hero Br'er Rabbit's famous words: *Oh, please, Br'er Fox, whatever you do, please don't throw me in the briar patch,* as he found himself sailing through the air on his way straight into the briar patch.

During my early teens, my ballet studio in Boston had two support poles from floor to ceiling that had to be avoided when my fellow students and I practiced lines of *piqué* or *chaînés* turns from one corner of the room to the other. I kept an eye on those poles in an attempt to circumnavigate them, and I kept sailing right into them. One day, my teacher said, "If you don't want to hit the poles, don't look at them." I averted my gaze, and I never banged into them again. The point being that whatever you focus on, you're sure to magnetize straight to you.

So it was with writing about Jerry. My struggle to escape this part of my history was like an invitation because he was embedded so firmly in my psyche. He was, unfortunately, an integral part of what shaped me. There would be no way *not* to write about him, so I might as well go for it, I reasoned, which brings me to this story that happened so long ago.

I met Jerry in an era when these were among the most popular lyrics and adages:

Love is all there is.
Follow your bliss.
If you can't be with the one you love, love the one you're with.
With love, all things are possible.
Remember, be here now.

During the late sixties, when I met Jerry, magical thinking was at its peak, saying no was unpopular, and saying yes was considered hip and cool. Falling into bed with someone you hardly knew was not looked upon as slutty or dangerous behavior, rather it was called "going for it" and "letting the love in." There were no AIDS or herpes as yet, as far as we knew, and back then, falling in lust was constantly mistaken for falling in love. In fact it was encouraged, as we believed that one thing might lead to the other. Or that you couldn't have one without the other.

I can say now, without hesitation, that although I thought I did, I never loved Jerry, the man that I married for a stunning reason: I was afraid not to. I was far too needy to be capable of mature love back then. I was nineteen, a member of the Harkness Ballet, and Jill and I were visiting Los Angeles for a week. We were crossing Sunset Boulevard in front of the Playboy Club (which is now long gone), when a midnight-blue car made a point of coming to a screeching halt in front of us, letting us pass.

Nice convertible, I thought.

At the time, I was well versed in the difference between British Freeds and American Capezio pointe shoes. I understood the advantages of flat over raked stages in Europe where I had performed for princesses and multimillionaires. I could carry on a reasonable conversation in French, and I knew my muscles intimately, how to isolate each one and heal the strains and sprains that a ballet dancer inevitably sustained. I was disciplined and focused way beyond my years. But when it came to cars, I didn't know the difference between a Chevrolet and a Ferrari, and this deep-blue convertible happened to be the latter. Neither did I know the difference between a well-meaning suitor who respected women and a predator disguised with a smile, a come-on, and a dark agenda.

Jill and I shared a laugh as we continued our walk across the boulevard, stepping safely onto the opposite curb as the man in the Ferrari roared down the street past us, made an illegal U-turn, and pulled up beside us.

Why did the ballerina cross the road?

To fall into the snake pit on the other side.

The handsome, self-confident man behind the wheel grinned, driving as slowly as we were walking. "Are you staying at the Sunset Marquis on the third floor overlooking the swimming pool with an empty field between your hotel and the Empire West apartment building?" he asked us.

"Yes," I told him.

"How do you know that?" Jill asked.

"I've been watching you two get undressed through a telescope for about a week," he said. "I live in the penthouse of the Empire West." He pointed up where, sure enough, a telescope was visible, propped up on the patio of the highest floor, facing our hotel. At the time, there were no structures between the buildings like there are today, and he'd had a bird's-eye view. "Since I already know you, sort of, would you like to come over and meet my roommate?" he asked with a good-natured laugh.

Here's the part that will forever make me cringe. Jill stepped back, and I stepped forward. I was oblivious to the danger; in fact, I was pretty much saying, "Bring it on," while Jill recoiled from it.

Sisters

I wish now that I had allowed my sister to save me that afternoon, but at the time, I didn't want to be saved. I never even knew I was in harm's way until years into the future when I needed to escape from a life that was systematically and brutally breaking my spirit and damaging my trust.

I didn't know I was starting a descent when I accepted the invitation to meet Jerry and his roommate, Ben, that day. They told me that when they first met, they found out that they'd been born on the same day in the same year in the same hospital. "What if they switched us at birth?" Ben said, smiling. "What if Jerry is the heir to my family's fortune instead of me?"

He told me he had decided to take Jerry into his penthouse, have him as a confidante, and give him access to his riches. I listened, rapt, to their story, which they took turns telling, moving so seamlessly from one to the other that it was more like a performance. They had obviously told it many times before, but if they were making the whole thing up, which was a strong possibility, it really didn't matter. I was hooked, and I didn't feel the danger when I slept with Jerry that night, the first time I'd ever had sex with a man on the first date. It was also the last. I wonder why I so willingly gave myself to this self-admitted Peeping Tom who lived in a seventeenth-floor penthouse that his roommate, Ben, paid for, complete with a six-foot-six Jamaican butler named Rashan who served breakfast each morning on a silver tray.

I just didn't know the kind of darkness that abided in Jerry. I wonder if he even knew, this man who had his pick of his roommate's extraordinary car collection. Ben was an odd combination of a big spender and an agoraphobic, and the more Jerry drove his roommate's cars around town and showed up at parties and clubs, the better Ben liked it. While this kind of life was heady, luxurious, and over-the-top, an irresistible draw for many women, I cared little for the cars and the other accoutrements. My crime was not one of lust or greed. My crime was in wanting someone, anyone, to make me feel beautiful and desirable and to have the means to take care of me.

I became dependent on Jerry almost immediately. Although I'd been running my own show, traveling the globe, and living by myself since I was fourteen, I hadn't lived in the real world. I had stayed safe in the fold of the ballet, dedicated to my art and my training and loyal to my disciplined lifestyle. Beyond that, I knew nothing about straight men and the ways of the street, and so I clung to Jerry, masked lord of the underworld, a shameless liar and a guileful manipulator who had grown up playing stickball on the streets of Brooklyn. He seemed to know all the right things to say and do, and I took my cues from him as I struggled to make my way in a world that was not defined by ballet classes, pink tights, pointe shoes, and tutus.

I was wildly naive, and it didn't help that Jerry compared me incessantly to his former wife, who had apparently been a saint of some sort.

If she was so perfect, I wondered, why did they break up? According to him, I didn't cook as well as she did, I didn't dress as well as she did, and I was devastated to overhear him telling his brother on the phone that my blow jobs did not measure up to those of his ex. Yes, he was rude and disgusting, and all of these things were warning signs, but I was a needy woman and a slow learner, since I had arrived at the party late. I had done next to no socializing and no dating when I was in the ballet, so I had no experience to fall back on, no mentor to take my hand and save my soul as I dove headfirst into the fray.

Jerry dressed me up like a doll in expensive clothing, put jewelry around my neck, wrists, earlobes, and finally on the fourth finger of my left hand, as he showed me off, wining and dining me at a different restaurant every night. I had no idea I was sleeping with the enemy, a street hustler, a shyster, a retired thief, and a dangerous control freak. But there were signs, like the time Jerry tried to teach me to drive a car. I had lived in New York and traveled the world as a ballerina, so I really didn't need to drive. I was nineteen when Jerry and I got into the car for my first driving lesson. I drove straight for a while, forgot to stop at a STOP sign once, and then twice, when he began to yell, demanding I pull the car over. As soon as I stopped the engine, he laid into me. "For most people, learning to drive is a piece of cake," he said, "but there are a few people who can't do it. They just can't get it right. You're one of those."

I went to driving school and managed to get my license, but Jerry never missed an opportunity to put me down or tell me what I should do. "A woman needs to be there for her man whenever he wants sex," he told me.

I nodded my head and did as I was told, as he charged my new floor-length fox fur coat and diamond earrings on his roommate's credit card. I didn't know the extent of his self-hatred, the way his parents had abused him and his brother, or that his two favorite uncles, one by birth, the other by affection, had done jail time and currently fenced stolen property out of their jewelry store in Beverly Hills. When we went to The Roxy on Sunset to hear the latest rock-and-roll band, or The Climax on La Cienega, a dance club that opened at midnight and closed at six in the morning, I thought it was funny when Jerry pretended to be his roommate, Ben, tipping the valets with hundred-dollar bills and chatting up the waitresses with hits of cocaine. Most of all, I had no conception that giving up my heart and my innocence to fit into Jerry's dark and destructive world was leaving me empty and broken.

Drugs were one of the catalysts that took me by surprise and left me with irreparable damage. I started out innocently enough with a little pot smoking here and there. Then it was every day, and then Jerry began badgering me to try some cocaine. I resisted at first, but soon enough, I was sniffing copious amounts of white powder, swallowing quaaludes, and losing myself and everything I valued in the process. In a short period of time, I was in a living hell, hardly sleeping, barely eating, bone thin, spending most of my time with drug dealers and hard-rock musicians, snorting as much cocaine as I could get my hands on. During that time, I hate to admit that I lied and stole, taking hits of coke from friends who left their stashes lying around like an invitation—as if they knew I would help myself when they walked out of the room, which I did.

I wrote poetry, my form of journaling about the crazy drug-filled reality in which I lived, but deep down, between the lines and rhymes that filled the pages, were my bloodcurdling screams to be rescued. When I read through my poems now, I can hear my pleas for help disguised in lyrical descriptions of the way pharmaceutical cocaine floated upward when you blew on it, what great music my friends made between inhaling substances of different sorts, and how tingly and sensual I felt when I took a quaalude.

I also continued to do my crafts, knitting beautiful garments and making fringed leather bags and hand-laced book and script covers, which seemed like a saving grace. But I needed a much deeper kind of saving as I walked the edge of life and death. One time Jerry choked me so hard, his hands firmly gripping the tender skin around my neck, I realized that I had allowed it to go too far, that I might not return from this one. I didn't die that day, but I sustained serious damage to my neck as several tendons popped painfully when I turned my head in a particular direction, and still the psychological pain was worse.

After we got married one afternoon in Las Vegas on a whim, I realized I had sealed my fate. We were getting along so well right then, when Jerry proposed and suggested we tie the knot at the town hall in Vegas where we were vacationing, I went along with it. I just couldn't face what Jerry would become if I refused, which is what I meant when I said I married Jerry because I was afraid not to, and it all went downhill from there. Big surprise, right?

I remember one night when we were loaded, Jerry chased me around the house with a pair of police-issue handcuffs, threatening to call the cops on me. I managed to get one of my friends on the phone, but before I could ask for help, Jerry grabbed the receiver. In a cool and soothing voice, the devil personified, he told the friend that I was going crazy, I had taken too many drugs, and he was trying to calm me down. No, he didn't need any help, he assured the concerned person on the other end of the line. He had it covered, but if he needed anything, he'd be sure to let him know.

This kind of relationship could move in only one direction—downward and inward, until it imploded hard and fast, breaking me into a million pieces. The details of how I broke are not important. They are filled with physical and emotional abuse, imprisonment in a glass cell, manipulation of the worst kind, near-death misses, fear-filled nights, and large amounts of toxic drugs—the familiar story that often ends in an overdose or death. What matters is that I descended blindly and swiftly into the underworld of drugs and darkness, where I was raped, battered, demeaned, and disrespected in every way possible. Where were the sylphs and devas now, the glittering spirit forms that had shape-shifted outside my window when I was a child and kept me safe? Had they abandoned me or had I abandoned them?

I ran away once for a couple of days, but I might as well have stayed. I talked with Jerry on the phone a few times, and he told me he was house hunting. He was sure if we moved, things would get better. On the third day, he called me and said, "You have to come home now. I found a new house, and we have marble floors."

I moved back in—not because of the marble floors, which were cold and a pain in the ass to keep clean. I went back because Jerry cried and pleaded with me to come home, assuring me that things would be different. He would never hurt me again, he swore. I deserved better. It was true, I did deserve better, but a battered wife is not free, even if she has her own car keys and a group of friends. Whether the door to her cell is wide open or locked shut, whether she is alone or in a group, she remains imprisoned in an invisible cage, the glass walls sturdily built out of terror, shame, guilt, and self-loathing.

By the time I had done close to irreparable damage to my spirit, my self-confidence, and the inside of my nose, I broke the glass and made my exit in a mad dash. It could easily have turned out differently, but I was one of the lucky ones.

It was late one afternoon, neither of us had slept the night before, and Jerry was punching my upper arms as hard as he could, yelling that if I left him, I would end up in the gutter. I sat on the bed, absorbing the blows one after the other until he finally stopped. He looked exhausted, resting his hands beside him, panting to catch his breath, when I pulled back my arm and landed my right fist as hard as I could into the center of his face. The impact sent him staggering backward, and he fell to the floor. His hands flew up to his eye, and I stood and ran. It was over. I wanted to be anywhere else, even the gutter would do, as I rushed down the stairs to the driveway, started up my car, and drove away.

I never went back to him, and I left all of my things behind. I made a clean break and disappeared for a year with the help of a mechanic friend, who gave me one of his green work jumpsuits to wear because my clothes were bloody. An artist friend hid me first on a houseboat in Sausalito and then in a ranch house in the desert in the middle of a date grove. I called no one, not even a girlfriend, for fear that if Jerry ever found me, he would kill me or the man who had rescued me. And I began walking the long and rocky road back to sanity, vowing I would never return to the underworld again.

I kept my promise, nursing myself back to health, healing the outer wounds that I sustained from so much battering and fighting back. But it would be years before I found an outlet for healing the internal invisible wounds that this relationship had caused me. It began when an Academy Award–winning movie star left the following message on my answering machine: "Hello, Andrea. I'm an actress, and I read your book. I'd like to meet you. Please call me. Here's my name and number."

She was referring to the first book I ever wrote, *Awakening the Healer Within,* based on my many healing odysseys to the Philippines that began a couple of years after I left Jerry.

I was surprised that this accomplished actress was calling me and stunned that she felt she needed to inform me as to what she did for a living. She had won an Oscar a few years prior, everyone knew who she was, and I recalled her walk to the podium to receive her award in an elegant, sequined, black lace gown. I was gratified and surprised that she had liked my book so much that she felt moved to find my phone number, call me, and ask me to return her call.

Olympia & Me

Our friendship was born that day, and it took many forms over the years to come as we discussed sex, men, relationships, and creativity; practiced Pilates with a common teacher; did some writing together; and shared dinners both in Los Angeles and New York. But what tied me to her utterly and irrevocably was a workshop that she and several other extraordinary female elders gave for a group of about ten women in which I learned that I could not and would no longer silence my voice in this world. I had found a way to start healing the terrible internal wounds that my relationship with Jerry had made, and I learned that as a woman, I needed to speak out about what I saw and knew, no matter how painful my truth or the perceived consequences.

This wise woman and her cofacilitators used a myth to support their teachings, featuring the mythical Mesopotamian goddess Inanna and her dark counterpart, Ereshkigal. In the myth, Inanna is drawn to the underworld, a form of hell, to seek wisdom and understanding. As she leaves the light-filled domains in order to gain entry to the underworld, she is forced to give up seven of her most precious gifts: her connection with heaven, her magical ability to manifest, her rapture of illumination, her emotional heart, her ego, her will, and her sexual powers.

She enters the underworld, naked and bowed, deflated and empty, where she self-destructs and becomes Ereshkigal, her counterpart. Now she is nothing more than a bloody corpse, a piece of rotten flesh hanging on a meat hook, hopeless, unable to save herself, trapped in a cage of her own making—until her sister, Innana, arrives to save her. She returns to the realms of light and goodness but is permanently stained by her foray into the underworld, no longer innocent. Along with her magical powers she now also embodies the primal qualities of rage, fury, greed, possessiveness, and self-hatred. She claims the right to survive, but she has been permanently changed, carrying the abysmal truth that attaining growth and wisdom demands unthinkable sacrifice.

My above explanation of the myth of Inanna is simplistic at best, but the work we all did was not. During several days, I struggled to retrieve the broken pieces of my psyche and fit them back together. I learned, amid the desperate sobs and triumphant screams and wails from various women in that room, all who had gone through their own version of suffering, that giving voice to my full expression was not only my birthright, it was my mission and, in a sense, my obligation to the world, to women in general, and to the time in which I lived. I would never again allow a man to hurt me, disrespect me, or get in the way of my true expression. I would speak my mind and my heart as I took communion with my soul. I was finally one, united with myself, determined never to be torn apart again.

Up to that time, Jerry had appeared in my dreams at intervals with a recurring theme. Always the villain in the story, he was cornering me, screaming at me, trapping me, and choking me, while he talked at me with such speed and intensity, I awakened terrified, holding on to my neck. I prayed for the dream to stop, and then I had it once again, several weeks after the workshop. This time, I was on a houseboat like the one where I'd hidden away, and there was Jerry, yelling at me, abasing me, and reaching for my neck. This time, however, I stood my ground, pushed him easily to the side, and walked away. I don't know if he watched me leave because I never looked back. I was finished with him, and I never dreamed about him again.

It was at least ten years and several best sellers later when I next heard from Jerry. He wanted to have lunch, he told my answering machine. Would I be willing to see him? To talk about a few things? The mere sound of his voice threw me into a state of PTSD. I wondered how it would feel to sit across from him at a restaurant. I had dated quite a few men since Jerry had waged war against me. While none of them were what I'd consider a good match for me, each of them seemed like prince charming in comparison.

I decided to have lunch with Jerry. I would do the courageous thing and face the villain. Friends told me that he had remarried and quit drugs and that he owned an antique store. That was all I knew about him when I arrived at the restaurant on Melrose Avenue where we had agreed to meet. He was already there, and when he got up to hug me, my appetite flew out the window like it had seen a ghost. I felt like following it, but I was there to see this thing through.

"You didn't get fat" was the first thing he said to me. Was he disappointed? Why had he even considered such a thing? Couldn't he have worded that differently?

"No, I didn't," I said and sat down. Jerry was uncomfortably thin, and time had not been kind to him. He was prematurely wrinkled, and he told me he had suffered a serious back ailment, a slipped disk that had caused him a great deal of pain and discomfort. I nodded and had very little to say about it as I pretended to read the menu. It was a marvel to me that I had awakened beside this man every morning for years, our lives and our bodies entwined, and I had wanted the best for him. Now, years later, he felt like a stranger to me. I couldn't remember what it felt like to have sex with him, I didn't want him to touch me, and I didn't care about his aching back. He boasted about his marriage and his bank account, but I didn't care whether or not he was happily married, I didn't care how much money he had, and I didn't care how he treated his current wife. I probably had been canonized to her like Jerry's ex was canonized to me. I expected that in my absence, according to Jerry, I'd become the greatest cook in the world, I'd dressed like a runway model, and I'd been the best lay he ever had. I pitied his current wife, but I was grateful that how he treated her was none of my business.

I ordered a turkey sandwich with fries. I have no recollection of what Jerry ordered as he began talking quickly, the same thing he'd always done, more so when he was nervous about something. Was he remembering the way he had treated me? Was he trying to find a way to apologize? To ask for forgiveness? I listened, the same thing I'd always done, wondering where this was going. It would have been nice if he'd wanted to say he was sorry, but it was unlikely as he waxed on about how great his life was, how many big celebrities bought his antiques, and how many exotic cars he had collected.

It all could have been true; he very well might have become a collector of Ferraris like he claimed. Jerry always had been good at acquiring material things, and he had been partial to Ferraris when I met him. And he might have been selling antiques to people like Michael Jackson, Cher, and Ann-Margret. This was Hollywood, after all, and his crooked uncles from Beverly Hills could easily have steered some wealthy celebrities in his direction. Still, I didn't necessarily believe what he was saying because he always had been prone to exaggerating. If he had found a thousand dollars in cash in the street, he would have told everyone he'd found double the amount. He was that kind of guy.

I was getting bored and exhausted pretty fast when the waitress brought our orders. I was wishing he'd get to the point and say what he had to say, when he began to talk about me. He said he'd heard I had a new career, that I was writing for a living, and he wondered if I was doing any writing about the past. And wasn't I glad that neither of us did drugs anymore?

So there it was. Jerry was afraid that I was writing about him, about us, about the terrible things he had said and done. That was why he had asked me to lunch—not to apologize, but to make sure he was safe from possible shame or embarrassment.

He began grappling for words. He was becoming tongue-tied as I sat up straighter. I began to feel in control, and my appetite came roaring back. While Jerry hemmed and hawed, trying to get me to discuss my writing career, I gave him one-word answers and began to eat. His incessant chatter was picking up steam, but to me, his voice was getting softer and softer, and the only thing that interested me was my turkey sandwich—and the fries, which were cooked just how I like them, crisp on the outside and soft in the middle. I interrupted his gibberish to ask him to pass the mayonnaise, which I didn't really like, but the sandwich needed something. I spread a little mayo on the bread, took a big bite, and told him how good it was.

When I ponder Jerry's attempt to save himself from the written word, my written word, I remember dating a guy for a short time who was so freaked out by intimacy that when he decided to get a pet, he asked the pet shop owner which animal was likely to die the soonest so he wouldn't be stuck taking care of it for too long. He bought two hamsters, guaranteed to have short life spans. Unbeknownst to him, one of them was pregnant, and then there were six. He returned them all to the pet store pretty quickly. One night soon after, when we were having dinner, he asked me, "Are you ever going to write about me? I wish you would. Please write about me."

"You'll be lucky if I don't," I told him.

Jerry would be lucky if I didn't write about him either, but unlike Hamster Boy, Jerry knew it. He *wanted* to be left out. He was praying to be left out, looking for reassurance that I would leave the past in the past. He wanted me to forget about his meanness and his drug-fueled behavior. He wanted me to assure him that whatever he'd said or done so many years ago, I would let bygones be bygones, that I would not embarrass him publicly, remind him about or reveal what he had done, or hold anything against him.

He didn't come right out with it though. He didn't ask me directly, so he didn't get what he wanted. Which means that I didn't reassure him. When we parted company, he must have been frustrated, but I felt empowered by my new position in life that gave me a platform to say what I wanted to say and to expose what I wanted to expose. I dedicate this chapter, then, to Jerry, who most likely won't read this book because reading was never his strong suit. If someone else gives it to him and he reads this chapter, he can assume I forgave him since I did him the ultimate kindness by changing his name. Apart from the name, though, this is the whole truth, nothing but, and I feel redeemed that he knows who he is, even if nobody else does.

Chapter Six

THE CAPTAIN

All our dreams can come true,

if we have the courage to pursue them.

— Walt Disney

I was alone when I stepped onto the stage in the empty theater. I could sense apparitions from the forties hovering like breezes that never blew away: the director planning his shots; the sound man listening intently under his headphones; the cameraman choosing his light angles; the gaffers and gofers; the makeup and wardrobe people doing what they'd been hired to do as the star of the movie pirouetted from one side of the stage to the other, her red satin pointe shoes gleaming in the spotlight.

She was ballet dancer/actor Moira Shearer, the star of the 1948 classic movie *The Red Shoes*, parts of which had been shot on the opera house stage in Monte Carlo, right where I was standing. Adapted from a Hans Christian Anderson fairy tale, *The Red Shoes* was about an up-and-coming ballerina who was given her first lead in a ballet in which her red pointe shoes were imbued with magical powers that would not allow her to stop dancing. I was particularly touched when, in the film, the ballet impresario asked the young woman during a rehearsal, "Why do you want to dance?"

"Why do you want to live?" was her answer.

At the end, torn between her love of the ballet and her love for a composer, with her red pointe shoes laced up and leading the way, in a moment of uncontrollable despair, she jumped to her death from a balcony overlooking the train station where her great love was about to board a train and leave her forever. Her dying words were, "Take off the red shoes." They were no longer of any use to her; the magic was gone, and she would never dance again. The film ended with the ballet company performing *The Red Shoes*, a spotlight following the empty space where the ballerina would have danced.

It was 1963, and I was sixteen, a member of the Harkness Ballet Company, when I stood on that stage. A few hours earlier, our plane had landed in Monaco, where the company would be rehearsing and performing, and I went straight to the theater. I walked upstage and down, envisioning the making of the production that had been shot the year before I was born, that had so inspired me when I was a very young girl with big dreams. I looked out at the empty chairs upholstered in red velvet in the ornate opera house located in the legendary Monte Carlo casino with its marble-paved atrium, ionic columns of onyx, and the opera house itself decorated in red and gold with bas-reliefs and sculptures.

As a child, that movie had been real for me—not so much the plot, which described a woman torn, having to choose between her love of the ballet and her love of a man. I'd been too young to fully comprehend that kind of choice, and really, it was no longer necessary; women were finding ways to have it all. But the dancing part was real for me, as were the beauty of the costumes, the red satin pointe shoes, and the choreography that Moira Shearer performed, technically perfect and artistically breathtaking.

I stood quietly gazing out into the empty opera house as tears welled up in my eyes and ran down my cheeks. I had made it. I had lived the ballet, eaten it, drunk it, and dreamed it since I was young, inspired by the classic movie. Now I was there, right where it had been shot, living my dream. I would remain in Monte Carlo with the other members of my ballet company during the next year, renting my own flat, passing by the tracks of the train station that was no longer in use, rehearsing in the underground studios of the casino, performing for Princess Grace and Prince Rainier in an international music festival, and visiting all the locations of the movie that had underscored my young life.

Everyone has a dream, whether or not we ever bring it to fruition or even remember what it was, as life evolves. I wrote a book in the year 2000 for a South African long-distance cycling champion who had realized his dream of creating an indoor cycling training program that would prepare athletes for the rigor of riding on the road. I interviewed him multiple times, surprised and gratified by his rare gesture of inviting me to be the sole author on the cover of his book, since I was doing the writing. For this project, I had graduated from being a "With" to being a "By."

In the book, he explained the kind of freedom that bicycles had symbolized to him when he was growing up. Among many other life experiences, he offered his readers a detailed account of the revolutionary training method called "Spinning," which he had created while recuperating from a failed attempt at a long-distance race in 1987. It was called The Race Across America, an arduous ten-day, 3100-mile cycling competition from Los Angeles to New York City. He had burned out a couple of hundred miles from the finish line, where he had stopped, unable to keep pedaling. As he lay on his back for several months afterward, trying to heal, he came to understand that although his body was wracked and exhausted, it was not a physical problem that had stopped him from reaching his goal. He had stopped because his mind and spirit had failed. He needed to find a way to strengthen his mental faculties and spiritual resolve in order to finish the race. Out of that desire, he invented the concept of this indoor training method he called "Spinning ™," which would be practiced on a customized stationary racing bike with a weighted flywheel in order to emulate outdoor road cycling. Training on this bike would allow riders to alternate between high and low resistance, to sprint as if they were cycling in the flats, to climb as if they were on a hill, to jump in and out of the saddle repeatedly to strengthen their quadriceps and increase their endurance, and to close their eyes while they pedaled, meditating on their breath and their heartbeat.

The idea for his invention was inspired by the rugged, violent sport of "roller racing" in South Africa, where he lived before he came to the United States. When the weather became prohibitively cold for outdoor training, dedicated cyclists would drag a piece of equipment into a bar: a set of rollers that looked like a treadmill about a foot and a half in width with a speedometer, a distance gauge, and three very slippery drums—two at the back and one at the front with a band that linked the wheels.

After downing way too many beers, the men took turns balancing a bicycle on top of the rollers, jumping on, and pedaling as hard and fast as they could. While onlookers placed bets on who could go the longest and the farthest, the rider pedaled his heart out, doing his damnedest not to get thrown, similar to riding an electric bull. The sound was fearsome when a man went flying off the rollers and crashed into the walls. He numbed the pain by downing more beer. When the weather changed, they abandoned this indoor sport and went back outside to ride once again, a lot worse for the wear.

And so, Spinning was born, along with the first prototype of a bike called a Spinner. Once it was introduced publicly, the popularity of this sport mushroomed so fast and furiously that it was adopted by a large number of gyms, both nationally and internationally, in the first few years. Each teacher puts his or her personal "spin" on the training, sometimes a far cry from what the athlete originally had in mind. But whether it is presented as an aerobic exercise or a moving meditation technique, it remains popular to this day, a dream that was manifested through dedication and stamina.

The simple word "spinning" transports me to my childhood, when I immersed myself in fairy tales like *Sleeping Beauty*, who pricks her finger on a spinning wheel and drops into a slumber that lasts for a hundred years. In *Rumplestiltskin*, an imp-like creature magically spins straw into gold. The training exercise Spinning, which I practiced under its creator's tutelage, was also magical for me, as I learned how to create the illusion of high-speed motion on a stationary racing bike, indoors, with my eyes closed, in a meditative state.

Embracing this training method designed to prepare cyclists for the road was ironic for me because I'd never ridden a bicycle. I had no interest in being on the road. During my childhood, when the rest of the kids took their training wheels off their bicycles and rolled down the street on their own steam for the first time, I avoided it. A young girl on my block had had a bike accident, and I'd been traumatized by seeing her humerus bone sticking out of her arm and hearing her bloodcurdling screams as they carted her away. I left bike riding to other people—my parents never pushed me into it—and although I did manage to get on a bike once as an adult and ride it down the path in Venice Beach just to prove to myself that I could do it, I never got comfortable with it. That was all the more reason that I was attracted to Spinning, where I could recreate the sensation of riding a bike without actually doing it. My muscles got stronger, and my endurance increased as I trained diligently with the cycling champion while I wrote for him, continuing my training long after the book was finished.

In 2002, before he departed Los Angeles to live in Santa Barbara permanently with his family, I upped my training and entered his twelve-hour Spinning challenge, which I managed to complete with a couple of short breaks. He led this charity event, his last hurrah in Los Angeles, by riding his own Spinning bike on a stage in front of the rest of us all day long, intermittently soothing, goading, and encouraging us to push our limits and keep on Spinning from eight o'clock in the morning until eight o'clock at night. I was no stranger to discipline and hard work because of my ballet days, and I took on the task with enthusiasm. I trained diligently throughout the year. I was triumphant in the final attempt, and it will forever remain a treasured memory. When it was over, those of us who had finished the twelve-hour race that went nowhere collapsed into a pile on the stage and lay there on top of each other, smiling, too exhausted to talk.

A few days after the challenge, I was sitting with the athlete and his wife just before they were scheduled to leave town, when he said to me, "You didn't need to train so hard. You could have finished that ride with less effort."

I smiled at him and said, "Finishing the ride wasn't enough for me. I wanted to get strong enough to enjoy it all along the way, and I did." He and I both understood that it had required consistency and an elevated level of fitness.

During our interviews for the book, among our many discussions and debates was the difference between the terms "discipline" and "consistency." For me, "discipline" was a hard word, suggesting a rigid structure that one took on with unswerving diligence, steadiness, and fortitude, staying on track when the going got rough, never veering off the path. It described a kind of impeccable focus, where a person never stopped until the goal was reached. I can still recall mornings way back when my mind tried to seduce me into skipping my ballet practice—just for today—but I didn't succumb. The constant internal debate—should I or shouldn't I, will I or won't I—was like a distant voice yakking in my ear as I used my discipline to get me to class and rehearsals each day, committed to my career and dedicated to the training that came along with it. While I couldn't stop my mind from engaging in the debate, I used my discipline to keep it at bay, as if I were listening to somebody else's argument.

"Consistency," on the other hand, was a softer word that suggested allowance and surrender, a way of transcending the battle altogether. It seemed to me that after a while, discipline flowed into consistency as a natural progression. After I had danced for many years, and I was consistent with my training; at some point, the struggle ended and the flow took its place as I showed up to practice every day as naturally as my eyes opened in the morning. I no longer had to drown out the inner struggle because there *was* no struggle. I simply embraced my practice as surely as the sun rose in the morning and set in the evening.

During my ballet years, it took healthy doses of both discipline and consistency to become successful. Really, nothing was ever harder physically, mentally, or spiritually. When we went on our tortuous one-night stand tours for weeks on end, we had a bus for the forty or so dancers, a truck for the costumes and pointe shoes (as many as eighty customized pairs for each woman), and another bus for the forty-piece orchestra that went everywhere with us. We arrived at a new city almost every day and we rehearsed, performed, slept, and got up to get back on the bus.

But there were sweetnesses along with the trials. On a ten-week, fifty-city tour, I struck up a friendship with the lead clarinet player, who managed to find a rose in each city where we performed and give it to me while I was putting on my makeup. Then there was my friend Lar, who bought each new Beatles release when it came out and sat in the dressing room with me while we listened to it for the first time on a ghetto blaster. And of course, there was the incomparable joy of performing choreography to glorious music that elevated my soul and made me happy to be alive. There was also the feeling of being different in the best kind of way, surpassing the mundane and spending time in the highest echelons of personal achievement. There was all of that, and still, the physical demands, the punishing repetition of practice, rehearsal, and more practice were unequalled.

On the other hand, during my short and unexpected stint as an actor after I'd stopped dancing, the resolve required to step onto a set and perform in front of the camera was almost ludicrous by comparison. I'm not saying that acting didn't have its unique challenges and obstacles. I needed self-confidence, endurance, and the ability to immerse myself in the character I was playing, but I never needed the same kind of relentless discipline. I had that down, because when you perform on stage, there are no redoes. You have to get it right the first time or suffer the humiliation. Making movies was so much more forgiving. If you put your foot in the wrong place or flubbed a line, there were retakes and camera tricks to hide certain things and to illuminate others. Even the day-long audition for my first movie in 1969 stands in stark contrast to the day-long audition that was required to become a member of the Harkness Ballet in the sixties, about four years prior.

Imagine this: In response to a newspaper ad in 1964, my mother and I leave Hartford, Connecticut, before first light to show up in New York City at nine o'clock at a theater on Broadway that's freezing cold and poorly lit. In the company of a load of other girls, I use a makeshift dressing room to change into my practice gear, a pair of pink tights, a black leotard, and a thin black sweater that adds no bulk to my sixteen-year-old body and provides as little warmth. Putting on a pair of soft pink ballet shoes with elastic sewn across the arch and carrying with me a pair of pink pointe shoes with satin ribbons, I am one of 250 hopefuls who crowd the table in the lobby where several assistants are taking names and giving out numbers with stick'em on the back. Once we've registered and pasted our numbers on the fronts of our leotards, we walk into the theater, where a group of instructors and producers are seated side by side in the center of the ninth row, facing the stage. We can see only the backs of their heads, and rumor has it that among them is Rebekah Harkness herself, founder of the Harkness Ballet. No one tells us how many dancers are needed. It could be one or fifty.

The overhead lights are off, and several large spotlights are switched on and pointed at the stage, arranged so that they light up the contenders from head to toe while keeping the faces of our deciders in the dark. According to our assigned numbers, we're broken up into groups of twenty-five, the first group stepping onto the stage and taking their designated places. The rest of us scatter around the theater, hovering close to our parents, awaiting our turns, avoiding each other's glances, doing our best to warm up in the chilly air, using an arm of a seat as a ballet barre, doing what we can to control and direct the adrenaline shooting through our young bodies.

A ballet teacher stands at the front of the stage, leading each group through a few preliminary exercises, at the end of which are eliminations.

The first to go are the ones who are untrained and unable to perform or remember the most perfunctory exercises. After eight separate groups have performed and we are initially culled, about half of us remain to continue the audition.

No one leaves the theater for lunch, as if stepping out for even a moment might ruin our chances or bar us from coming back in. During the thirty-minute break, we eat what we've brought from home: a sandwich, some fruit, a few carrot sticks, whatever is the least bloating but might give us a little energy. I've brought some raw vegetables and a few apple slices, which I force myself to eat because I'm not the slightest bit hungry.

Throughout the afternoon, the remaining dancers are broken up into smaller and smaller groups as we are put through various routines, some *en pointe*, some modern dance, and a little jazz to see if we have the ability to remember the steps, follow directions, and adapt to various styles. This is important because the Harkness Ballet is a contemporary ballet company open to experimentation and diversity.

By early afternoon, I've managed to remain standing while others have been eliminated on all sides of me. "Falling like flies" is the apt cliché. And equally apt is "crying like babies" when contenders are let go. The eliminations are brutal as they call out the unlucky dancers by number, each of us praying *not* to hear our number being called. I go from style to style, hardly remembering how many times I've been on the stage, dancing my heart out, feeling relief when several people in my group are sent home and I'm still there. And then I feel almost guilty when at three in the afternoon, girls on either side of me are told to gather their things and leave. I'm sure I can't bear it any longer now that our ranks are so diminished and each routine we go through feels final and deadly. But I keep on going for two more hours.

It's about five o'clock in the evening when I am among six dancers standing in one line, side by side. The faceless judges in the darkened theater seem to be buzzing among themselves as we all stand there, not looking at each other, feeling the dread of yet another upcoming elimination, when a teacher steps up onto the stage. "This is it," she says. "Congratulations! You made it."

We look at her face to make sure she means it. Then we shyly look beside us, breaking into smiles as we nod at each other. We have something in common. We have passed the audition, and we will all be working together. The overhead lights in the theater are switched on for the first time all day, and they blind me. When my vision clears, I can see the faces in the row of directors, including a blond woman I am sure is Mrs. Harkness—something about the way the others are treating her, deferring to her as she gets up first and begins to leave. Squinting, I look out at the audience to scan the few remaining parents seated at the back of the theater. When I find my mother there, smiling broadly, I smile back. I'm exhausted, but it's over. I've made it. My old life is ending, and a new life is beginning.

Now compare that to this: It's 1969, at one o'clock in the morning (I'm nineteen), when my boyfriend, Jerry, and I walk into Sneaky Pete's on the Sunset Strip, an old-world Italian restaurant where Hollywood types mingle with tourists after hours. Rumor had it that a week earlier, John Lennon and his bud Harry Nilsson had gotten very drunk, caused a scene at the bar, and were asked to leave. Tonight, Jerry orders the surf and turf, I order a filet mignon, and he heads to the men's room while I remain at our table, listening to the piano player, tapping out the rhythms on my empty dinner plate.

"Excuse me," someone says. "May I speak to you?"

A polite man in a straight-looking business suit stands beside me. "Yes," I say.

"Are you an actress?"

"No, I'm a ballet dancer."

"Well," he says, "I'm a film producer, and you look perfect for a role in my movie that we're shooting in San Diego. I auditioned women all day today, and no one was right. We're already in production, and we lost our leading lady. She kept arriving on the set drunk and stoned." He pulls a business card from his inside jacket pocket and begins to write something on it. At that moment, Jerry returns to the table, and I say sarcastically, "This is Mark. Give us a minute. I'm being discovered."

It doesn't escape either Jerry or me that this clichéd approach in the wee hours of the morning reeks of being a Hollywood casting-couch scam, but I'm intrigued. I go to the audition the next morning anyway, with Jerry in tow so there can be no hanky-panky. We are the only ones there as an assistant ushers Jerry and me into the back room. Mark, the producer I met the night before, dressed much more casually, hands me a couple of script pages. I read them silently and then, with Mark taking the male role, we read them out loud together. When we're finished, he asks me to wait while he walks into an adjoining room to make a phone call.

He is gone for about five minutes. When he comes back, he asks me, "Can you drive out to San Diego right now?" He says he likes me for the film, a Vietnam protest movie (it's 1969, and the war is on) called *Captain Milkshake,* and the role is a hippy girl named Melissa in her early twenties. Captain Milkshake? I have no idea what that means, and I don't ask. This is all too surreal, especially since Mark is asking Jerry to drive me straight to the San Diego set a couple of hours away, where they're shooting, and read for the director and the leading man. I've never acted in my life, but I decide to give it a go.

I'm scheduled to fly back to New York later that afternoon to start rehearsals the next day for a new set of performances. We're preparing for our first season in New York at a Broadway theater, a pivotal run since the New York critics are the toughest and can make or break a ballet company. I'll get in trouble for missing even one day of rehearsals, but I boldly cancel my flight anyway, and Jerry and I drive the two hours. I have on a pair of denim shorts and a white T-shirt, and when we walk onto the set, I feel underdressed and deeply intimidated. I've never been on a movie set before as an actor or an observer, but I've been a performer for years, and as anxious as I feel, I know how to fake it. Feigning confidence on a movie set, I discover quickly, is far easier than covering up extreme pain or performing on no food and almost no sleep, all of which I am familiar with. I get in touch with a kind of abandon as I am defiantly breaking the ballet rules to which I've adhered faithfully since I first joined my company three years earlier.

When I meet Richard, the director, and Geoff, the leading man, something in me relaxes. They are not foreboding at all. In fact, they seem to really want me to do well as I begin the day-long audition. The main difference is that I'm not competing with anyone, and what a day it turns out to be! Before I read the same lines I read with Mark that morning, Geoff takes me aside and says, "Just read it like we're talking. OK?"

We practice a few times, I get used to answering to the name Melissa, and after we've read for the director, he suggests that Geoff and I get into his car. Jerry comes along for the ride, and we spend the rest of the day cruising from one beautiful venue to the next. The weather is fine as we stop at the seashore in La Jolla, where Geoff and I run through the tides and walk along the beach. We go to a lake in Balboa Park, where we climb up onto a raised cement wall and watch our reflections in the lotus pond just below us. We go to the San Diego Zoo, where we "goof off" together, looking at animals and talking to some people in our immediate area. We end up in front of a Baskin Robbins 31 Flavors ice cream parlor, where Richard directs me to say something silly or amusing to the merchant. I walk inside and ask him if I can have all thirty-one flavors on one cone, please. We all laugh and leave the ice cream parlor holding two-scoop ice cream cones, laughing and teasing each other all the way back in the car.

Before Jerry and I leave for Los Angeles, I explain to Richard that I have no time to waste, that if he chooses me, I will have to ask for a two-month leave of absence from the ballet company, and I'll have to do it first thing in the morning. They are expecting me. He has no extra time either, Richard assures me. The film is in production, and they're on a tight budget and a deadline. They'll let me know as soon as we get back to Los Angeles. After the two-hour drive, we've been at Jerry's penthouse no longer than fifteen minutes when the phone rings. I stare at Jerry, and he gestures for me to pick it up. "Hello?" I say.

"Is this Melissa speaking?" the voice at the other end asks.

Once again, it's over. I've made it. My old life is ending, and a new life is beginning.

I called New York first thing the next morning to speak to the Harkness Ballet artistic director. I'd had a sleepless night, excited about the start of my film career and in dread about this phone call. I had always been a good little ballet dancer; I didn't make waves; I was on time, good-natured, and dependable. But not today.

"Hi, Larry," I said, stumbling over my words. "I'm in Los Angeles, and you know what? I auditioned for the lead in a movie yesterday. I really did, and I got it. I mean they want me for the movie. Can you believe it? I start this afternoon, that is, if I can stay here in Los Angeles. I want to know if I can have a two-month leave of absence from the company to star in this movie. It won't take much longer than that. At least they don't think so. I'd really like to do it."

Larry must have thought I'd lost my marbles somewhere on the Sunset Strip, and he refused to give me the time off. He deemed it "out of the question," partly because of the importance of the performance season we were facing, but also because he didn't want to set a bad example for the other dancers. "What if someone else decides to go on an audition and thinks she can take time out of rehearsals if she gets lucky?" he asked me. "Where does that leave the company?"

Being a member of a ballet company is like being a soldier or a professional ball player. First and foremost is the team, then come the leaders, who command great respect. And there are tons of rules and regulations. No way can someone waltz away for a couple of months to do something fun and think she can just come back and pick up where she left off with no harm done. I could see Larry's point. I understood all too well what it took to be a member of a unified group where we all depended on each other as we rehearsed, performed, and traveled together, working toward the same goals.

Rehearsing

I knew how it felt to support someone who had sustained an injury and needed me, her understudy, to take over. I also knew how it felt to support someone who had just gotten a role that I desperately wanted. I could see why a leave of absence was inappropriate for so many reasons—so I quit the company. Just like that.

After dancing and performing all my life, enduring constant criticism and injuries, getting teased about having large breasts, rare among ballet dancers, and dancing till I dropped, quite literally, I walked away that Monday morning, abandoning one dream for another as I remained in California, broke my ballet contract, broke my mother's heart, got thrown out of the dancers' union (AGMA), joined the Screen Actors Guild, and embarked on a new life and a new career in a new city. And I began calling Jerry's penthouse home. All in one day. I never looked back. Why should I? I was about to become a movie star, have my face plastered on the big screen all across the country, and live in a gorgeous home on top of the world with a butler and a maid and someone who said he loved me. Who could walk away from that?

In the film, a Vietnam vet named Paul with a case of PTSD is on a three-day leave to help his mother bury her husband, his stepfather, after which he has to return to the war. A pot-smoking hippy girl named Melissa who lives in a commune meets him at the airport, gives him a ride home, and shows up at the funeral for his stepfather. She and Paul become lovers. During his three-day leave, Melissa introduces Paul to her friends and to the antiwar effort in which she is deeply involved, and their love affair flourishes as he begins to question his participation in the war.

It doesn't have a happy ending. Nothing did back then during the drawn-out Vietnam conflict that lasted from 1959 to1975. Despite the odd title, *Captain Milkshake*, the movie was serious, and the issues raised were provocative, as was my wardrobe, because I was never allowed to wear a bra. As a ballerina, I was accustomed to having my chest flattened and tucked into tight-fitting costumes, wearing tons of exotic makeup with my hair plastered down, the excess pulled into a tight bun at the back of my head.

In contrast, Melissa, the role I was about to play, was a free-wheeling, breast-bouncing, hair-tossing, war-protesting, peace-loving kind of girl. Now, my breasts were being celebrated instead of being hidden. My character wore loose clothes, laughed a lot, and smoked pot every day, which couldn't have been more opposite to how I lived at the time. But I quickly embraced this life philosophy with the help of one of the original San Diego hippy families in the movie, who took me on as a project. They were bound and determined to get me high and keep me that way.

I'd smoked pot occasionally in New York over the last few years, but to these weed-ingesting, acid-dropping hippies in San Diego, Anchovy, Thesp, and Viv to name a few, I was the straight girl from New York who lacked any real pot-smoking experience. In their opinion, I needed to "get my head," as they called it, and they made sure to hand me a joint whenever I was in their vicinity. I only indulged when filming was over for the day. I couldn't risk being high during working hours because I needed to be crisp and clear. There were just so many new things to learn and memorize.

I have a favorite memento—a still photograph of my director, Richard, now a dear friend, and me when I first arrived on the set. We're sitting together on a bench, Richard is talking to me, and I'm staring at him, listening so hard I can almost see my brain receptors vibrating.

Richard & Me

I had so much to take in and remember—no hard blinking or moving frenetically during close-ups; no missing my mark, and no looking at it either; never looking directly into the camera, in fact, pretending the camera wasn't there at all; stopping in the middle of what might feel like a perfect take because of a technical problem and reshooting with enthusiasm and energy as if it was the first time; articulating my words without sounding tense or allowing the tone of my voice to rise unnaturally; matching my action from long shot to close-up. And on and on. Most of all, I needed to relate to my costar as if he were my lover, when in truth we had only just met.

After Richard and I finished whatever we'd been discussing in that photograph, I vaguely recall being shuffled off to the makeup trailer on my first day, taking off my bra, getting into my wardrobe, being made up, and having my hair brushed and fluffed around my face. I took to it all surprisingly naturally. Over the course of filming, I was never late to the set, and I rarely flubbed a line or missed a mark. While the dream of being a ballerina had been ethereal and idyllic, the act of striving to master ballet technique and enduring the daily physical demands of the craft for years on end had made me a hard-core realist. As a result, my focus and concentration were so highly developed, you could almost call me overqualified. I embraced my role completely. I did what the director told me to do; I leaned on my costar, Geoff, for trade secrets, support, and feedback; and I watched dailies to see how I looked and how I moved. I was OK with it all—until the first time I heard my voice played back.

The first scene I filmed took place in the "hippy pad," where I lived with a bunch of my pot-smoking friends. Paul was waiting in the living room, and I was brushing my hair in the bedroom and talking to Viv, who was nursing her baby. With my back to the camera, I got up, took off my denim cutoffs and my T-shirt, changed into a dress, and headed out into the living room to talk to Paul. All of that looked fine when they showed me a playback, but when Paul and I started to speak, and I heard my voice, I was appalled. I had no idea how my voice sounded, and I judged it as being so wrong, I was sure they were about to hand me my walking papers. I wouldn't have blamed them. But when I looked around, no one else seemed the slightest bit disturbed by my voice. I didn't say anything; I acted like it was OK, and I kept on going.

From the day I walked away from the ballet and began shooting the movie, my life started changing so much and so quickly, I could hardly recognize myself. It seemed like the film world at its worst was far more rewarding, appreciative, and supportive on a day-to-day basis than the ballet world at its best. In fact, it felt like I had gone from the Bates Motel to the Ritz. Back in New York, I had lived in a roach-infested, sparsely furnished, one-room, fifth-floor, walk-up apartment built over a corner café in the area that would become Soho several decades later. I did everything for myself there, from grocery shopping to cooking dinner, from sewing pointe shoe ribbons to washing out practice clothes. I took the bus or subway to the studio to rehearse each day, and I did the same thing in reverse when I was through.

In California, on the other hand, on weekends when we weren't shooting, I lived with Jerry in his roommate's Los Angeles seventeenth-floor penthouse with a maid and a butler who doubled as a chef. Jerry and I had dinner at wonderful restaurants like Chasen's or Le Dome. We usually spent the later part of the evening clubbing, and when we got home in the early hours of the morning, we would drop our clothes on the floor and fall into bed. When we woke up, the butler arrived at our bedside with eggs Benedict on a silver tray and freshly brewed coffee, and our clothes were already at the cleaner's. We got up, had breakfast, and then we started all over again.

Jerry drove me to San Diego each Sunday night in Ben's Silver Shadow Rolls Royce or the Ferrari he'd been driving when I first met him. I stayed on my own in a nice enough motel in La Jolla during the week, and I arrived at the makeup trailer early each morning, sipping coffee while someone made me up and fixed my hair. I kissed a man I hardly knew on the set pretty often (good thing I liked him), pretended to make love with him in front of the camera, and lolled around and shot the breeze with my fellow actors. I had breakfast when I was hungry and ate a catered lunch every day. I memorized a couple of pages of lines very quickly, tried to remember not to walk like a duck, and spent my free time reading books or taking walks. I liked everyone making a fuss over me, daubing at my face, checking my wardrobe, making sure I was happy, and complimenting me when a scene went well.

At the end of each day, when we wrapped, a professional costumer washed and ironed my wardrobe. I went to dinner with my fellow cast members at a nearby restaurant, took a look at my lines for the next day, got to sleep early, and got a hefty paycheck each week, more than four times the amount I'd made in the ballet. And I didn't have to stress over getting it right the first time. There were takes and retakes. I might try saying something one way and then another way to see what sounded and looked best. The luxury of retakes relaxed me and gave me a new-found confidence.

So did the fact that I knew my body inside and out. When we shot a nude scene in which Geoff and I smoked pot (we rolled up catnip in cigarette papers, and it made me sneeze) and we simulated sex, it took me some time to get used to being naked in front of a director, a camera-man, and a new friend, Geoff, who was becoming like a brother to me. But I wasn't plagued with the usual insecurities that nineteen-year-old women suffered. Granted, I wasn't convinced I was pretty enough to be a movie star. I hoped my makeup was good enough, and I wished that my cheekbones were higher and my eyelashes longer. But I didn't stress much about my body. I was an athlete with an athlete's body, and I had always been much more concerned with physical function, power, and endurance than I was with how I looked and how my clothes fit. My body was my ally, not my enemy. I knew I was in great shape, and I didn't fear how I looked from behind in my cutoff jeans. Or without them.

My days went relatively smoothly as I settled into my new life. Jerry was tame at this point because I was completely embroiled in my new career, and he stayed away during the weekdays. But I struggled at night with a number of recurring nightmares about my past life as a ballet dancer. I'd dream I was in an unfamiliar theater in a town I didn't know, it was show time, I was in the lobby, and I couldn't find the stage door. I'd rush round and round, trying the handles on a number of locked doors, while I could hear my music playing, and I couldn't figure out how to get to the stage. Or I'd be backstage, looking everywhere for my missing makeup case, trying to borrow some from someone else, but they didn't have the color shades that I needed. I might be standing in the wings and not know the steps to the ballet I was about to perform. Since sitting in costume had always been a no-no, I'd dream I was sitting on the floor in my tutu while the wardrobe lady raged and yelled at me.

Or I'd be in costume and makeup, tying my pointe shoe ribbons around my ankles and watching them come untied when I stepped onto the stage, the ribbons flapping, afraid that my shoes would fall off or that I'd trip myself or someone else.

These nightmares went on for years; the pressure of being a live performer had made a permanent stress indent in my psyche, and there was a great deal to unravel. But my movie, *Captain Milkshake*, was and still is a shining symbol of the sixties to my psyche, with its light shows, its energetic depiction of political activism so prevalent at the time, and its music from greats like Steve Miller and Country Joe. There was no stress attached, I loved the people involved, and it was and remains a dream come true.

About a year after we wrapped, when the editing was done, the movie was released in selected cities, mostly college towns. Students were deeply affected by its antiwar message, since many of them were losing their friends in the killing fields, or they were taking off to Canada to avoid the draft. But as enthusiastically as the film was received, it never enjoyed mass release because of a producers' quarrel over ownership. The struggle for the rights became a movie in itself, bizarre and unbelievable, where one of the men involved in the feud was taken out into the desert and shot. I kid you not. Richard was bereft, since he had loved this movie and put his heart and soul and all of his money into it. In the end, the movie itself was the victim, disappearing underground and surfacing many years later when Richard finally earned back the rights to his love child. He labeled it a revival film, rented theaters, and had private showings, and it earned acclaim in various international film festivals. It still does.

I have no film or video of myself as a ballet dancer. All I have are a few still photos from performances and the pictures that were printed in our souvenir programs. In the late sixties, we didn't use video as a study tool like athletes do today. Back then, we had to feel our way, study ourselves in the mirror, and trust other people's opinions about what we were good at and what we needed to master. But I have a copy of *Captain*

Milkshake, a DVD that I watch about once a year. I call it "hauling out the old Captain," which I do when I'm craving a sixties flashback or when I want to remember a magical time in my life when I lived my dream for an entire summer.

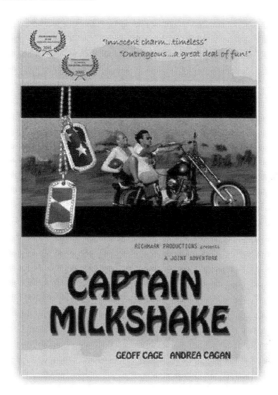

The Captain

When I first viewed the film, and for many years afterward, although I remembered how much I'd loved shooting it, I found quite a few scenes to be cringe-worthy. I had to walk out of the room or fast-forward through a strange facial expression here, an exaggerated hand gesture there, some awkward dialogue and some really bad acting on my part. But as time has passed, I've become kinder to myself, and my self-criticism has turned into appreciation.

My most stunning revelation when I view the movie these days is that when I was younger and was so busy judging my every move and everything I said and did, I was as lovely, pretty, graceful, and exciting as I wished I'd been. But I missed it. Too bad I couldn't see myself for who I really was when I was young and beautiful and fertile and filled with energy, light, and hope. Why did it take getting older to appreciate my youth? Why did it take getting wrinkles to appreciate the way my complexion used to look? Why did it take a sore hip and osteoarthritis to appreciate what it felt like to get up pain-free, eat whatever I wanted, and fall asleep at the end of an active day as soon as my eyes closed?

It's a real treat to see myself as a nineteen-year-old during the sixties, speaking her mind, making out with her boyfriend, tossing her hair, kicking up her heels, and running around San Diego, celebrating life and protesting the Vietnam War. I was happy during that period of time, but from what I've seen, happiness is a dicey concept. Feelings are fleeting, subject to chance and to change as they slip and slide and, like cloud formations, dissolve into a past yearning or a future desire when you least expect it. But when I allow myself to live the dream right now, whatever it is in this moment, fully embracing and acknowledging the hard-core reality of what it took to get there and what it will take to stay, I am deeply rewarded in this lifetime.

Chapter Seven

ISOLATION

Even the technology that promises to unite us, divides us.

Each of us is now electronically connected to the globe,

and yet we feel utterly alone.

— Dan Brown, *Angels & Demons*

Remember when groups of teenage girls used to sit together, giggling up a storm, and talk endlessly about boys? They had their local meet-up places, a coffee shop or an ice cream parlor, where they pushed a few tables together or sat in a semicircle in a large booth, ordered root beers, milkshakes, and hot fudge sundaes and made high-pitched sounds while they whispered secrets in each other's ears. One girl was all smiles because her heartthrob had just invited her to a dance. Someone else was in tears because her steady boyfriend had just suggested they date other people.

Back in the fifties, when my family spent summers at the Tide Rock House in Old Orchard Beach, Maine, each night before bed, I watched my older sister, Jill, a teenager at the time, wind her shiny, brown hair around metal rollers lined with paper inserts and pink rectangles of foam. When she had brushed her teeth and washed her face, she lay down in bed, curlers surrounding her head like a metal halo, and slept the entire night on her back, geisha-like, never turning over or moving so she wouldn't mess up her "do." As uncomfortable as it was, all her friends did it too, because wavy hair was in vogue, and, as yet, curling irons and heat rollers were only for movie stars or the swankiest of hair salons. Jill's fashion efforts were a fascination to me, as were my mother's, who wrapped toilet paper around her beehive hairdo before she went to bed. Her hairdresser had suggested it. He said all the women were doing it, and wrapping it would allow it to last for a week, at which time she would get her hair washed at the salon, and he would redo the beehive. In the mornings, my mother unwrapped her papered head and patted her bouffant do in place with her hands while Jill carefully removed her rollers, combed out her perfect curls, and sprayed some awful-smelling sticky stuff called Spraynet on her head to keep her tresses from swaying in the breeze. Then she met her girlfriends at the beach at the end of our street.

I had long, straight hair, and I was in awe of my sister's picture-perfect waves, her slim, tanned legs, her small waist, and the way her one-piece bathing suit fit her lean body so well. She and her friends picked a spot equidistant from the ocean and the hot dog stand to spread their towels on the sand. Then they turned on the radio and slathered suntan oil on each other's backs, ogling the lifeguards sitting high up on the lifeguard stand, so serious-looking and official in their tight red bathing suits, scanning the ocean through binoculars, ready to save lives.

When enough time had passed (all the girls knew exactly when that was), they casually took off in a group to hang around at the hot dog stand, where the neighborhood boys worked summer jobs so they could buy a girl of their choice a Ferris wheel ride and some cotton candy at the pier in the evening. The girls flirted and laughed, and when they'd spent the appropriate amount of time there (again, they all knew exactly when), they returned to their towels, shook the sand off, sat down, and reapplied their oil, giggling and gossiping nonstop about who liked whom, who already had a girlfriend, who was breaking up with whom, and who was the cutest and had the best hair. Jill had a mad crush on a tall guy named Dave, until one day she had her heart broken when she saw him on a beach blanket, kissing his girlfriend under her big, floppy hat.

These days, teenage girls still meet up in groups at the beach or at a local coffee shop, they still rate the guys as hot or not, but they go where there's Wi-Fi, they drink coconut water, their snacks are gluten-free, and all you can hear is the click, click, click of electronic keys as they endlessly send and receive text messages. Pierced and tattooed, they remain oddly silent with their heads bent forward, their thumbs flying as they send off texts and listen for the *ping* when someone texts them back, which might be the person seated beside them or someone in another country and a different time zone whom they met on Facebook. It's as if they've taken an oath of silence, never giggling, hardly reacting, butchering the spelling of common words as they key in messages like this:

r u still in bed? Sup? saw u the other day. did u c me? wut were u doing? idc but omg, u looked so sad. r u ok? idk wut u want. do u? btw, if u don't understand wut I'm writing, u aren't coo. lol.

OK, I'll stop, but teenagers have created their own shorthand, punctuation has gone out the window, and I wonder if they remember how to spell the simplest of words, like "you" and "what" and "by the way." And we thought Ebonics was hard to understand.

In an attempt to keep up with social media, I joined Twitter not too long ago. I asked a friend the other day in all seriousness, "Can I use hashtags when I post a retweet?" Sounds impressive, all the right words are there, but while I may be a quick study in picking up the dialect, it doesn't feel natural to me, and it probably never will, which only accentuates my sense of being isolated and out of the loop—unless that actually means I'm *in* the loop because these days, isolation has become alarmingly common.

Even when kids are together, they remain isolated, staring into electronic devices, developing rounded backs before they reach their twenties, and unable to make conversation with adults besides a groan and a head shake. The tattoos and piercings are forever, but grunting and texting is hopefully a phase they'll outgrow. It's hardly a surprise that when "electronically raised" kids reach young adulthood, they often have a hell of a time leaving the house, interviewing for jobs, and articulating their personal feelings, even among themselves. They are so unaccustomed to meeting people face-to-face, they don't know how to make eye contact or answer questions without the use of a keyboard.

While isolation has taken on epidemic proportions in our society, for a writer, isolation has long been an occupational hazard. So many of our great writers were alcoholics, like Ernest Hemingway, Truman Capote, William Faulkner, and F. Scott Fitzgerald to name a few. I wonder which came first. Did drinking help them write? Or did writing drive them to drink? Not all alcoholics write, so maybe tipping the bottle takes the edge off isolation and loneliness, and writing has nothing to do with it. Or maybe if they didn't have to face the blank page, they wouldn't have to drink to calm their nerves.

I was never a drinker—it didn't agree with me, and it still doesn't—but I found my own way of combatting loneliness. I was eighteen when marijuana and I were introduced, and, like meeting someone new, I remember it being a fresh and exhilarating discovery, filled with possibilities. I was a ballerina living in New York City at the time, when a group of my dancer friends and I strolled down Broadway one evening in a delightful smoke-induced glow. We window-shopped along the Boulevard, marveling at how shiny things looked, when suddenly, without a word to each other, we took a detour into Tad's Steakhouse en masse, salivating at the aromas and giggling through the entire meal. A love affair is always so great in the beginning, isn't it? The way it enhances the senses and transforms the ordinary into the extraordinary?

Marijuana relaxed my mind, sparked my creativity, and allowed me to appreciate taste, touch, and music in a whole new way, encouraging me to hold my concerns lightly, rather than obsessing, as I was prone to do, about things that I couldn't control. I was definitely my mother's daughter when it came to fretting.

Fretting

When I was in the ballet, I smoked pot only on rare occasions, abstaining for long stretches, but I started indulging much more regularly when I got together with Jerry, since he and his friends smoked pot all the time. They called it "wake and bake," when you got up in the morning, emptied your bladder, sipped some coffee, and lit up the first joint of the day. Not necessarily in that order. But it was new for me to wake up and not have a ballet class to attend or a performance that required rehearsals. It felt like I was free-falling, and smoking pot seemed to take away the panic.

When I made my getaway from my abusive husband, I smoked a lot less, but years later, when I became a working writer and spent long hours alone each day at the computer, I picked it up again to feel more grounded. Once I realized that smoking marijuana after a writing session took the edge off and helped me relax, I knew we were a good match. That was when we started going steady. We moved in together almost immediately, and the thought of being without my friend was more than I could bear. I spent unconscionable amounts of money to obtain the highest quality available, and I was always sure to have some on hand. I knew I was taxing my lungs, and I developed a cop phobia since it was illegal. Still, pot and I stayed together for decades, my longest relationship to date. It brought me a lot of ease and companionship, lightening up the loneliness that seemed to be unavoidable in my chosen profession.

When my favorite illegal alien went legit, circa 1996, I got a prescription, which was meant to punctuate its validity, but it actually did the opposite. Shortly after it was dubbed "medical marijuana," someone I don't remember handed me a business card with the word "DOCTOR" written on the front in bold capital letters with a phone number and an address. That was it. No name, subheading, or explanation. I called the number and was told by a polite young man to just drop by. No appointment was necessary. I drove over to the address on the card. I knew I was in the right place when I saw a dubious-looking storefront over which the word "DOCTOR" appeared on the protruding awning, matching the one-word title on the business card. Was his name Dr. Doctor? I wondered as I walked into an outer office and signed in with the receptionist, who asked me about my ailment.

"I have trouble falling asleep," I said.

He frowned. "Is that all? Isn't there something else?"

"OK," I said. "My neck hurts."

"That'll work." He wrote that down, said, "Please wait," and gestured toward the waiting room. I took a seat among an odd cast of characters, including an aging vet in camouflage, two teenagers with spiked hair and matching nose rings, and a painfully thin man, about thirty years old, with sunken eyes and purple spots on his calves that sometimes appear on people with AIDS. We were called in one by one, and each person emerged from the back office after about ten minutes carrying a piece of paper. It looked like no one was being turned away, and I felt pretty confident I would get what I came for.

When it was my turn, I found the doctor to be a pleasant man, slightly overweight, probably in his forties, and as we sat in his small office, I told him I had trouble falling asleep and constant pain in my neck. Both were true, all except the "constant" part. He jotted a few things down, used a stethoscope to check my heart, and I left in record time, $150 lighter (the fee has gone way down by now), holding a prescription in my hand that was good for a year.

Next I was on my way to a local dispensary on Sunset Boulevard where the doctor had directed me, with the appropriate papers to buy legally what I had bought and used for decades illegally. I parked my car and stood in front of the locked door with the name "Organic Superstore" written on it in green block letters beside a green cross, located between a nail salon and a coffee shop. I rang the bell, and an armed guard, his middle straining against the buttons on his uniform, met me at the door to check my paperwork. The kind of authority figure whom in the past I would have avoided at all costs was approving me for entry. I handed him my brand-new prescription and my driver's license, and while he jotted a few things into a computer, I reminded myself that he was there to protect me, not arrest me.

As soon as he ushered me into the back room, the musky aroma of cannabis hit me. I inhaled deeply and stood, awestruck, in front of a counter with glass jars filled to overflowing with numerous varieties of marijuana strains, twenty-five or more. They were all different prices and strengths, ranging from the strong knockout type to the kind that would gently hold your hand as you tiptoed through the creative inner recesses of your mind. I turned in a slow circle, taking in the jars of buds, live plants, and clones for people who wanted to grow their own (under the current regulations, a person could grow six plants at a time for personal use), edibles like brownies, cookies, and candy, and glass shelves stacked with paraphernalia like assorted rolling papers, bongs, pipes, and vaporizers—the kind of stuff that used to get you arrested if the cops found any of it in your car.

"Fuck Disneyland," I was mortified to hear myself exclaiming out loud. "*This* is the happiest place on earth." You could hardly blame me after having to hide my relationship for so many years. I had never expected to find myself in a legitimate shop where former pot dealers, now called "merchants," legally sold dozens of varieties of pot, now called "medicine," to be consumed by potheads, now called "patients." Everything had changed, and nothing had changed.

A very young man with a very wide smile standing behind the counter proceeded to walk me through the various strains and their costs. This one helped you sleep, that one activated your brain, this one eased your pain, that one stimulated your appetite. Was I interested in sativa? Indica? Hash oil? What was my price range? How about a prerolled joint? As a first timer, I could get one for free. Having so many choices was revolutionary, and there was even an ATM at the entrance in case I had forgotten to bring cash. I remembered a time when my choices were limited to "Mexican Horse Shit" from Tijuana, "Maui Wowie" from Hawaii, "Tiesticks" from Thailand, or "Da Kine" from Humboldt County. If it looked fresh, had purple tinges, and smelled skunky, I put up my money.

Now all that had changed, and I couldn't get over how knowledgeable the seller was and how underage he looked. I chose a quarter ounce of buds of a strain that would allegedly help me relax my mind and allow me to sleep when the time came. It would also work as a painkiller/muscle relaxer, he told me. After I paid (the cost was similar to the street cost), the young man punched a hole in a card with a dozen numbers printed on it as well as the dispensary name and handed it to me. "Don't lose this," he said. "After you rack up enough points, you get an eighth for free." What *was* this, the car wash?

I nodded to the armed guard as I exited Disneyland, already feeling some affection toward him, and I headed for my car, clutching my brown paper bag filled with the odorous stuff I was now training myself to call "medicine." I locked it in the trunk—*better not take any chances, I* thought—and as I drove home, I had to wonder: If what I had just purchased was legal, why did my heart race and the tiny hairs on my arms stand on end when I saw a cop driving beside me on the road? When you consider the fact that up until 1967, it was illegal for blacks and whites to marry, and to this day, the stigma hasn't fully disappeared, it's easy to see that old habits die hard, if they ever die at all.

When I try to understand why I was willing to put myself at risk when illegal pot equaled jail time, it all came down to loneliness. Being *alone* in and of itself was not so bad. I liked silence—I often preferred it—and I had gotten used to doing what I wanted to do when I wanted to do it. But when I was alone for extended periods of time, I began to feel an emptiness in my core, a sense that something important was missing, something I needed and couldn't find. I felt like it was my fault that I was alone, that I must be doing something wrong or I'd be in a great relationship. On top of that sense of incompleteness, of having missed the boat or arrived late for the train, I also suffered from what the Buddhists called "monkey mind," which escalated when I was by myself.

Imagine a monkey in the jungle, skipping and leaping, hanging from its long, hairy arms, flitting from branch to branch, only settling when it finds something compelling or aggravating enough to hold it hostage. My mind felt like that monkey as it flitted randomly from topic to topic, stopping and digging in its heels only when it arrived at something annoying enough to command my full attention. It drove me crazy because it focused on the severity of my crime of being alone as it conjured the appropriate punishment.

However you define it for yourself, and whatever you decide to do about it, loneliness is a dreaded state that strikes males and females of all ages from all social registers who spend enormous amounts of money, time, effort, and creativity trying to get rid of it. Lonely children create imaginary friends. Wealthy women join charities, donate large amounts of money, and go to luncheons, feeling like they're doing good in their free time. In the film *Castaway*, the lead character animates a volleyball he names "Wilson" to cope with being isolated on a deserted island.

Solitary confinement is about as bad a punishment as anyone can imagine, and people are willing to suffer extensive physical and mental abuse to avoid feeling lonely.

For me, marijuana was an antidote to loneliness. It quieted my brain and calmed me down when I was obsessing. Ironically, however, the more I smoked, the more antisocial I became. The very thing that was saving me was also keeping me trapped. In other words, when I was using it regularly, marijuana and I just wanted to be alone. We got so close, I thought I had found my Forever, that pot and I would be together until the end of my days—that was before I started suffering from side effects due to overuse.

I ignored them at first because they snuck up gradually, a little cough here, a memory lapse there, a little dullness here, some boredom there, a little hiding in my bedroom here, saying no to a perfectly nice invitation there, until one day, I was overindulging, I had become a hermit, and I had to call it quits. Marijuana and I had been seeing too much of each other, so unfortunately and also fortunately, I ended the relationship, and we split up. Thankfully and surprisingly, it turned out to be an amicable separation. I didn't suffer much withdrawal, and there was no drama or recriminations or insults. I missed it at first, especially when I was lonely, but it had outworn its welcome. I had to face the fact that while marijuana hadn't changed, I had. I had lost interest, outgrowing it like a baby outgrows her pacifier. When I decided to quit, I stopped taking it with me everywhere, I began to ignore it when we were home alone, and finally, we went our separate ways. These days it still shows up from time to time and I enjoy a puff or two, but it isn't the main event any longer, and I stopped judging myself for feeling lonely when I understood that people in relaionships and marriages are lonely, too. Being older and wiser now, I've seen how prevalent loneliness is and how painful it can become. It's understandable, then, why we try to mask it, saturate it, or smoke it out. It's such a common malady, in fact, musicians have been writing hit songs about it for years, like *Lonely Street, All By Myself, Only the Lonely, Are You Lonesome Tonight?* and many, many more.

Isn't it ironic, then, that although everyone is lonely, we feel like we're alone in it? And it often feels the worst when we aren't actually alone.

I never felt more lonely than on Sunday, November 24, 1963, when I was standing on Pennsylvania Avenue in Washington, DC, one among thousands and thousands of people. I was fourteen years old; President Kennedy had been assassinated two days earlier in Dallas, Texas; and grief, anguish, and disbelief hung heavy in the air. I'd been in the middle of a ballet class on Friday morning when someone tiptoed in and whispered something into our ballet master's ear. He stopped the class, said, "Someone killed the president," and dropped his head into his hands. No one ever stopped a class, we were trained like soldiers, and we were stunned as we stood there a moment, wondering what to do. We slowly shuffled out of the room, speechless and unsure where to go. We ended up in front of someone's television, watching silently and crying softly when we saw Lyndon Johnson getting sworn into the office of president with Jackie Kennedy by his side, her pink Dior suit stained with her husband's blood.

I was living in DC pretty much on my own (a stunning reality in itself), and I called my parents sobbing, telling them I wanted to fly home to Connecticut for a few days while the funeral was taking place. It was too much to bear by myself. But getting in or out of Washington right then was impossible, and my father said rather harshly, "You want to leave Washington, and everybody else is trying to get there. Go out and watch history being made." I suppose he was trying to strengthen me, kind of like tossing a baby bird out of the nest or throwing your kid into the water to activate her self-preservation instincts. Or maybe his harshness came out of feeling helpless since he couldn't grant my request. Whatever his reasons, conscious or unconscious, I had to stay right where I was.

On Sunday, two days after the tragedy, I stood for hours out in the street, feeling desperately alone in the midst of unfathomable sorrow. It seems as if someone, maybe another kid my age, must have been standing there with me, but I don't remember being with anyone. All I can recall is how alone I felt among masses of people who were speaking in hushed voices, almost whispers, all of us struggling to absorb the enormity of what had happened. It was disturbingly quiet for such a large gathering of people, and no one spoke to me or noticed me while I waited for the procession to show up.

Uniformed military police officers stood facing the crowd that had gathered all along Pennsylvania Avenue, guns and bats in tow, their arms behind their backs, their fingers clenched, their faces grim and unmoving. When the muffled drum corps approached, announcing the imminent arrival of the procession, the police officers did an about-face. They raised their hands to their foreheads in a long salute while the caisson was wheeled by, pulled by a team of white horses bearing the enormous burden of the slain president's flag-wrapped casket. The crowd went silent; all we heard were the muffled drums and the clip-clop of horses' hooves as we watched our beloved first lady, Jackie Kennedy, walk by in her black dress, her face veiled, flanked by her brothers-in-law, Bobby and Ted, with newly minted President Lyndon Baines Johnson just behind them, making his first public appearance as president with his wife by his side. President Charles de Gaulle of France, six feet five, towered above 220 other foreign dignitaries from ninety-two nations, all gathered together to honor our fallen president. Finally, a saddled, riderless horse with brown boots in the stirrups facing backward took up the rear. He was skittish and straining at his lead as if trying to break free of the constraints and bolt off down the street.

The procession was on its way from the East Room of the White House to the Capitol Rotunda, where the president's body would lie in state while lines of people, ten miles long, would view the casket before the president was buried in Arlington National Cemetery a few days later. As the procession continued to pass me in the street, the silence of the crowd was broken when a black woman standing to my right lifted her head, opened her mouth, and began to wail. Other women's voices joined in, keening out their shattered hopes and dreams. The sound of their sobs rattled me. Despite my youth and political naïveté, I understood that something irreversible and deeply tragic had occurred. The president had been shot, and I, along with everyone else, would carry the wound for the rest of our lives.

I'd had the privilege of seeing Jackie Kennedy in happier times at my ballet school on Connecticut Avenue where she brought her six-year-old daughter, Caroline, for dance classes every Wednesday afternoon. Some of the other schoolgirls and I stood around in our gray wool uniforms whenever the first lady was there, trying to look casual as we watched her peer through a peephole into the studio to watch her daughter leap and twirl.

I was in the eighth grade at the time, and I lived across from the school in dormitory-type housing in a place called Mclean Gardens on Wisconsin Avenue, where I was largely unmonitored. So were the other eight or nine girls from out of state who boarded there with me, joining the day students who made up the majority. An elderly, gray-haired woman, supposedly our housemother, checked in on us boarders at random times, but she didn't live on the premises, so I was mostly alone—waking up in the morning to my alarm, getting dressed, going to the cafeteria for breakfast, and taking my first ballet class of the day at nine o'clock. Then I had French and math. After lunch, I had English, another dance class, and I rounded out the day with history and science. I ate supper in the same cafeteria, and I spent the evening washing out my sweaty practice clothes, sewing ribbons on pointe shoes, and doing my homework, struggling with math, which, for me, was like trying to solve the mysteries of the universe. Finally, I went to bed, more often than not, crying myself to sleep. The depth of my loneliness was staggering, and I thought I was the only one who cried and felt alone because I never saw the other girls crying. But then, they never saw me crying either, because we all hid our sadness from each other.

When I first heard about this school that my mother had discovered in the newspaper, I had been enthusiastic about attending. Constant rides back and forth from Worcester to Boston for ballet training four times a week were taking their toll on both my mother and me. I had checked out the School of American Ballet in New York, taking a summer course, but I opted not to have my scholarship renewed for the fall and winter. I felt too alone there, I didn't want to live with an aunt I hardly knew, and the cutting competitiveness among the students there was hard for me to handle.

The school in DC seemed to be a softer choice. It probably was, but I had no idea how lonely and devastating it would be to leave my parents at fourteen years old to live in a tiny room in a hotel-like atmosphere with no adult or parental figure to turn to or get comfort from. Apart from when I was in ballet class, I felt isolated, and when I told my parents how lonely I was, they said I could come back home if I wanted, but I didn't want that. I wanted my mother to come and stay with me for a week or two to help me adjust, but apparently, the idea of being on her own in Washington without her husband even for a week was too scary for her. So my father bought me a goldfish.

I tapped food into the water and watched Goldie swim, eat, and defecate in her small fishbowl, looking pretty lonely herself, while I wrote a letter each morning to my mother, pouring my heart out about how much I loved the ballet and how sad I was. When she wrote back, she red-penciled any grief-filled words I had misspelled and used them in a sentence. After a year in the dormitory (I found Goldie dead one day, floating at the top of her fishbowl) and another year sharing an apartment with a fellow dancer when she and I were both fifteen, I left DC a great speller, a learned grammarian, a highly trained ballet dancer, and a lonely young girl with a broken heart.

My therapist says I left home "before I was cooked." But when I was home, I felt raw and unseen most of the time, so it really didn't matter where I was. It certainly would have been easier to manage my life if I had been older, but my mother had meager skills when it came to nurturing, and loneliness has remained a challenge that seems to outweigh most others throughout my life.

Now that I understand myself better, I know I can do something about isolation. Even though my lifestyle as a writer requires so much alone time, there are ways to reach out and be with other people, like going to dinner, listening to music in a club, walking in beautiful places, and inviting friends over to enjoy my home and the uninterrupted view from my picture windows. Where people gather, isolation disappears, and there's a lot of comfort available in sharing laughter, food, and ideas with friends.

I once went to an AA meeting, invited by an acquaintance who was celebrating twenty years of sobriety. Everyone cheered as he received his twenty-year chip, and he thanked his friends for their support. But when he got back to his seat, he whispered to me that he had never been an alcoholic. He went to AA meetings because he was lonely and he liked hobnobbing with the celebrities who showed up there. *To each his own,* I thought, but I got a lot of insight that night when a famous rock star got up and went to the front of the room to speak about his life. "We're all lonely here," he said in his thick Northern English accent, "but we can't tell that to everybody we meet. When I pick up the dry cleaning and the woman behind the cash register asks me how I am, I can't very well moan at her, 'I'm lonely.'"

Even rock stars get lonely, and I know I'll never heal my loneliness because it isn't a disease. It's the human condition, and loneliness torments everyone of any age and class. Whether someone is wildly famous or almost famous, married or single, wealthy with tons of Facebook friends or a loner who shuns social media and holes up in bed, we are all lonely. Both the best and the worst of us. We get short reprieves, suspended moments of grace when we forget about ourselves and our feelings, placing our focus on someone or something outside ourselves. But like a boomerang, no matter how far you throw it, loneliness always finds its way back.

After all these years of trying to exile, abandon, and throw loneliness away, I've learned that whether I try to snub it, eat through it, drown it, shoot it, burn it up, stuff it down, run the car over it, steamroll it, or fly it to the moon, it isn't going anywhere. It's always there, resilient as a cockroach, ever faithful, and no amount of praying, drinking, meditating, breathing, distracting, stomping, or fucking will banish it. The only alternative is to make friends and learn to live with it, like an annoying relative you're stuck with during a holiday gathering. While I still get lonely from time to time, as uncomfortable and permanent as it feels, the truth is that it's temporary, and it's perfectly safe. It won't kill me. But trying to find a way to eradicate it just might.

Chapter Eight

UNCHARTED TERRITORY

I've been absolutely terrified

every moment of my life—

and I've never let it keep me from doing

a single thing I wanted to do.

— Georgia O'Keeffe

nspiration can show up in the most ordinary places. I was in bumper-to-bumper traffic on the 405 freeway during rush hour one afternoon, bored and aggravated, wondering what would happen if I suddenly needed an ambulance. What if a fellow driver shot me in a fit of road rage and there was no way for anyone to get through? I looked up and saw a news helicopter making slow circles above the traffic, and I had a vision of a rescuer dropping down on a line from a chopper, pulling me out of the car, strapping me into a basket, and having me airlifted and whisked away to intensive care.

I used that image as the opening scene in a novel, and I wrote a story around it. Although I've always been an avid reader of fiction, I had never tried my hand at novel writing. I was much more comfortable writing nonfiction, usually someone's memoir that had a fixed beginning, middle, and end, with an already established roster of personalities. Their individual speech patterns had been developed over real time, they had inherent characteristics, and they were living lives of their own choosing, lives that I had nothing to do with. I was simply a reporter, listening to my clients' stories, writing them down, and checking for authenticity on Google pages, Internet fan clubs, scandal websites, and published discographies and filmographies. I would ask questions, listen to the answers, do the research, and slowly chip away at the hubris to bring out the deeper emotional content in a private life that had been lived publicly for a very long time.

As a ghostwriter, I honed my interview skills over the years, encouraging a client to recall intimate details of his or her life. It wasn't always easy to mine those depths, especially if my subject had made decisions along the way never to reveal the treasures that were stored there. Maybe the events were too painful, too personal, or just too far in the past to recall them in detail. But I've developed methods over the years to unearth these treasures. My clients sometimes resist me, but it's my job to keep digging deeper, even when it puts them off.

And it does. I was once sitting with a movie star in her luxurious bedroom that looked like every girly girl's fantasy. There was lace from Limoges, crystals from Swarovski, lampshades from Tiffany, etched glass from Steuben, and bedding from Ralph Lauren. She was talking about her childhood and how much her parents' divorce had impacted the family, especially her younger brother. After a while, I said, "You told me how your mother felt about the divorce and how your father and your brother felt about it. But what about you? How did it affect you?"

Her hand flew up to her right temple as she closed her eyes, winced in pain, and let out a groan. My question had triggered an instant migraine, and our work was over for the day as I left her lying on her back in her darkened bedroom, her eyes covered, her personal assistant hovering close by. I had touched the tip of her deepest pain, which she had stored away on purpose a long time ago. Who was I to start digging it up and performing autopsies on what she had so carefully and deliberately covered up and stashed? She eventually backed out of the project respectfully; both she and I agreed that writing a memoir was a bad idea for her. It hadn't even been her idea in the first place; her overzealous agent had told her it would be good for her career.

With a few exceptions, like the one above, I'm pretty lucky at maneuvering clients' recall skills, deciding when to come forward and when to hang back, how much to push, and when to let go in order to be effective and productive. Once I've gathered together as many parts of someone's history as I can find, I organize the events, fitting pieces of his or her life puzzle together as seamlessly as possible so a reader won't get seasick from navigating choppy waters or drowsy from the tide slapping lazily against the shore for too long. I enjoy the process as I soften behavior when need be, punching up interesting tidbits and revealing previously hidden triumphs and lessons among the comings and goings of someone's day-to-day life.

Writing fiction, however, is something else altogether. Creating characters from scratch and giving them appropriate dialogue and personality traits is only a part of the challenge. There's a plot to map out, events to dream up that have the right amount of tension and release, peaks, valleys, emotional arcs, and precipitous occurrences that will throw readers off balance, leaving them teetering on the edge, like walking a tightrope with certain disaster waiting on either side.

In a welcome change from being a reporter, I spent chunks of time over several years writing my novel and living in my imagination, creating characters and assigning them everything from how they looked to what they liked and disliked, from what they wore to how they were raised, from their eccentricities to whom their parents were. I created childhoods for them when it wasn't even relevant to the story, making sure that their roots informed their psychological makeup, which in turn informed their dialogue, so conversations would sound logical and connected. I regarded each of them individually, issuing them physical and emotional characteristics of someone I knew, someone I wished I knew, someone I wished I didn't know, or in rare cases, someone I had yet to meet. I created every little thing about them, placing them in dubious situations, guiding them along, until eventually they took on attitudes of their own as they turned the tables and began guiding me.

"I would never say that," one of them critiqued me when I'd been struggling with a page of dialogue for hours. "I don't speak like that, and I would never be that direct or pushy. No wonder you're having trouble. Try this instead." I didn't tell anyone that I was taking advice from my made-up characters. They would think I was crazy, that I was imagining things. I kept it to myself, and when I was invited to dinner, nobody knew that six invisible people tagged along with me.

In the beginning my characters showed up only when I invoked them. In fact, there were times I couldn't summon them no matter how hard I tried, a state commonly known as "writer's block." Even though I had created them in the first place, shaped their bodies, filled their minds with thoughts, and breathed life into their psyches, they wouldn't let me in. It was as if their existence was a closed system, and they didn't need or want any further help from me. "Go away," I imagined them telling me. "I've got this, and I don't need any more of your ethical considerations or your personal preferences."

I was persistent though, and once I'd written them into multiple chapters, they took up permanent residence in my mind and began following me wherever I went—to meals, when I went to the movies, and most tangibly, when I went to bed. I'd drop into that twilight place between waking and sleeping where disjointed words and phrases floated in the ethers, and I would hear them talking among themselves. It felt like I was eavesdropping on my characters' conversations, and I wanted to write things down so I wouldn't forget what I heard. But if I roused myself enough to grab a pen, they would disappear. They seemed to have minds of their own, personal opinions about me and about right and wrong, and they had distinct speech patterns that varied from character to character. When I think about how long it took me to fashion each of them, to prod them into existence and breathe real life into them, I can see why I was so bereft when they disappeared.

I had finished the manuscript and submitted it to my agent when they took off in a group, all at the same time, leaving me to grapple with a serious case of "empty mind syndrome." I was filled with nostalgia when I recalled how they'd acted early on, begging me to give them more to do and say. When they were initially emerging and taking shape, no matter how much attention I gave them, it was never enough. Give a guy a line of dialogue and he takes a paragraph. Give a girl a paragraph and she takes a page, and the next thing you know, she wants a whole chapter. So even though they'd been demanding and shamelessly acting out, I was surprised at how much I missed them when they went away, even Troy, the old son of a bitch, the aging news anchor/antagonist in my story.

For years I had listened endlessly to his lies and watched his ruthless invasion of other people's privacy. I'd suffered my protagonist, Daphne's, fear of just about everything, and I'd been in awe of her ability to cook a great meal. And then there was her friend Sami, a Desert Storm veteran, the polar opposite to Daphne as she executed risky helicopter maneuvers for hours on end and showed up at dinnertime, hungry, because she didn't know how to boil an egg. I had compassion for Daphne's mother, Judith, a sixties casualty, even though she was always loaded and conniving, pretending she was being upfront and honest. At least Troy admitted to his lies and manipulations. Young Hummer grew up in the street speaking Ebonics and spraying his graffiti tags in public places in the dark of night. His friend, Tooey, didn't speak at all, and Bobby, Daphne's lover, broke into my dreams because he was an insomniac and didn't have any dreams of his own.

Still, despite their horrific behavior (my fault, I should have given them better parents), when they left, I ached for each of them like lost pieces of my heart. It's tricky business creating characters for a novel, learning to love and accept their weaknesses as much as their strengths and giving them names that seem appropriate. A pushy friend once took me to task for the names I'd given my characters, suggesting new ones she thought were better. I was insulted for each of them. Their names were simply their names, which I felt they had chosen themselves. There was no way I would change them according to the whim of someone who was meeting them for the first time.

I sometimes imagined a room filled with odd characters auditioning for a part in my book like they were trying out for a TV talent show. They would introduce themselves, and then they'd pull out all the stops, emoting, singing, even tap-dancing with a hat and cane, saying, "Over here. Choose me. You won't be sorry. I'm infinitely interesting, and I'll come through for you."

I usually skipped over the more obvious ones and inevitably found myself attracted to a sad, wounded girl sitting over in the corner, hiding behind a newspaper, hoping I wouldn't spot her. "You," I'd say, pointing at her. "I want you."

"Oh, no, you don't want me," she'd try to reason with me. "I'm shy and scared and I don't like crowds. I'm not very interesting."

The actual writing occurred at intervals, when I was between my bread-and-butter projects. There was nothing better than going to sleep at night with my characters in my head, reviewing what I'd be writing in the morning. Not the actual words; that only happened when I was at the computer. Rather, I'd get a topic in my head, kick it around and play with it while I was falling asleep and find it there in the morning, waiting for me to put my fingers on the keyboard and let it rip.

As I worked on the novel year after year, I once asked an agent how I would know when it was finished. "There comes a time," she said, "when the agent has to take the book out of the writer's hands, or you'll end up editing it for the rest of your life."

I could see what she meant. When I pick up a book I wrote many years ago, I can open it to any page and decide what rewrites I should have done. It could go on forever, but it doesn't, since life comes in and demands other things, and the relief of finishing something is pretty great. Well, it's great for a minute, right after the book has been "put to bed." The writing is done, decisions have been made, and it's in someone else's hands to take it to the next level. I feel like I can breathe easy again. But all too soon, I make the inevitable death-defying dive into a pool of fear and anxiety, and my inner dialogue sounds like this: *Will they like it? How long will they take to read it? Will I have to rewrite it again? And again? Will there be time to do the rewrite? Right now, what do I do with the hours that are stretched out in front of me? I know I prayed for this project to be over, but now that it is, I have nothing to take its place, and I'm oh so lonely.*

I was feeling this emptiness after I had finished writing a memoir for a celebrated black actress. My novel was tucked away in a familiar place on the shelf where it naturally gravitated between rewrites, and with my palette empty, I headed off for the weekend to a desert spa. I'd been there before; it was a tried and true place for me to unburden my mind and heal myself inside and out, but I had no idea that, this time, I would end up in uncharted territory.

I came of age in a "go for it" generation, in direct opposition to the fifties rigidity, where certain things "were done" and other things "weren't done." In the spirit of the sixties, if I could imagine it, and it appealed to me, I tried it. Intent on breaking through the armor of the boundaried reality into which my peers and I were born, a reality that offered no room to innovate and little incentive to drop old habits and form new ones, we rebelled by taking LSD and psilocybin mushrooms and exploring inner worlds that had been hidden beneath the rules and regulations so prevalent in the fifties. In the spirit of "anything goes," we dared to imagine a world that was receptive to new ways of doing and being. And we dared to be the people who introduced and investigated them.

Sexual experimentation was *en vogue* in the sixties and seventies, and as I recall that period, I see that the nature of the experimentation was shaped by the particular drugs we ingested at any given time. I asked a friend who lived in Haight-Ashbury during the height of psychedelia what had turned the Summer of Love into the Winter of Hate. Why did he leave after a year, and when did the love graffiti on the sidewalks and walls turn into gang-related homie tags and death threats?

"When we were taking LSD and smoking marijuana," he explained, "we were feeling the love. But when cocaine and speed infiltrated the ranks, when these angry, aggressive agents penetrated our minds and hearts, good became bad, peace turned into anxiety, empathy became aggression, and openness and sharing morphed into clenched fists and hoarding. That's why I left. The love was gone."

I felt the difference, myself, pretty dramatically, as I followed the drug trajectory that he described collectively in Haight-Ashbury from my own vantage point. When I was smoking pot and ingesting psychedelic compounds, I was open and filled with compassion, which was reflected in my sexual experiences. They were all about love, inclusion, and sharing. But when I fell into the stress and isolating effects of snorting cocaine, my bed became a boxing ring, and it was every man and woman for himself or herself. I have no intention of detailing the things I did or said. There is no reason to offer up sordid details or shuffle back through speed-fueled actions that were painful, harmful, and so contrary to what I allow into my world now. But the shift from receiving to grabbing, from acceptance to revulsion, from delighting in a partner's pleasure to seeing how far you could push him before he crumbled, was apparent and clearly fueled by sinister substances coursing through the blood, causing a reversal of empathy and compassion.

When I made my getaway in my late twenties, abandoning stimulants, bad men, and opting for a softer, easier way of life, my sexual habits followed suit. I embraced intimacy and caring, exiting a world of anonymity and emotional numbness, enjoying the rewards of openness and kindness. I stopped chasing the highs and losing sleep night after night, and I began meditating, eating healthily, and practicing yoga. My life was filled with breath, and my breath offered me a better life.

It was in the early nineties, I was over hurting myself or anyone else and way over drug abuse, when I went to a desert spa to meditate, heal, and contemplate the next phase. That was when Gabriella showed up on a motorcycle. She was a Brazilian goddess, attractive and playful, and she carried with her a strong presence and a sense of aliveness. I didn't get it right away, how much she resembled Sami, the helicopter pilot from my novel, the part of me that had almost no fear and was up for anything. Gabriella's smile was sparkly, and her energy was a combination of male and female, well contained in a small-boned body with thick eyebrows and long, brown hair falling down her back.

We arrived at the spa at about the same time. She was visiting with three female friends who were staying there. We spotted each other outside. I was in a bikini, sunbathing, and she was sitting in the shade, fully clothed in her biker gear, paging through a magazine. She smiled at me, I smiled back, and she disappeared for a few minutes into one of the rooms, returning in an aqua-blue bikini and taking a dive into the pool. Her body was tight and muscled as she splashed a few of her friends who were lying on rafts. They laughed and so did I; it was so much fun to watch Gabriella playing in the pool like an otter, upturning a raft and diving beneath the surface for some underwater laps. She looked a little bit like trouble, the fun kind, and I felt drawn to cool off in the pool where she was quietly kicking her legs behind her, her eyes closed and her hands holding on to a step at the deep end.

I swam a little bit, floating and enjoying the beauty of the women who were relaxing in the healing artesian spring waters that bubbled up from underground. I'd met a variety of people at this spa, many of whom were healers and light workers of different sorts, mostly from Los Angeles and surrounding counties. But I had never seen this Brazilian contingency because this was their first time there. They lived in Los Angeles and made their livings doing massage therapy and other forms of healing, all but Gabriella, who lived in this desert oasis, enjoying small-town life and studying nursing at a local hospital.

I went into my room after my swim and dozed for a while, and before I knew it, the sun was setting. The aroma of beef and chicken sizzling on the outdoor grill wafted in through my open window, and I realized how hungry I was. I walked out of my room, car keys in hand, ready to head over to a local Italian restaurant when Gabriella stopped me. "If you want, come and join us," she said. "We have plenty of food, too much, and maybe you'd like to try a caipirinha."

"What is that?" I asked.

"It's a rum drink from Brazil, guaranteed to knock you on your ass. I'm Gabriella, by the way. Call me Gabby."

"I'm Andrea." We smiled at each other; I liked her. I followed her poolside, where her friends were pouring drinks from a large pitcher into individual glasses. I took one, we toasted, and I sat on a chaise lounge, sipping and listening to them quipping in Portuguese, the decibel levels rising the more drinks we had.

And so began my friendship with this group of uproarious Brazilian women, and particularly, Gabriella. Gabby. We spent the evening eating, talking, laughing, and sharing stories. Gabby stayed overnight with her friends, and we all met back in the water the next morning. We soaked, sunbathed, munched on the fruit I'd brought with me, and drank strong Brazilian coffee. We all hung out for the rest of the day, and they asked me to join them for dinner again. I agreed. I was in my room, reading, when there was a knock on my door. I opened the door and smiled. It was Gabby.

"Dinner?" I asked her. "Is it time?"

"Soon," she said. "Can we talk?"

"Sure. Do you want to come in?"

She looked into my room and then behind her. "No," she said. "Let's just sit in the chairs outside here."

I put down my book, grabbed my sunglasses and a bottle of water, stepped outside, and sat down. She looked a little bit nervous as she cleared her throat, and finally she said in heavily accented English, "So what are we gonna do about it?"

"About what?" I asked her.

"About us."

There was an "us"? I stared at her a moment, and I realized that she was right. There *was* an "us," but I hadn't been looking at it that way. I'd always had lots of girlfriends.

Juliet Green and Me

I got along really well with them, and they had been my emotional rocks ever since I was a child. I was what you would call a woman's woman, even when I was living with a man. I loved and needed my women friends; we were always there for each other, and I can't imagine how I would have gotten throught life without them. We used to say that men could come and go, but women were forever. I understood those kinds of relationships, but with this woman sitting beside me, I had to admit that something was different. It felt intimate and, yes, it was exciting, and it felt sexual. Hot. Seductive. No different from the chemistry I felt with a man. I was stunned by this, that I was drawn to her in that way. There was sexual heat between us, and her question about "us" hadn't come out of left field, although it had seemed that way.

I thought for a moment and said, "I've never had sex with a woman. I kisssed one once, but that was a long time ago, so let's not do anything about it. Just let it be, and when we all go home tomorrow, that'll be that."

"That might be fine for you," she said, a look of concern on her face, "but you're giving me a heart attack."

We both laughed. I really didn't want to do anything about Gabby. And then, suddenly, I did. I wanted to kiss her. Really kiss her. But I was afraid to start something I didn't want to finish. Or maybe I was afraid that I *would* want to finish it. Did I really want to go there? I could just let it go. That would be easy. Or I could venture into virgin territory, so to speak, and see where it led.

We didn't talk about anything more that night. We just ate, drank, and smiled a lot. When we said our good-byes the next day, we exchanged numbers, and, a few days later, on a Friday evening, I puttered around my house, vacuuming, cleaning the coffee table, and dusting off my collection of shimmering quartz crystals, waiting for Gabby. When I first bought my dream house in Laurel Canyon and moved in, I had imagined a romantic evening there, lighting candles, fluffing pillows, and burning incense while I waited for a lover to arrive. But I had never pictured that lover to be a Brazilian woman, fifteen years my junior, arriving on a motorcycle.

A part of me didn't want to open the door to that unexplored world. My attraction was probably a momentary wrinkle in time, I rationalized, a trancelike state fueled by the desert winds that had blown in a bevy of South American goddesses. But what if it was something more? I had invited Gabby here, and she had agreed to come, but now it seemed unfair to her. What if it didn't feel right to me when she stepped inside my world? It probably wouldn't. What would it be like without the desert night skies filled with stars, the healing pools that felt like silk, and the sweet goodness of fruity caipirinhas? I actually hoped that I would find out I'd been mistaken, that I'd been temporarily enchanted like Hippolyta in a *Midsummer Night's Dream*, and now, several days later, it would all be gone. It would feel flat and ordinary, the magic would have left, and I could pretend I had felt nothing.

The gods must be laughing, I said to myself as I heard the roar of Gabby's bike arriving in front of my house. She had ridden there all the way from the desert. I showed her where to park her bike in my garage next to my Lexus. They looked conspicuously mismatched. Then I took her hand and led her inside, wondering if the neighbors were catching my act. I felt self-conscious, even though two gay men lived in the house across the street and the people next to them had just moved in, and we didn't really know each other.

Gabby removed her leather jacket and her boots, and I brought her something to drink. She looked so small in my house, so alien to my world, I thought I should have made up the bed in the spare room—until she smiled at me. There it was, I thought, as I leaned in and kissed her very slowly. We kissed for a while, and I lost the sense that she was a woman. She was a person—her gender was immaterial—and I was thrilled to be kissing her as I felt her hands exploring my body. That was when I stopped and said, "Wait a minute. I need to say something."

She looked at me sideways as if she knew what I was about to say and wished I wouldn't. I spoke anyway. "I'm doing this as an experiment because I'm attracted to you," I told her. "I don't know why; I've never been sexually attracted to a woman before, but I'm pretty sure I'll be going back to men. This is an aberration for me, but for you, this is the norm. You could get hurt, so maybe you want to think this thing through. I'll understand if you decide not to do it."

I put it all out there, but it was a stretch to imagine that she knew what the word "aberration" meant, since Portuguese was her first language. She looked at me and smiled. She had no intention of backing off. Whatever will be, will be, she was basically saying. I led her downstairs to my bedroom. I was intimidated at first, afraid of doing it wrong, unaccustomed to the folds and curves of a female body and feeling unsure of myself. But when I finally let go and immersed myself in the experience, it felt as if I were making love to myself, exploring my likes and dislikes and reading hers as well as I could.

Later, when I lay quietly in bed, Gabby at my side, I felt content in my body, but fears were dancing around in my head. What if I were actually a lesbian? Was that why I hadn't found the right man? Was I ready to embrace a new lifestyle that so many people were against? Was I ready to be a pariah in a world where I was used to being accepted? I eventually dropped off to sleep. I awakened in the morning to a sight that was so beautiful, I held my breath. The light was pouring in through the open window, and there lay Gabriella, still asleep, breathing deeply, her dark brown hair falling in waves on her narrow shoulders and across her right breast, her eyelashes catching the glow of the rising sun. What had I started? Part of me wanted to get her up, get her dressed, and send her on her way. The other part wanted to nuzzle into her side and fall back to sleep.

She began to stir, and the corners of her mouth turned upward. She was familiar with awakening beside a woman. It didn't feel odd to her, but I got up quickly, heading upstairs to make coffee while she showered and got dressed. We engaged in some small talk, and when she kissed me good-bye and headed out to get on her motorcycle, I knew we weren't through with each other. She came back to visit me a few more times, and I visited her once or twice. I got more comfortable in her presence, but the getting-to-know-you phase was fraught with inconsistencies and confusions.

For starters, I had to wonder if I was finished with men. There was a kind of relief in that, in never having to deal with their denseness, their egos, and their penises that were always running the show. Was he satisfied? Was he not? Did he get hard? Did he not? Would he look elsewhere to find someone prettier, younger, or less powerful than me? Apart from all of that, though, I adored Gabby. I loved her low voice, her accent was irresistible, and she laughed heartily. We always had fun when I wasn't busy trying to find something wrong with her, and I loved jumping on the back of her bike and speeding with her into the wind. I felt at home with her adventurous spirit, and I liked that she always made sure I was happy and comfortable. She was a nurturing kind of person.

But I had the sense with Gabby that something was missing, because something was. *Where's the beef?* I asked myself each time we made love. After the first few times, I started missing penises, which had given me a lot of pleasure in my life. Gabriella was a virgin. From her vantage point, everything was in order because she had never been with a man. I had, and I knew what I was missing. And there were other things that bothered me. Like the time she arrived at my house in a bad mood, and I asked her what was going on.

"I have PMS," she said. "I'm getting my period in a few days, and my hormones are all messed up. You know how it feels."

Resentment flared up in me. Men didn't get PMS and didn't have the emotional swings that women had. I was the one who got PMS, that was *my* space in the relationship, and I didn't want to share it with anybody.

And then there was the social aspect. She brought me to a friend's house in the desert one weekend to introduce me to some of the women she hung out with. That was reasonable, I wanted to get to know her friends, but I never expected to meet a female UPS driver with a crew cut, her girlfriend, a lipstick lesbian who worked in the adult sex toy trade, and a hardware store worker who made keys and sold pocket-knives. It felt like a room filled with aliens, and although they were all women, there was very little femininity.

On top of that, I found the fact that Gabby stared at me a lot to be off-putting. I must have been fulfilling some sort of fantasy for her, the blond-haired, blue-eyed, straight American woman whom she'd considered unreachable and had placed on a pedestal. That was never a soft place to sit; it had a hard, thin edge, and it required vigilance and a balancing act to stay upright. I felt like I was being objectified as Gabby showed me off to her friends, and I couldn't wait to leave. On the way home, she said, "You looked uncomfortable at Ellie's house just now. Why?"

"I'm not a lesbian," I said, "and it was a strange reality for me."

"Right," she said. "You're not a lesbian, but your girlfriend is. I've heard that one before."

The pressure was building because nothing felt right or normal to me. What was I doing? I didn't feel like myself, but not because I was unwilling to face the truth. I knew the truth about myself, that I was a heterosexual woman exploring my sexuality with another woman. Men were still going to be in my life, so I better learn how to get along with them.

One day, after we had sex, I told Gabby we needed to talk. "It's clear to me this isn't going to last," I told her. "I want to give you a head's up so you can—"

"Are you leaving right now?" she interrupted me, a look of irritation clouding her face.

"No, not right now. But I feel like—"

"I don't want to talk about it," she said. "When it's time to go, just go."

"Are you sure? Maybe if we discussed it, you'd understand and feel better about it."

"No," she said. "I already understand. When you're done, just leave. I don't ever want to talk about it. Let's talk about something else."

Over the next few weeks, we saw each other twice more. I made an overnight trip to the desert, and she came to Los Angeles for a night, but I had one foot out the door. She felt it, but maybe she hoped she was wrong. It had been three months from start to finish, and we'd seen each other a few days a month when I backed away. Part of it was that I was an avid reader. She wasn't, so we didn't really have a meeting of the minds. Our upbringings couldn't have been more different, and there was the fact that our sex was incomplete for me, and so was our emotional connection. I remembered what she had said, that she didn't want to talk about it. When the time came, she had told me quite clearly, I should just leave. So I gave her what she asked for. I canceled my next trip to see her and told her I was taking some time for myself. I broke her heart.

I sometimes wonder if I picked the wrong woman. If she had been older, wiser, more mature, and if she were a more experienced lover, would I have fallen in love and gotten more deeply into a same-sex relationship? There's no way to know, but I seriously doubt it. All I know for sure is that I hurt sweet Gabby a lot. She took it really hard. I learned from a friend that she couldn't believe I had turned on a dime, that I had gone away with no warning. How could I do such a thing? She was a human being with feelings. Why didn't I talk it over with her? It was miserable timing, she told her friend, and she was devastated.

There's never a right time or a pain-free method of ending a love affair when one of the parties doesn't want it to end. It didn't matter that I had done it the way she'd asked. There was no right way. I didn't try to contact her, and she didn't try to contact me. She had too much pride.

I've been on both sides of that one, and the person who does the leaving has a much easier time of it, gay or straight. In retrospect, I probably should have sent her a letter, something tangible that might have meant something down the line, expressing my thanks for her kindness and how open she was and how she taught me to understand my body in ways I had never known before. I wonder how often gay women fall for straight ones and if it ever works out. I have no examples in my life. I only know how it was for me. As attracted to Gabriella as I was, I don't think I'll take a woman as a lover again. But who knows? Like late comedian Richard Pryor once said, "I ain't dead yet."

Chapter Nine

THE AGONY OF PARADISE

God hides the fires of hell within paradise.

— Paulo Coelho, *By the River Piedra I Sat Down and Wept*

I used to imagine that Paradise was a tropical island somewhere in the South Pacific with balmy nights, swaying palm trees, warm ocean waters, perpetual sunshine, and ripe fruit you could pluck right off the trees. I envisioned it as an enchanted garden of peace, prosperity, and happiness, devoid of misery and human suffering. A realm of contentment and acceptance. A world of light and purity without fear or regrets. But I've been to Paradise; it didn't deliver, and I have no interest in going back. In contemporary vernacular: been there, done that.

I know I sound spoiled and ungrateful. I'm aware of how many people would have traded places with me when Paradise opened its doors and invited me in. But there were no toilets or running water there, palm trees dropped ominously heavy coconuts without warning, the trade winds blew bloodthirsty mosquitoes into my face day and night, the wild chickens never stopped squawking, the roosters crowed all night long, and the cuddly looking kittens had fleas. The ocean floor was strewn with thick black slugs that made swimming an exercise in ickiness, the ground was filled with *tupa* crabs scurrying into their holes and attracting mosquitos, the woven thatched huts needed constant maintenance, and the warm tropical sunshine caused the fruit on the trees to heat up and rot.

This was not what I had pictured when Nick first told me about his island paradise. Who owns his own island in Tahiti? This man, an Oscar-winning cinematographer, nominated many times over, had dated movie stars and world-class photographers before I met him, and his private island was part of his charm. A framed photograph of it, a circular bevy of several hundred palm trees, sat beside his Oscar, which he adorned every few days with a fragrant necklace of fresh flowers. He was what you might call "to the manor born" when it came to fame and fortune as his mother was full-blooded Tahitian and his Caucasian father had written, among many other noteworthy books, one of the most famous classic novels of all time, *Mutiny on the Bounty*.

The story goes that one night when Nick was very young, his mother cooked up a shrimp dish that was so savory and delectable, a wealthy dinner guest raised a glass to her and bequeathed a small island, one of the many he owned, to Nick. When the man died many years later, and they read the will, Nick was stunned to find out that the gentleman had made good on his promise. He was the proud owner of his own private island.

Located about six hundred yards off the South Pacific coast, the island was a third of a mile around and about a ten-minute boat ride from the mainland, Papeete. Nick went there between movies and whenever time permitted. The island had no conveniences whatsoever, which didn't bother him. He had no trouble sleeping under the stars, his olive-colored Tahitian skin naturally repelled mosquitos, and he didn't care a whit about plumbing. But he spent his days there building rudimentary shelters, including a romantic sleeping house protected with mosquito nets, a small kitchen fired by propane, a large chicken coop, and a living space with a thatched roof, striving to make the island somewhat livable so his children and his girlfriends (he was divorced) might enjoy it as much as he did. Plumbing and electricity were still in the future, but he fully intended to bring the little island into the twenty-first century, and I heard that he did so before he died in 2003.

I had high hopes in 1980 when I headed for Nick's Paradise. I had been living with him for a few months in his luxurious Hollywood penthouse with shiny hardwood floors, a vaulted living room, magnificent American Indian rugs, native artifacts, and window seats in every room where I could curl up with Nick or a good book or both. He showered a great deal of love and attention on me at the time, complimenting and appreciating me and introducing me to fascinating people. He was twenty-two years older than me, which made me the younger woman, but I was not an arm piece. Nick wasn't that shallow. Rather, he saw me as a way to stay in touch with a younger generation, which suited me fine because he was very handsome, nimble, strong, and full of creativity. He ran circles around men and women his age, he liked my original poetry, and our conversations were exciting and stimulating as he knew so many artists, writers, photographers, and filmmakers whose work was of the highest caliber, and these people made great dinner party guests.

When Nick asked me to join him in Tahiti for two months, I pictured romantic nights on the white sand beach at the point of the island, making love under the stars, and skinny-dipping beneath a full moon. I imagined sailing to neighboring islands, visiting his friends. He knew Marlon Brando—he had worked with him in a movie—and I expected at some point, we would head over to Brando's island so I could meet the legend himself, his Tahitian wife, and a few kids in the actor's favorite milieu. None of that happened. Once we arrived at Nick's island, he refused to leave for just about anything and he wouldn't stop his constant construction in order to spend time with me. His obsession had switched off of me and onto the island. I had rightly pegged him as a monogamous kind of man when it came to women, but I never imagined I would have to compete with a South Pacific island.

When we landed at the airport in Papeete that first morning after flying all night from Los Angeles, Nick took me on a wild and dangerous ride in a rental car to where his motorboat was docked. I was terrified as he kept nodding off behind the wheel because he had drunk too much champagne. He wouldn't allow me to take over for him—he was too macho, and I had no idea where we were going anyway—but that uncomfortable ride spoke of things yet to come.

We miraculously survived the drive, probably because ours was the only car on the road that early in the morning. Once we were at the dock, we boarded a little motorboat with our small bags, some kitchen supplies, and several gallon jugs of drinking water. Nick steered the boat, sobering up when the tiny island and the lush palm trees came into focus. Three baby kittens mewed at us amid a brood of squawking chickens, and there was Henri, an old Tahitian man with dark skin and bow-legs that looked like tree roots. He caught hold of the boat line, pulled it closer, and wrapped the rope around a post. Offering me a hand, Henri helped me out of the boat. He looked like he was a hundred years old. He and Nick began conversing in the strangest French I'd ever heard. The Tahitians spoke a French dialect in which they pronounced every letter in each word like they did in their native Malaysian language, so although I understood French reasonably well (I picked it up when I lived in Monte Carlo), it took me a while to understand what they were saying.

Henri took our suitcases off the boat, and I unpacked my meager belongings—a pair of rubber clogs, a couple of books, several bathing suits, a journal for writing, a few pairs of shorts, some T-shirts, and three *pareos*—pieces of native cloth that tied around the waist to make a skirt or a dress. Nick had told me that was what everyone wore in Tahiti, himself included, so at least I would appear fashion forward. But to whom? There was no one on the island except a rooster and a bunch of chickens, Henri, and a few of his workers who rowed over each day and left at sundown.

I put on a fresh T-shirt and tied a *pareo* around my waist, and Nick walked me around the island, which took fifteen minutes because we walked slowly while he described what he wanted to build and where. It was truly beautiful there, pristine and untouched by civilization, as the waves lapped against the shoreline all around the island, depositing strange sea creatures on the shores and other debris that Nick stopped to study. I felt so small, I took his hand for reassurance, but his attention was already moving away from me as we made our way around that tiny piece of land jutting up in the middle of the Pacific Ocean. When we got back to where we had started, Nick grabbed a quick cup of coffee, and he and Henri took off for the other side of the island, where they began doing some repairs on the chicken coop. I watched them go and huddled in the kitchen next to a burning mosquito coil, swatting at darting bloodsuckers, talking myself down. We had only just arrived, I reminded myself. I would get used to it, and surely Nick would spend some time with me after he took care of immediate concerns.

I was wrong. He was distracted and obsessed with his palm tree heaven, and within forty-eight hours I had a full-blown case of island fever. Word had spread among the mosquito population that my white American flesh was irresistibly tasty, coils be damned, and the bites on my face became swollen and infected while huge black, armored, roach-like bugs felt entitled to crawl all over my body. I understood they were there first, but I felt like I had been duped by false advertising. Where was the realm of contentment and beauty? Where was the world of light and purity without fear or doubts? The brochures had lied. Paradise was not what it was cracked up to be, and I was filled with misery and regrets.

First and foremost, I regretted that I was in supposed Paradise and I didn't feel the slightest bit blissful. Not even when we dined on fresh hearts of palm called "millionaire salad," scooped out of a recently toppled palm tree or when topless dark-haired beauties floated by on wind sails. That was a man's fantasy, not mine. But as I look back, Paradise really didn't have a chance with me because I had given myself up to live

Nick's life. My suitcase may have been light and half empty, but my head was heavy and full of upsets, judgments, and shame, starting with the fact that I was so desperately lonely, I couldn't even be happy in Paradise. What the hell was wrong with me? I'd thought that simply being there would signal my insecurities to take a hike, but that was not the case. I was stuck with myself and my overactive brain, and I abandoned my soul, left myself in the lurch, and tried to deny my feelings because they didn't fit into someone else's idyllic world. In short, I gave myself away, hardly for the first time.

An average day in Nick's Paradise went like this:

Wake up with the light at six o'clock and watch a magnificent sunrise.

Have coffee and fresh papaya at six thirty.

Take a walk around the island at seven o'clock to see what the tides had washed in.

Get back at seven fifteen.

Wave good-bye to Nick at seven thirty as he proceeds to work with Henri.

Occupy my overactive brain for the next twelve hours and deal with mosquitos without going mad.

Watch a magnificent sunset at seven o'clock in the evening.

Eat dinner at seven thirty and talk about what Nick intends to build the next day while he drinks too much wine and passes out.

Drag him into bed at nine o'clock, pull the netting around us, and watch the thirsty mosquitos find a way through the mesh to use Nick's back as a springboard to jump onto me and drink my tasty white blood while he snores, exhausted from a hard day's work.

The next morning, wake up with the light at six o'clock and start all over again.

The above included weekends. When I try to recall what I did during the days, I have no memory besides using *tupa* crabs for target practice. When Nick identified them as culprits that attracted mosquitos, I took a BB gun and shot them on sight.

Crab Killer

Sometimes I put the nose of the gun directly into their holes and pulled the trigger. At other times, I plugged up their holes, hoping they might suffocate—but none of it seemed to decrease the mosquito population at all, and after the first few days, I felt like I was committing crabocide, so I stopped.

My respites occurred only twice in four weeks, when Nick took me to Papeete to visit his elderly mother. We passed the Gauguin museum both times—the artist had lived right there—and I tapped Nick on the shoulder, but he didn't stop. When we were heading to his mother's house, Nick wanted to get there before lunch, so we didn't have time. On the way back, he was trying to beat the sunset, and besides, it was just a museum.

Nick's mother still lived in the house where Nick had been raised, and I was allowed to wander into the study where his father had written his timeless classic novels with a cowriter. Hundreds of books lined the floor-to-ceiling wooden shelves, and I stood at the desk where he'd written, running my hand over his original blotter and trying on the glasses that sat on the desk, untouched for these many years. What manner of brain used a beat-up, rusted typewriter to produce literature that was so brilliant that it would never become old and would outlive and immortalize its creator?

Nick's mother had lived all of her married life in that same house where she had raised Nick, and she had vigorously opposed a new thoroughfare that would run between her main house and her smaller one on the beach below. She knew that the noise would disturb her personal paradise, but the city won. The construction began, and on the morning that the thoroughfare was scheduled to open to traffic, Nick's mom woke up stone deaf. She couldn't hear a thing. Most of the family blamed it on a course of antibiotics that she had reportedly taken, but Nick looked at it as divine intervention.

She never got her hearing back, and when we sat down to lunch, Nick smiled at her and said aloud to me, "Aren't Mother's tits huge?" Unaware, she smiled at her son, picked up the silverware at her place setting, and heaved it onto the floor with contempt. Her Javanese maid picked it up and put it back in the kitchen. It was a Tahitian custom to eat with one's hands, even at formal dinners, and she didn't care that we were using silverware. She would have none of the newfangled ways. She proceeded to eat the pork chop that she correctly called "pig" with her hands, while she warned us to stay away from parts of the island where they had "eels with ears" and other strange and odd wild animals with singular characteristics.

Beyond those two visits, we didn't leave the island for the rest of the month. I was terribly lonely during that time, and I think it would have been nice if Nick had prepared me for the isolation before we left (he hadn't) and if he had checked in with me during the day when he buried himself in his building projects (he didn't do that either). I tried meditating, but Nick made fun of me, so I stopped. I tried cuddling the kittens, but the fleas left their marks on my body beside the mosquito bites. As I sobbed all alone on the white sand beach, scratched my bites and made them bleed, and wallowed in my loneliness, yearning for my friends back home, I might just as well have been anywhere else. I was learning the hard way that Paradise had little to do with my surroundings. It was about my insides, how I felt about myself and my life, and how few tools I had developed to comfort myself and deal with the boredom and loneliness that was eating me alive worse than a mosquito ever could.

I'd been in Paradise for a month—I don't know how I'd made it that long—and I was looking at another month when I went to find Nick in the middle of the day. I interrupted him as he was sawing the center out of a palm tree that he and Henri had just felled to make room for a guesthouse. What wouldn't I have given for a guest right then? Anyone to end my isolation. "I need to talk to you," I told him.

"Can it wait until later?" he asked, the sweat dripping off him as he worked the saw.

"No, I need you right now," I said, tears pouring down my cheeks, which were red and swollen from insect bites.

He looked at me, stunned. "What's wrong?" he asked me. "Aren't you happy?"

He had no idea. He had slept beside me for a month of nights, made daily meals for me in the tiny makeshift kitchen, and made love to me on the nights he wasn't too exhausted or drunk, which were far too few. And this was the first time he'd noticed that I was unhappy. What did he think I did all day? Did he think about me at all? Did he care? He was not an unkind man, but he was deeply self-centered, and while he worked himself to the bone, he was being so profoundly nurtured by the island, I guess he thought I was having the same experience. What else could he think, because I didn't tell him? I was afraid of being demanding and upsetting him.

When I told him that day that I had to leave, that there was no way in hell or in Paradise that I could stay for another week, never mind another month, a cloud of disappointment washed over him. "They can't wait to get here," he muttered almost under his breath, "and then they all want to leave."

I guess I wasn't the first woman to get island fever here. Clearly it had happened before, but it hadn't occurred to Nick that his women's discontent had anything to do with him. Did he ever consider that squatting over a hole in the ground every day was deeply unsettling for a woman, and getting bitten from head to toe was discouraging and painful? I suppose he figured he had brought me to this magical place, he had paid my way and fed me and slept beside me every night. He gave me no cause to be jealous—there were no other women—and he made sure there was plenty of food and that I had no financial burden. What more was he expected to do?

I now understand that Paradise is not a place; it's a state of mind that can exist anywhere. Right here, as I write these words, Paradise can be my soft, furry, flea-free cat suddenly jumping into my lap or an inspired sentence that I happen to write. Or it can be under the covers where I like to burrow after I write, a moment of clarity in the office of my wise therapist who really loves me, or in the heartwarming embrace of a good friend. For Nick, Paradise was his little Tahitian island where I spent a month of my life, but I couldn't find it there. It was hiding behind my self-loathing, my extreme isolation, and my fear of speaking up, being true to myself, and asking for what I needed.

When I returned to Hollywood on my own to find a new place to live, I had a premonition one night the moment I got out of my car—not specifically about what was to happen. I just felt something ominous in the air, and my body contracted. I'd been apartment hunting unsuccessfully all day (Nick was still in Tahiti), and I'd had dinner with a friend. When I got that odd feeling in front of Nick's building, I figured I was just tired as I locked the car. It was half past ten at night, not terribly late, and the street was empty of people. That was not unusual. It was a residential district on a Sunday night, and most people were already in for the evening. But something still felt off.

I was on the corner of Fountain and Sweeter Avenues in the heart of Hollywood, a neighborhood that was reasonably well lit. Tired and discouraged, I felt defeated as I stood under the street lamp, wondering how I would ever find a decent place to live, fishing around in my purse for the penthouse keys. A habit. I usually located my keys before I got to the front door of the building, so I was holding them when I raised my head and saw two dark forms in the distance ahead, rushing down the street toward me, one behind the other. They were two African American men, and they were getting closer, not looking to their right or their left, coming straight for me. I did the only thing I could think to do. I looked directly into the eyes of the man in front, who was now just a few feet away. I had heard that looking into the eyes of an attacker might cause him to back down. "Stand firm and don't look like a victim" was the conventional wisdom.

His eyes were black holes of hatred—free-floating, nonspecific, generic hatred. In retrospect, it wouldn't have mattered if I looked at him or if I didn't. He and the man close behind him didn't see me as a human being. They didn't care if I was nice or mean, strong or weak, they didn't need to know my name or my history, whether I was a racist or a saint, how old I was or if I was broke or a fat cat. In that moment, I was every white woman with blond hair who lived in an upscale neighborhood and had a car and a purse with some cash in it. Causing me bodily harm probably trumped stealing my purse for them, even though they were set on doing both.

As the front man's very large fist connected hard with my face, I literally saw stars, and I felt my purse being deftly slipped out from under my shoulder. It was a tidy, well-timed operation; they had done this before. I somehow stayed on my feet as I took the blow on bent knees. My hands flew up to my face and covered my left eye as the men ran past me, down the street, and around the corner. There was a hundred dollar bill in my wallet along with two twenties. I didn't mind losing the money; I just didn't want *them* to have it.

I ran toward my building blindly since I could see only out of my right eye. I thanked God I had taken out my house keys as I ran up three steps and fit the key into the lock of the heavy front door that led into the lobby. It opened. I walked in quickly and let the weight of the door close behind me. I looked around, but there was no doorman or building guard. I didn't carry a cell phone back then. I rushed down the hallway of the first floor, randomly knocking on three or four people's doors. "Help me," I called out. "I just got mugged." I could feel my voice vibrate in my body, raspy and sharp-edged.

No one opened a door or spoke a word. I stumbled back down the hallway and rang for the elevator. I removed my hand for a moment, saw a pool of blood in my palm, and placed it back over my left eye. Now I was a mugging statistic. When the elevator reached the ground floor, I stepped into the very small cage and pushed number eight. I was breathing in gasps, and as I began slowly ascending, it seemed as if the walls were caving in. When I finally stepped inside the apartment, I slammed the door behind me and rushed to the telephone to call someone to take me to the emergency room.

I dialed a couple of friends and got two answering machines. They were either out or they'd settled into bed and weren't answering their phones. On the third call, I reached a girlfriend, Susan, and she told me to try to stay calm. She and her boyfriend were on their way. I sat on the window seat, crying, as I dialed 911. I hadn't looked in the mirror; I was afraid to see my face as I reported the mugging to the police while Susan and her live-in boyfriend were dashing over to help me. Ironically, she would end up living in this very penthouse apartment many years in the future, with Nick as her second husband. The gods must be implicit in these kinds of things that seem so impossibly random.

"I would have given them my purse if they had just asked," I told the woman who answered the 911 call. The police would find me at the emergency room, she told me, after they scoured the neighborhood. If the muggers were still loitering or attacking anyone else, the police would find them and stop them as quickly as possible. She asked me if I needed an ambulance. I didn't, I told her. Friends were coming to get me.

While I waited for Susan, I cried softly, shivering. Up until that night, I had naively believed that if I lived my life with grace and generosity, this kind of thing wouldn't happen to me. Like a naive New Ager, I believed that bad things didn't happen to good people, so my anger and disappointment about having to move out of the penthouse, I deduced, had to be at the bottom of this. I needed some kind of an explanation, because if I hadn't asked for this, if I hadn't caused it, and if it truly had been random, how could I ever feel safe again? It was easier to blame myself and my behavior because that was something I could change. How could I accept the idea that that my mugging was as random as being in the wrong place at the wrong time? And then, blaming myself was hardly foreign to me.

Susan and her boyfriend took me straight to the emergency room at Cedars Sinai Hospital. When the police found me there, they returned my empty purse; it had been discarded in a trash bin near my building. My assailants had taken my money and credit cards, but they themselves were nowhere to be found. The police said they would most likely get away with it. I went home that night with a blood clot in my left eye and a fractured nose. My nose would heal, and the blood clot would slowly dissolve over the next few weeks, but the emotional wounds, the fear and insecurity, would take much longer.

In fact, it was decades later when I directly addressed these concerns at a friend's graduation from a six-week program called Impact: Model Mugging. This was a form of self-defense in which men dressed up in padded suits to protect their body parts and pretended to attack women who were being trained to beat the living daylights out of them. It scared me to watch the graduation demonstration because I had the mugging and my battering husband lurking in my past. I signed up for the course before I left that night, one of the bravest things I've ever done.

The hardest part was getting myself to each of the six classes. When we were in session, it was so difficult to stand up and fight, I spent hours before each class in dread, wondering how I could get out of it. Finally, I'd pull into the parking area of the meeting place where the classes were held. I had to talk myself into putting one foot in front of the other as I joined ten women who looked exactly like I felt. We sat in a circle on the first day, the ten of us, one female instructor, and two men who would serve as our padded attackers, and I will always remember what our instructor told us. "Women are natural nurturers," she said. "It goes against our natures to have to fight. It's the saddest thing in the world that we have to learn to defend ourselves against the very people, the men in our lives, who were meant to be our protectors. But we do. So let's get on with it."

Before each class, we stood with our arms interlocked in a tight circle that looked like a sports huddle, and together we stamped one foot three times in a row, shouting as loudly as we could, "No! No! No!" *No* was our motto and we learned to use our voices and our bodies to protect ourselves against potential attackers. The padded suits the men wore made them look like deformed monsters and allowed us to hit them in the crotch, the throat, and the eyes with full force, so we didn't have to pull our punches as we learned to go against our feminine natures and use all of our strength to defend ourselves.

I learned that the average male attacker is about five foot eight and a coward, afraid to pick a fight with a man, so more often than not, he attacks a woman from behind. Our padded monsters emulated attackers and rapists by walking behind us and throwing their arms around us, climbing on top of us and calling us filthy names to make us react. It was terrifying, but we had to learn to fight when our adrenaline was shooting because in a real-life situation, that was exactly what would be happening. These highly trained men could instantly evaluate each woman's strengths and weaknesses, meeting our self-defense attempts with exactly the right amount of power from week to week, so we would always win the fight while we got stronger and more confident with each training session. Finally, during our last session, they fought us full out, and each of us was successful at stopping them.

I remember these padded monsters looking at times like my attackers who'd punched me in the street and at other times like my ex-husband as I learned to fight back with all my strength. I was no longer leaving myself or any part of me behind. And neither were the other women. Like me, each of them had her own demons that haunted her and ultimately had gotten her to the training. But we never told our stories because they didn't matter. What mattered was that we were ready and willing to stand up for ourselves in an upside-down world where men so often threatened women and children, randomly or otherwise, and we were no longer willing to be victims. A true story circulated around the training rooms about a woman who had taken the course and had hurt a potential rapist so badly that he took her to court and tried to sue her for bodily damage. Of course he lost, but his sense of entitlement was staggering.

In my class, a mother had brought her daughter, and she told us that a neighbor of hers had scolded her for subjecting her child to such violent training. "You're taking away her innocence," the neighbor had said.

"Better me than a rapist," the mother had answered.

Besides learning to fight, which was the main objective of the classes, we were also given training in de-escalation, as they taught us how to talk down a potential attacker if that was an option. We were taught to run for our lives, as well, if that was an option. If there were no outs, and we had to fight, they made sure that by the time we graduated, we knew how to do it effectively so we could save ourselves.

I invited a number of friends, men and women, to my graduation to observe what I had learned and to cheer me on. I hadn't realized how much fear I'd been carrying around until I took that course, but how could I have avoided it? Fear was spoon-fed to me in my childhood. Up to today, I am still fighting to release it in what feels like a never-ending battle as I recall a huge family gathering, a Thanksgiving many years ago, when safety and danger were the topics of conversation. An aunt spoke about kidnapping, an uncle mentioned how unpleasant flying had become, and my mother looked up, waited for a break in the conversation, and stated quite simply, "The whole world is dangerous." And she went on eating.

Since that was my early programming, what chance did I have to feel safe after being battered by a husband and falling victim to a mugging? But after my self-defense training, my step was lighter, more grounded and solid. I felt less afraid because I stayed alert and aware when I was alone. I looked around and trusted myself when I felt something in the air. I made sure to listen to my instincts instead of shaming myself, and as a result, giving myself away.

I think it should be mandatory for all children, male and female, to learn self-defense in school when they're still young—both the physical aspects and the mind-set. What a lot of pain and suffering we could eliminate. Maybe this training would have given me the self-worth and alertness to avoid my abusive marriage. I hope I would have looked at Jerry, evaluated him, and side-stepped the relationship, like my sister did, holding out for something better. As far as the mugging, there was no way I could have de-escalated the situation, and fighting two men was daunting. But if I had taken the self-defense course before it happened, maybe I would have trusted my instincts and gotten back into the car when I felt something ominous in the air.

Getting rid of old programs, particularly the ones in which I devalue myself, has been an ongoing theme of my adulthood. It seems like I spent the first half of my life meeting new people, inviting in new experiences, finding love, buying things, filling my home with stuff, and appreciating what I have. And then I've spent the second half of my life letting things go, sort of like having an epic garage sale and laying all my stuff out on the lawn to see what really matters. These days, it has become more important to let go of things than to hold onto them. It has become more important to give love than to get it. It has become more important to free my spirit than to be "spiritual." It has become more important to be healthy than to look pretty, as I work hard to uplift my mind and heal my body, until one day, in a final exhalation, I let go of them too.

Chapter Ten

SEX WITH THE EX

You never really know a man until you have divorced him.

— Zsa Zsa Gabor

I did that thing you're not supposed to do. I had sex with my ex. Well, some of us aren't supposed to. I know women who are more than capable of having sex with an ex, or just about anyone else, and leaving it behind once it's over. Like most guys, these women can fuck and run, and what happens in the bed stays in the bed, which sounds like an enviable ability to me. They can have fun and keep things uncomplicated. But that has never been me. The only thing I leave in the bed after sex is my underpants.

I spoke with a friend, one of these women, the other day after she'd had a tryst with an old lover in a remote hotel in Malibu. Even though they were both in what they called "good" relationships, they'd done the deed for old time's sake. They had parted quite happily, and within an hour of leaving the premises, my girlfriend had moved on to the business of the day at her real-estate office, carrying with her only a sense of feeling refreshed, appreciated, and filled with energy. No abandonment. No guilt later when she got back home. No wondering when or if it might happen again. No fretting over why it had happened at all or what was wrong with her current relationship that made her want to act out. She didn't think of it as acting out, and for her, it wasn't. When she and I talked about it a few days after the fact, I realized that I was much more concerned about the possibility of a next time than she was, and it had nothing to do with me.

My reunion with my ex (I'll call him Ethan), as opposed to hers, was a disaster, and ever since, I've been trying to write about it. But I keep writing *around* it and completely missing the point. I like to blame Ethan's and my divorce on the fact that he was so much younger than I was (I speak about him in the past, as if he doesn't exist any longer), but although our age difference was notable, there were a host of other contributing factors. Let me try again, and maybe this time I'll find the courage to tell the truth.

I met Ethan, seventeen years my junior, when a young friend of mine brought this sandy-blond, buff, good-looking Englishman to my home back in 1993. It was convenient or not, depending on how you look at it, that someone delivered him to me instead of my having to go out somewhere to meet him. I wouldn't have done it. At the time, I'd been living out the most unhealthy traits of writers: staying home alone a lot, brooding, smoking too much pot (thank goodness I didn't like drinking or I would have been doing that too), editing and reediting my work ad nauseam, riding the emotional waves that I was streaming onto the page, embodying some of my characters' worst habits, heavily obsessing on the idea that my life should be different and less lonely than it was but refusing to do anything about it.

When Ethan walked through my front door, I was instantly intrigued. There was just something about him…which is what people say about other people when their pheromones are stirred up. After he had pored over my music collection (good thing I had the requisite Beatles CDs or he might have walked right out), he took in the panoramic view from my living room, looked me up and down shamelessly, and then smiled broadly at me. "You're gorgeous," he said, taking a seat on the couch.

"You look like an angel. I knew there were women around like you. We should get together. I have some things that you need, and you have some things that I need."

I pegged him as a gigolo then and there, and I told him so. He laughed. Then I promptly buried the information because it was inconvenient, considering the gap that I wanted him to fill. I have since learned that "gigolo" was too sophisticated a term for Ethan, as it suggested premeditation. A more accurate term would have been "opportunist," since he didn't think things through. He just naturally showed up when and where it would do him the most good, and he was absent when he was most needed. I hear tell he's still that way, as a few women have reported to me in recent years. But I was a sucker for a foreign accent, and I got swept away by his charisma, his good looks, his strong body, and his blindness to our age difference, which I handily interpreted as his European sensibility. In truth, his blindness came not from his place of birth but rather from his obliviousness to others and his sixties-like attitude in the nineties that he would never grow older and neither would I. Then there was his "unfinished business" with his mother, a cliché for sure, but there's a reason for clichés, as they ring painfully true. How much more obvious could his mother complex have been? Did I need him to call me "Mom" in order to catch on?

For my part, I had become largely unresponsive to men of my own generation; my peers felt like they were over-the-hill even though we were the same age. I guess if you meet someone when you're both young and then you grow old together, you overlook the obvious because it happens gradually, like sagging skin, a balding frontal lobe, political exhaustion, and a weariness from having slayed too many dragons in the big city. Ethan's skin was taut, he had reasonably good hair, and he had avoided politics and dragons, scorning them both. I chose to ignore the fact that he was searching for someone to slay the dragons *for* him, and then later, when I did smooth the way for him on several occasions, he interpreted my support as meddling and used that as a reason to separate from me.

If only I had acknowledged his codependent and devious bent. If only I had understood that my success as a writer satisfied his need to walk beside someone who had claimed her place in the world because he had not yet claimed his own—which also became the source of his bitter resentment toward me. If only I had stopped long enough to notice how entitled he felt to spend my money on fancy clothes and knockout marijuana and to give so little in return. If only...

When we first got together, I was blissfully in denial, thrilled that a gorgeous younger man found me irresistible. I was in awe of his imagination and belief that the world was his to mold into whatever shape or form he could dream up. I loved making love with him, and I liked the idea that he could have any woman he wanted, and he wanted me. It was a somewhat pathetic period in my life when knowing that a man desired me was enough. Whether or not I wanted him was pretty much beside the point. I was a slow learner when it came to men, which I like to blame on having had no brothers. Or being in the ballet and growing up around mostly gay men. There's always someone or something else to blame, isn't there? Mostly I wanted and needed to be wanted and needed, Ethan had the same stumbling blocks, and our coming together masked the emptiness in both of us. Temporarily, of course.

It's easy to fall into these kinds of traps in the heart of Hollywood, California, where financial disparities and age differences between couples are common and accepted, whether the woman is richer or poorer, younger or older. In fact, there's an unspoken admiration, a "you go, girl" attitude, when an older woman is in a relationship with a younger man, even if he's broke and not very bright. There's that Lady Chatterley fantasy of being the woman of the manor and getting down and dirty with the gardener or the contractor with the fabulous tool belt. Or anyone else along those lines.

"If you want to be cool and hip, date younger," the tabloids tell us in capital letters. In the next breath, however, they call women who date younger men "cougars," formerly a pejorative term that morphed into a well-accepted, even enviable description of a confident, strong, single woman over forty-five. So which is it? Does the word "cougar" refer to a desperate woman on the hunt for younger men to distract her from the fact that she's aging? Or does it mean she's so alive, attractive, and self-assured, younger men find her alluring, and she can meet their energy, thrust after youthful thrust? I guess it all depends on who's doing the translating.

The truth is that age gaps are so common here in La La Land, we actually have cougar websites devoted to the phenomenon, and there are cruises designed for older women and younger men to sail the seas and mingle. Which brings me back to the fact that although Ethan's youth was a contributing factor to our demise, it wasn't the main reason we imploded. While he had some endearing qualities, like his boyish exuberance, his ability to speak several languages fluently, and his hunkiness, he also had some weaknesses that had nothing to do with age disparity that I carefully managed to skip over. I'm talking about blatant immaturity for a man of any age and his staggering sense of entitlement that only an Englishman could pull off, like his habit of reading the last page of a book first. I suppose I shouldn't have cared, but as an author who works so hard to make a book interesting by creating arcs of tension and release and payoffs in the end, it really bothered me. It was like cooking a gourmet meal for someone, and he eats dessert first and skips the entrée.

In many ways, Ethan and I were poorly matched at the time we got together, but we did share some common ground besides our sexual attraction to each other. We were born into different religions, and we hailed from different countries, but I understood his European way of looking at life since I had lived in the south of France and Brighton, England, for extended periods of time. I had traveled and performed throughout the continent when I was dancing professionally in the sixties, and the people I met and the places I danced were enviable and exciting, the kinds of experiences Ethan would have given anything to have had for himself.

An elite clique of artistes, we ballerinas were known for our eccentricities, like working ourselves to the bone, hardly eating, and our strange-looking duck walk from overly rotating our hips outward. I wasn't even out of high school when I joined my ballet company and began to tour the world. While most girls my age were having their sweet-sixteen parties, I had my own flat in Monte Carlo and was privy to more than one sighting of Rudolph Nureyev, the Russian ballet star who had dramatically defected from Russia to Paris in 1961.

In fact, there was a constant presence of a group of luminaries around us dancers who were truly out of this world and brought home the point that we were not ordinary people living ordinary lives. I remember one day during rehearsals, when the door to the studio swung open a few inches, and a pale, white-haired, sad-eyed face peered in. It was Andy Warhol, a friend of Rebekah Harkness's, our founder.

On another occasion, during the grand opening of the townhouse on Seventy-Fifth Street that Mrs. Harkness renovated and converted into ballet studios and called Harkness House, I turned a corner at the bottom of a large, gilded staircase. When I looked up, there was Salvador Dali floating down the stairs, his thin, black mustache corkscrewed at both ends, his black cape trailing behind his slender frame, a baby ocelot gracing his left shoulder.

There in Harkness House, where we had our daily hour-and-a-half class every morning and rehearsed our repertoire for the remainder of the day, Mrs. Harkness put on display a priceless gold, bejeweled urn—a container for her ashes "when the time came," created by Dali himself and protected behind bulletproof glass. The urn had been sculpted into a large golden chalice in the shape of an apple, and it slowly rotated, its gilded butterfly wings fluttering open and closed to reveal priceless sapphires, emeralds, rubies, and diamonds. Mrs. Harkness's prized possession and future resting place lived in the hallway of Harkness House between the elevator and the staircase, under the watchful eye of a full-time security guard. We passed it every day, nodding to the guard and making our way up the staircase to Studio B, our toe shoe ribbons dangling behind us.

One of the wealthiest women in the United States, our illustrious founder had been a renegade ever since she graduated high school in

1932. She and a group of her well-to-do female friends had formed what they called "The Bitch Pack," a subculture of local debutantes who liked to shock people by attending parties where they laced punchbowls with mineral oil and performed stripteases on banquet tables. She was still wild and unfettered, and we never knew what she would do next, from taking a gay lover who did choreography for us to spontaneously appearing with us on the ballet stage one night.

Mrs. Harkness had homes in the most sumptuous places, like Gstaadt, Switzerland, where I once visited her picture-perfect chalet in the mountains when we were on tour in Europe. When she bought property in Watch Hill, Rhode Island, a coastal village with a reputation for housing the extremely wealthy in sumptuous estates they modestly called "cottages," she also bought the old fire station in the center of town, complete with a shiny, red fire truck. The first summer I was with her company, she took her dancers, our teachers, and our choreographers out of the stifling heat in New York City and relocated us at breezy Watch Hill on the ocean. We spent that summer living in the rooms above the firehouse as well as in apartments up in the hills, rehearsing six days a week on the bottom floor of the converted fire station with the pole intact, smack in the center of the room. On weekends, we climbed onto the back of the fire truck and were transported to the Harkness estate, where we lounged poolside, drinking champagne and eating caviar and hors d'oeuvres.

There in Watch Hill, where we lived for two months, I held the rare distinction of becoming an item in a scavenger hunt. In this town of old wealth with huge yachts and Victorian-style castles, I was in a phone booth (remember them?) just outside the fire station, talking to my parents, who were living in Connecticut, when a tall, lanky teenager with longish brown hair slowly ambled up and knocked on the door. I opened it, still on the phone, and said, "Yes? Do you want something?"

He answered in a slow drawl, "Hi, my name is Perky. Are you a ballet dancer?"

I nodded.

"Great," he said in a monotone voice, "you're an item on my scavenger hunt. See? It says right here, one ballet dancer. I already got a gull feather and a sailboat mast. But I need a ballet dancer. Would you mind coming with me?"

"If I can bring my girlfriend," I bargained. He agreed. I told my parents I needed to go (I didn't tell them why), and Perky waited while I ran inside, stunning my girlfriend with the news. She was game, and we both accompanied him to one of the larger mansions in town. The only kid in Watch Hill who had managed to scavenge not one but two ballet dancers during the hunt, Perky was an instant star among his friends, the offspring of some of the wealthiest landowners. These kids were so bored, they listed human beings as items on their scavenger hunts. As for Perky, he was richer than rich, outspoken, and pretty gutsy, but "perky" he was not. I never saw a more relaxed, nonchalant teenager, so his name must have been an antonym the other kids had given their laid-back friend.

During the three years that I traveled and performed with the Harkness Ballet, I had so many unusual experiences and met so many amazing people, I can hardly recall them all. What I'm trying to say is that I was a member of a dedicated, disciplined group of obsessive women and mostly gay men who had every reason to believe we were special. This was what Ethan wanted to believe about himself too, maybe because he left his small English town when he finished high school and began living in other countries, picking up languages, and figuring out how to get along. Or maybe he felt so ordinary, the opposite of special, he couldn't maintain his sense of self around me. The way I see it, the main difference between us was that I toiled for my daily bread and the right to hobnob with royalty, while Ethan searched for sponsors—a delicate way of saying that he was on the prowl for women who would reward his good looks and virility with a luxurious place to hang his hat and an introduction to interesting, famous people. The perfect prey for a cougar.

During the four years he was with me, I rewarded his beauty and charisma with money, nice clothes, good pot, and the promise of a green card. You could say we had a shotgun wedding—not because I was pregnant. Ethan's visa had expired, he was running in fear of the INS, and I was afraid if I didn't marry him, he would get snatched away and deported, forever exiled from the United States. At the time, I was forty-six, he was twenty-nine, and his unremitting energy reminded me of how I used to be. Connecting with him was like plugging into a high-frequency electrical socket, and I felt reborn and excited about life. I just couldn't get enough of him, and I didn't want him to go away.

After we were married at the luxurious home of one of my clients, I took the requisite trip to his birthplace, a sleepy little town in south-western England, to meet his parents, who still lived in the house where Ethan grew up. I was pleased to find them completely welcoming—my age didn't seem to bother them—as we settled into Ethan's old bedroom located downstairs in their small home. I put some of my things in the drawers, feeling as if we had traveled back in time, imagining his high school posters on the wall featuring champion soccer players and hot-looking movie stars. His relatives and friends could not have been kinder when we all met one evening in a cozy pub in the center of town, play-ing darts and drinking beer. But it was at the wedding party his parents threw for us where the reality of my situation came to light.

Family and friends gathered at Ethan's birth home to eat some typi-cally English, heavy, meat-laden dishes and to raise a glass to us, the newlyweds. I ate and drank and met a bunch of lovely people, all of them ignoring the fact that I was old enough to be Ethan's mother. I ignored it too, until everybody left and we were two couples—his parents and Ethan and me. We were chatting about where I was born and grew up, sipping some wine, when Ethan's dad looked at me, and for a moment his face lit up. "Don't tell me that you were at Woodstock," he said, hop-ing that I was.

I wasn't. Never mind, he indicated with a hand gesture as he got up and headed for the garage, returning with some CDs. He put one into the tape machine. The sound of Crosby, Stills, and Nash wafted through the air as Ethan's dad and I began singing along. Ethan looked kind of pouty, and I got the terrible realization that his father was age-appropri-ate for me since we related to music from the same era. I felt intensely uncomfortable at that point and excused myself as I went downstairs to get some sleep. But I couldn't sleep. I had made a strange, irreversible error, I thought to myself, and I turned away from Ethan when he came to bed.

I got over it when we returned to California, where anything goes, and we carried on living together as a married couple. But I had seen what I had seen, and that night changed me, even though I tried to keep things light, telling some friends I was writing a sitcom called *Married to Children*. It was just too easy in Hollywood to live an unconventional lifestyle with an unconventional spouse.

The details of Ethan's and my relationship are no different from other people's stories of finding love and sexual excitement with a partner and then losing it. What is relevant here is that after four years together, a little less than two of them married, he was ready to flee from me and my house late one afternoon.

I didn't know that he had already met his new squeeze, whose claim to fame was her close relationship with several prominent celebrities. That must have produced plenty of pheromones for Ethan, who thought he was in love, and now that his next woman and home were lined up, along with the promise of hanging out with the rich and famous, he told me, "I can't be with you anymore. You're swallowing me."

He was telling the truth, at least from his point of view. It was easy for him to get lost in the shuffle when we were together, since I was enjoying an upward surge in my writing career. I blamed our split on the fact that he was young and inexperienced, but that wasn't the elephant in the room. The real pachyderm was the fact that I had chosen someone who, even before he moved in, was already figuring out what he could get without a thought about what he had to give. He was narcissistic; he felt so overpowered by me that he spent all of his energy trying to keep himself together and in the center of other people's attention. It didn't work.

If I had studied his behavior more carefully, I wouldn't have been surprised when he was getting ready to move on. I was in too much denial, hoping he would settle down, but the truth was that he'd been moving away from me for at least six months. When he announced his plans to move on, I sat on the edge of the bed, trying to absorb what was happening. I staggered to my feet and surprised myself a moment later when I impetuously flung my body to the floor of the bedroom, sobbing and moaning, "No, no. This isn't happening. This isn't supposed to be happening."

It was, though, and his decision was irreversible. I knew that. He stared at me, paralyzed, unsure what to do or say as the muscles around my solar plexus tightened, and I could feel the tearing away of my treasured dream. My life with Ethan was about to become my life without Ethan. In fact, he was already gone. What had I expected? That our odd coupling would withstand the test of time?

I stood up and faced him, trying to pierce his psyche with my eyes. "Don't you leave yet!" I commanded him. He stepped back, a look of fear washing over him. I wiped the snot from my nose and chin with my sleeve. I staggered to my chest of drawers and ripped my sweats off. Sobbing all the while, I pulled out a soft yellow sweater and searched for the pants that went with it. I'm confounded about that now, that I felt the need to be color-coordinated as I was rushing to drive away before he did, so he wouldn't get the satisfaction of physically leaving me while I stood there, sobbing. Instead, I left *him* standing there and sped off into the night, upset not only that he was saying good-bye but also that he was allowing me to drive in such a broken state, as I headed for a girlfriend's house.

The first day I awakened without him, I had to face the humiliating fact that he had slid into another girl's bed on the day that he climbed out of mine. I don't know why that kind of thing is humiliating for the one who gets left, but it is. Later he swore up and down that he had left me *before* he slept with her, but how could I be certain? Did it even matter? Would it change anything either way? I lay there, desperately wishing it was three months into the future, when I expected the pain would be greatly diminished if not gone altogether. I wandered from room to room in my house, and it seemed like he had never even been there—my childish husband who had withdrawn so completely, it was as if he had lived alone in my house with me. The only thing he had purchased when we were together were several Beatles CDs, which he had remembered to take with him. He hadn't bought a decoration, a piece of furniture, not even a lamp, and along with the CDs and his toothbrush, he had taken most of his clothes. I went out and bought a few extra toothbrushes to trick myself into thinking I wasn't alone. Of course, that didn't work.

Besides a few expensive suits I'd bought him that he had left behind, everything else in the house had been mine, and it still was. There were almost no signs of him. It was one day after he left, and nothing looked different. Had he even been there at all? Had his beautiful, lithesome, athletic, toned body ever really reclined on the couch? Had we really laughed uproariously until we cried on so many nights? Had we really made love slowly descending the stairs together, not wanting to separate our bodies for fear that it might go away?

It did go away, and I had to face how much he *really* wanted to leave, because we hadn't lived together as a married couple for the requisite two years for him to get his green card. Just in case I was harboring any illusions about him coming back to me, the naked truth was that he had chosen the risk of deportation over staying with me for a few more months. And then, when he called a couple of days later to brag about a pair of high-profile celebrities with whom he had smoked pot and dined the night before, I understood the true meaning of the word "twerp." *A silly, insignificant, or contemptible person* is *Webster's* dictionary definition, and that resonated with me.

When I found out that Ethan had moved in with the other woman less than a week after he left, or maybe the same day, I summarily rolled up the suits he had left behind into tight little balls, tossed them into several black trash bags, and threw them into the garage for him to pick up when I wasn't home. All the while, I imagined dialing the INS, reporting him, and ending his stay in the United States. I had that option within my power, and I thought about how awful he and the new girl would feel when the authorities ripped him away from her. I even directly threatened him with it once when he was speaking to me like a rude child, reminding him that all it would take was one phone call, so he damned well better change his attitude if he didn't want to be hand-delivered back home.

I didn't make the call. In the end, I agreed not to block him from getting his green card as long as it didn't cost me any money or time, and he did what was necessary to make it happen. I just don't believe in revenge. I prefer to let things alone and allow karma to have its way, since it usually does a better job than I ever could. In the end, Ethan got his green card, his new relationship, and the chance to mingle with Hollywood royalty for a while. I got my independence back, a little worse for the wear, but at least my conscience was clean.

Years later, five to be exact, Ethan apologized to me. He called and asked to see me, and because he seemed genuinely contrite, I forgave him. It felt real, but I had a few things to learn about the nature of forgiveness, as Ethan and I started meeting once in a while to have dinner and a few laughs. One night, about eight years after we had separated, he suddenly became sexually attracted to me again. I saw it in his eyes— that look that I always hoped I would see again. I don't know how many times I'd imagined that he would wake up one day, understand what he'd lost, and try to get me back. And when he tried, I imagined that I would turn him down flat. Revenge would feel sweet, I thought.

That didn't sound like forgiveness, but I cut myself some slack, since I wasn't the first woman to fantasize about the glory of rejecting the man who had rejected her…but when the opportunity arose, I didn't go for the glory. Rather, his sudden desire for me lulled me into denial as I imagined how easy it would be to take him as a lover. I hadn't been with anyone else for some time, and Ethan and I were a step ahead because we already knew what the other person liked in bed. We'd been fulfilled with each other, and as immature and insecure as he was, he had been healthy sexually, so I figured it'd be a breeze reconnecting with him. There I was again, pretending to be someone else.

When we got into bed some days later and started to make love, it was no surprise that the anticipated breeze became a dark storm of memories and obstacles, and my body couldn't keep up with my mental desire. My mind was racing, reminding me of every negative thing he had ever said and the ways he had taken advantage of me. As a result, I wasn't wet, it hurt like hell, I couldn't get him inside me, and he stopped before we got past the initial penetration. This had never happened to me before, not with him or anyone else. But I had never tried to have sex with an ex. To make matters worse, I kept hearing the cruel words he had hurled at me a week or two before he'd fled from my home altogether. "All I can see are your wrinkles," he had uttered in abject cruelty. At the time, I wanted to retaliate by talking about his early male pattern baldness that was showing up on his frontal lobe, but I refrained. Instead, I pretended his declaration didn't hurt, but the mere thought of those words this many years later still stings.

We parted ways after our unsuccessful physical reunion, but he called a few days later, speaking with what sounded like a forced lightness, supposedly checking in on me. As if he thought he was supposed to. After a moment or two, he told me how desperately busy he had become in the last several days, much too busy to make another date with me. Finally, he admitted that even if he weren't that busy, he was done. I recall a bit from Andrew Dice Clay, a comedian who made his living by being a misogynist. He had just finished having sex with a woman who informed him, once the deed was done, that she had a live-in boyfriend.

"That's OK with me," said Andrew in his heavy Brooklyn twang. "I'm done."

In his own inarticulate way, Ethan was saying the same thing, hemming and hawing for a while, not knowing how to word it, since he got hopelessly tongue-tied around me, especially when he was making excuses. Finally, he blurted out icily, "Well, it wasn't exactly a freeing experience."

In his next few remarks, which were mostly jumbled, I was able to glean that he somehow believed that I expected him to be monogamous with me once we had gone to bed again. God only knows where he dreamt that up; it was so off the wall and conjured on his part that I didn't even address it. But it was clear that Ethan hadn't changed. If being with me after so long were to take any effort on his part, he was out of there. What else was new? Somebody once said, "Getting back with your ex is like taking a shower and putting your dirty underwear back on."

This time, I didn't take to my bed. And I'm relieved to report that when a new man came into my life, my body worked fine. I had shut down with Ethan because it was Ethan. I was fine with someone else. And I got one more reminder that my being a "fuck and run" kind of girl and a master at forgiveness were both figments of my imagination. Once again, I had put myself in a position to be judged and wounded by a twerp who was still wallowing in his twerpdom.

I decided to cut him off at that point—enough was enough—and to stop seeing him, contacting him, or responding to his calls, which was a big step for me. I remember a time when the social consensus was that cutting people off and refusing to make up with them was not acceptable or "spiritual." Back in the sixties, when we were newly embarking on the self-help path, we believed that forgiving, no matter what someone had done, was an ideal that an enlightened person was meant to live up to. But I've changed my mind.

Today I believe that forgiveness is a grand and wonderful thing when it's authentic and based in reality. But paying lip service to forgiveness is like sticking a knife in a wound on your own body and turning it. I had thought that if I forgave Ethan, or even if I pretended to, it would lighten my heart and allow me to think of myself as a good person. But I have since learned that forgiveness is dynamic, not stagnant. It was erroneous of me to think that if I forgave someone today, I would automatically forgive him tomorrow and would no longer be susceptible to the pain that his actions may have caused me. If only we could forgive once and have done with it, life would be a great deal easier. And so would relationships.

But forgiveness occurs in the heart, not the mind, so wishing doesn't make it so. Sometimes I forgive Ethan for the pain he caused me, and sometimes I still hate him for it. Sometimes I see that he was doing the best he could, and I forgive myself for falling into the trap of believing that it would be safe for me to open my legs and my heart to someone who had wounded me in the past. Sometimes I feel grateful that I can see my part in what happened, and at other times I'm angry for not protecting myself better. It flips back and forth, but it remains true that forgiving is not a one-step process. It is never set in stone—a real and valuable lesson that I learned from having sex with my ex.

Sister Helen Prejean, author of the profound book *Dead Man Walking*, reminds us that a little mercy toward ourselves would be a good thing, as she says, "Forgiveness is never going to be easy. Each day it must be prayed for and struggled for and won."

Day by day is the only way. And if forgiveness is your goal, I wouldn't recommend sex with your ex. Unless you happen to be one of "those women."

Chapter Eleven

SOB STORY

Down [the rabbit hole] Alice went…

never once considering how in the world

she was to get out again.

— Lewis Carroll, *Alice in Wonderland*

"If I start crying, I'll never be able to stop." Does that sound familiar?

When the floodgates opened a few years ago, and I shed the first tear of many, I had no idea that a storm was gathering momentum inside of me. I only knew that I'd come to the inevitable end of a hot two-month love affair that had no future, I'd stopped taking my antidepressants for some crazy reason that made sense only in my serotonin-deprived head, I was in a row with a close girlfriend, I was irrationally angry at my sister, and I felt isolated and unloved. Hardest to bear and at the foundation of it all, my mother was dying, and I didn't know how to reach her heart, how to make her understand that I loved her and how to know for sure that she loved me. I thought I'd released all hope of making a real connection with her many years back. I had just begun therapy when I called her and said, "I want to be closer to you. I want to be able to talk to you about the pain and difficulty in my life, not just the good stuff."

"Oh, well," she had answered in a singsongy voice. "I hope you won't have to."

Could she have been more clear? I thought I had dropped all unreasonable expectations back then, but I hadn't made a clean break. I'd remained hopeful, my mistake, and now, she was on her way out with no apparent desire on her part to make things right with me or with anybody. She seemed to think there was nothing to clear, that everything was fine and nothing needed to be worked out. For her, it didn't.

I remember telling a girlfriend that I had phased out my antidepressants.

"Why did you do such a ridiculous thing?" she asked me, a look of horror on her face.

"I think they stopped working," I said. "I'm meditating for an hour a day, and I'm in therapy. Shouldn't that take care of it?"

"I'm not stopping my antidepressants, ever," she said, frowning. "I think they should put them in the water supply."

I saw her point when the full force of my sorrow shattered me like a wrecking ball. I'd never had a full-fledged anxiety attack before then. I didn't understand that depth of pain until I began awakening each morning in dire anxiety, as if the attack had started without me. I don't know when my crying bouts turned into ceaseless sobbing, but I remember that wherever I went and whatever I did, my pulse pounded like I was having a heart attack, and I cried—in yoga class, in restaurants, in bank lines, at the auto body shop, at the post office, the pharmacy, the doctor's waiting room, and the hardware store. I felt so much despair and so out of control, so utterly inconsolable, that I would walk into a room and look behind me to see if the rest of me had followed. I was that disconnected. It seemed that my off switch was as broken as I was, and I had the wettest, snottiest, most vulnerable and unbearable year of my life since I ran away from Jerry. Yes, it lasted a year and several more months. I'm not sure exactly how many because after a while, I lost track.

I'd felt really good and centered about six months earlier when an old friend, Matt, suddenly remembered my last name. Apparently he'd been trying to recall it for years when he woke up one morning, sat up in bed, and said, "Cagan." Just like that. He got up, Googled my full name, and was directed to my website, which included my e-mail address. We hadn't seen each other for thirty-five years when he sent his phone number and a message that got my attention:

It's Matt. Remember me? I like your photo. You look very classy.

Of course I remembered him. We'd met in the early seventies in Los Angeles, years before we became lovers, when we were both married to other people. I dialed the phone number he sent, this many years later, and when he answered, I recognized the unmistakable Bronx accent that he had never lost. If anything, it sounded stronger, and I remembered a time many years prior, when I was high on LSD one afternoon at a friend's Beverly Hills mansion, tripping with a group of like-minded people that included Matt. I was standing by myself, gazing at a sunset with colors so penetrating they couldn't be named, when Matt came walking out of the backyard with a beatific smile on his face. "I saw God," he told me so matter-of-factly, I rushed into the garden he had just left in hopes that I might catch a glimpse of Him too. Apparently God hadn't waited for me, but that was my most vivid memory of Matt, one that he didn't remember.

His most vivid memory of me, he told me, came years later after we had both ended our marriages. We were sitting on top of a flat, massive moon rock in Joshua Tree in the high desert where we had taken psychedelic mushrooms. We were naked, the fronts of our bodies were pressed together, our arms were wrapped around each other, our legs were intertwined, and he was inside of me. That was one that *I* didn't remember. Well, I vaguely remembered it, but not in the burning detail that he did. He went on to tell me that ever since we shared that psychotropic plant-induced journey to another world and made love so close to the heavens, that moment was his most potent masturbation fantasy, providing comfort on many a lonely night when his marriage of twenty-something years was falling apart.

This ill-fated marriage had ended in a blaze of betrayal and addiction, when Wife Number Two had become a heroine addict and was in and out of more rehabs than Matt could recall. He had spent a small fortune trying to get her sober for the sake of their two kids, but no matter how much treatment she got, she still used, cheated, lied, stole, and abandoned her children and her husband, making a royal mess of their family. Matt had reluctantly moved his son and himself (his daughter was in college) to an apartment in Sherman Oaks, literally fifteen minutes away from my aerie at the top of Laurel Canyon.

The evening following our reunion phone call, Matt was on his way to my place with Chinese food while I was trying to choose the right outfit that would make me look good without being too obvious. Some years earlier I had done a book with the ex-wife of a politician who had reconnected with a lover from college. They had married and were enjoying their lives together after many years apart; she highly recommended reuniting with a past lover. In fact, she thought everyone ought to try it because the Internet made these kinds of reunions not only possible but easy and doable. I was taking her advice as I chose a pair of black skinny jeans and a white T-shirt. I stared at myself in the mirror, wondering if I would look sexy enough to him, nursing the secret hope that we might be attracted to each other once again.

I knew it was a long shot. A few years earlier I'd met up with another friend from my past, Gary, someone with whom I used to sneak out at odd hours and meet in dark places for lines of coke and secret trysts when I was cheating on my husband. I was thrilled when Gary was on his way over to see me after so many years—until he walked into my house sporting a huge potbelly and a gray pallor. It still warmed my heart to see him again, and I might have overlooked the physical changes, but when he opened his mouth he didn't make any sense, and I was repelled and disappointed. I got through the evening somehow, but I decided not to see him again, vowing from then on to leave the past in the past. Until now. I was determined to have sex with someone, hopefully with Matt if he fit the bill, so that Ethan, my insensitive ex-husband, would not be the last man with whom I had shared a bed.

When the doorbell rang, I was frantic with expectation. I forced myself to walk slowly, remembering to breathe, and I opened the door. There stood Matt. We had an awkward moment as he stepped forward to hug me while I stepped past him, wanting to close the door so my cat wouldn't run outside and get devoured by a coyote. I laughed nervously as I shut the door, turned around, hugged Matt easily this time, and introduced him to Lulu. Then we sat on the couch and stared at each other for a few minutes, unsure where to begin.

He broke the ice by reaching into his pocket and taking out a pipe, a lighter, and some fresh buds of marijuana. As if no time had passed, he filled the pipe and lit it, looking at me through the brown eyes that I recalled so well. But now, behind his eyes was a well of sadness that had not been there when I knew him before. He had always been carefree, someone who seemed to take everything in his stride when he'd been a pretty significant drug dealer long ago. At the time, he was young, naive, and slightly arrogant, a successful commercial producer boasting a lack of fear and a sense of "so what?" about everything. Now in his midsixties, he appeared scarred and scared, hungover from years of being lied to, eating too much fast food, and raising his kids without any active participation from his wife, the drug addict mother of his children.

We had a smoke together—he still had the best pot—and I watched him flick the ashes into my fragile, handblown glass bowl located beside the more obvious ashtray. "Why did you get married again?" I asked him, moving the bowl out of his reach and setting the ashtray in front of him. I recalled that his divorce from Wife Number One, a woman whom I had known, had been pretty painful for him.

"I really loved my first wife, but I was too young to hold a marriage together. I thought I'd never get married again, but I decided I wanted kids, so I changed my mind," he said.

"Really?" He appeared to be somewhat of a kid himself. "What made you decide you wanted them?"

"It was one of the few things I hadn't done," he told me.

Was that a good enough reason? I wondered. Well, it was what it was, and from what he was telling me, it was obvious how much he loved his son and his daughter. We spent the rest of the evening eating egg rolls and shrimp fried rice, sipping tea, chatting, reminiscing, smoking, laughing—the kinds of things old lovers do when they see each other for the first time after many years and are testing the waters. "You look great," he said more than once.

"You look great too," I told him. I meant it. Far from handsome but cute enough, he looked different now than I remembered him. He was trim—he always had been—and his full head of hair, although graying, was thick and unruly like I remembered. He had more wrinkles; that was to be expected, so did I, and I didn't find them unattractive. Neither his nor mine. In fact, his wrinkles looked natural to me. But his front upper teeth, which used to be crooked and yellow enough to give a Brit a run for his money, were straight and white. Too straight and too white, because his bottom teeth were the same kind of crooked they used to be. The new teeth significantly altered his appearance, not in an unflattering way, but they made him unrecognizable, and I would have walked by him if I'd passed him in the street.

Fragments of his history drifted back to me, like the year he had lived in Haight-Ashbury and taken acid every day. He had left the Haight, and I remembered the self-sustaining island in Canada he had described where he and a group of his friends went to evade the draft during the Vietnam War, growing pot and vegetables and waiting for the war to end. I also remembered his house in Laurel Canyon after his first divorce, where he had slept with a multitude of women (it didn't hurt having the best drugs in town), incidentally the place where he and I first made love.

Now, at my place in the canyon, as the evening was drawing to a close, we finally got up the nerve to kiss. He left pretty quickly after that, but I knew he'd be back, and we became lovers again in a few days. I was happy about it. I'd been celibate for years, and suddenly, this man and I were unwilling to take our hands off each other, hungrily inhaling each other's scents, wondering how we got so lucky at this point in our lives. I reveled in the things I had missed so much, like giddy laughter, pillow talk, sexual heat, and the feeling of being adored and admired, a great distraction from my work deadlines, my mother's ailments, and her motley crew of crazy caregivers who needed constant attention and discipline from my sister and me.

My love affair with Matt sizzled very hot for a few months, but I knew it would burn out. It had to, because besides pot and the past, we had very little in common. I was a writer, and he barely read. He had kids, and I was childless. And he kept telling me that our sex was too good to be true. It couldn't possibly last, he repeated over and over, and besides, he was going to move away from Los Angeles to Santa Cruz as soon as his son graduated high school. His daughter was in college there already, and the lure of living in the natural beauty of the ancient redwoods, having his kids close, and becoming a pot grower in a world that was swiftly shifting its stance on marijuana was infinitely attractive to him. He kept reminding me that our affair had an expiration date, which kept me slightly distanced from him. As delicious as it was, he was cutting out of Los Angeles as soon as he could, and he wanted to make sure I didn't forget it.

When things cooled off after a few months (it seemed like it happened overnight), I decided we should stop having sex. If this was going nowhere, I told him, I needed to disconnect so I wouldn't get hurt. To his credit, he honored my request that we remain friends. We both wanted that, and we saw each other from time to time to have some dinner—until I fell into the abyss and began to drown in a pool of my own tears. I believe it was more than dumb luck that when I went under and screamed for help, Matt was there to grab my hand, raise me up, hold me, comfort me, and help me get back on dry land. I sometimes wonder what would have happened to me if he hadn't been there, but that kind of mind chatter is a waste of time. The reality was that I needed him, and there he was, always ready to come to me, dry my tears, and help me sleep.

I don't ever remember him being unavailable or saying no, and I wonder where he found that kind of patience. Before fatherhood had opened his heart, he had hardly been a patient man, having been reared in the mean streets of the Bronx. The Vietnam War was in full swing in the early sixties when Matt left the New York business world, moved to Haight-Ashbury, and became one of the original hippies, growing his hair long and wearing the same pair of tattered jeans every day for longer than I care to imagine. He arrived in Northern California one evening, he told me, and he didn't leave for close to a year as he followed the advice of LSD guru Timothy Leary: "Turn on, tune in, and drop out."

That was easy to do when a person swallowed countless hits of acid all day long. During the famous rock concerts of that era, Woodstock and Altamont, Matt and a team of fellow drug veterans found themselves standing at the opening of a canvas tent, at the ready to assist those who had taken LSD, but instead of "breaking on through to the other side," they seemed to be facing in the wrong direction. Unsuspecting drug users learned the hard way back then that with a single swallow, the same drug that could swing wide the door to awareness could conversely sound a death knell to a previous state of awe and appreciation. It was all in the perception, something that could be transformed in the hands and direction of skilled guides—people like Matt and friends who showed up to help turn around the experiences of innocent ingestees who found themselves on a "bad trip," a horror show of sorts induced by the subconscious, a hearty onslaught of negativity that clung to one's psyche with a talon-like grip.

Not that anyone was forced to drink the Kool-Aid back in the sixties. Kids chose to gamble with their very souls back then, when the effect of LSD—either the light-filled revelations of a glorious rebirth or a slow demise by hellish fire—was like a deadly game of Russian roulette, varying according to a random assortment of internal chemical factors as well as external environmental ones. Once under the influence of powerful psychotropic drugs, youths discovered the real meaning of "good vibes" versus "bad vibes," of sanity versus insanity. It was all in the preparation, which included the environment in which you chose to park your body while your mind went for a roller-coaster ride.

It was also about how deeply you had delved into self-investigation before you opened your mouth and swallowed the drug. How large a dosage were you ingesting? Did you have any idea? What was the quality of the particular batch? Had someone you knew tried it before you took it? Were the people around you the type who saw the glass as half full or half empty? Was there a general sense of safety and well-being in the highly charged atmosphere? Or did a woeful pall hang in the ethers, sure to take aim at the most unsuspecting and vulnerable minds and bodies?

Despite the mud that covered the ground from nonstop rain, Woodstock is still touted as an archetype for group love and acceptance, a spark of beauty where half a million kids saw that they were part of a greater entity. But that was not the case in Altamont. In the words of rock star Grace Slick of Jefferson Airplane, who performed in both concerts, "Altamont was the hot flash of music festivals. I'm glad I forgot to put in my contact lenses."

There just wasn't much love and light going around, since the security team of Hell's Angels in Altamont were being paid in as much beer as they could consume. In the dangerous atmosphere of drunken aggression, there was nowhere to go once the LSD-filled mind had been altered beyond recognition and was pointing in a perilous direction. And so, the line at the entrance to the help tent was long, desperate, and continuous as misguided souls, fearful, confused, and addled with distorted images, were ushered lovingly inside and invited to lie down, to breathe, and to allow Mother Earth simply to cradle them in a loving embrace. "I'm dying" was the common complaint when someone had lost his or her way and was fighting inner demons. "I'm dying, and I don't know what to do."

"Just die," Matt suggested, touching a forehead here, a hand there. "Go ahead. It's perfectly safe." And die they did, one after another, not to the physical world or the earth upon which they rested their weary bodies, but rather to their inner perceived world that was misfiring messages and threatening eternal hell fire and annihilation.

"Just die," Matt and his fellow healing angels repeated to the casualties who lay quaking in fear and panic. "It'll be OK. You'll like it, and everything will feel good again." In the end, there *were* actual physical deaths in Altamont due to drunken violent behavior, but none of them occurred in that tent where good shepherds encouraged the flock to open their minds and hearts to a freshly minted world that spoke of hope and acceptance. In that tent, the staunch and hard-earned lesson of letting go into the pain was being offered and encouraged by drug dealers, draft dodgers, and hippies—the healers, poets, and philosophers of the time, the people who gave everyone permission to die to what was painful, old, and obsolete, survive the ordeal, and be reborn into something new and good. This was where I believe Matt got his training, or at least he got a lot of practice at sitting calmly and bearing witness to the most disturbed individuals, freaked out from strange hallucinations and terrified of obliteration.

When I lay in bed, a number of decades later, crushed, alone, and sobbing beyond redemption, without the encouragement of hallucinogens, gasping for breath, angel-less and beyond hope of finding a tent of shepherds to offer me a safe place to die out of my agony, Matt was there in the flesh, sitting by my side, repeating the words that he had told the LSD trippers so many years ago: "Just die." In my case, however, it was, "Just drown."

I remain impressed that this man, who by gender is not known for the ability to quietly observe a woman's pain without trying to change it, was able and willing to sit by my side (after we had stopped sleeping together!) and hold me patiently while I sobbed, slobbered, and shivered, never trying to fix me. Not that I didn't want to be fixed. I did. But when I finally unleashed the floodgates and "cried me a river," well, I was no Alice in Wonderland, a fictional character who would be saved by strange English-speaking creatures from drowning in her personal pool of tears. When I broke into a thousand pieces, just like Humpty Dumpty, neither the king's horses nor his men could put me back together. But there was Matt.

Perhaps the most unsettling part of my torment was the fact that after years of believing I was strong, powerful, and able to withstand any and all of what life had to offer, I faltered and collapsed as the invisible dam broke beneath me. I lost all semblance of control, and for the first time in my life, when I offered free rein to the bitter tears that would surely drown me, I came to a shocking realization. I was a vulnerable, susceptible individual, often unable to cope, who showed up everywhere in tears, red-faced and swollen, helpless, and as needy as hell. But I had to stop the pain somehow, and I had reached a point where the road went only one way—in, in, and further in, with no light-filled visions of redemption on the other side.

I opened, I entered my darkness, I screamed and moaned and drowned—for weeks and months, sometimes alone and sometimes with Matt or with someone else at my side. Each time I turned over my wracked body and fought the ever-present anxiety, as if underwater I watched the images that had eroded and finally broken the walls of my years of strongholds—my dying mother, my inability to touch her body or her heart and have her touch mine, my fear of her suffering and of my own, my extreme disappointment in how life had turned out, my searing loneliness, and then, from much further back, the isolation, blisters, strained tendons, and sprained ankles that had tortured me in my youth while I forced myself to smile when I performed on stage as a ballet dancer.

That was my US Navy SEAL training, in which I, a young, fragile, innocent ballerina with stars, music, beauty, and sequins in my eyes willingly offered myself up to the gods of the dance to become a tough, pain-resistant veteran who smiled when I was in pain, starved when I was hungry, and rehearsed endlessly when I was so exhausted I could barely hold my head up. A 103-degree fever was not enough to keep me off the stage back then. Neither was sleep deprivation, splintered toenails, caustic competition, and perpetual criticism, all of which arrived and dissolved regularly. That was then.

Innocence

Now, as I lay under the covers so many lives later it seemed, naked, phone volume turned off, shades drawn, afraid of everything, soaking my pillow and pleading for deliverance from myself and my tortuous thoughts, I finally had been taken down. All the way down. "Just drown," I kept repeating to myself between Buddhist mantras, the only thoughts I could hold in my head.

"May I be happy."

I turned my cheek to avoid the wet, salty patch in the middle of my pillow, wondering what being happy meant.

"May I be at peace."

I breathed in cat hair, as my little Lulu strained her six pounds of soft feline whiteness against me as if to staunch my flow of tears.

"May I be free from suffering."

I couldn't remember what that felt like. In fact, it sounded ludicrous to me as I repeated these mantras like lifelines, unsure as to whether they would save me or whether anything could. But there were no other cogent thoughts in my head. Nothing else I could think to say. No other words that held meaning. Nothing else to soften the sharp edges of my suffering that was punishing in its silence, taking up the hours in a realm where time had stretched far beyond recognition.

I continued to cry—anytime anyone hugged or touched me in a loving way. When I saw an elderly person with a walker. When I remembered my cat's advanced age. When I passed a homeless person on the street. Every time my mother told me she had lost more of her sight. When a friend asked me how I was feeling. When my mother didn't bother to ask.

Writing was out of the question during my long weep, and I only drove to the grocery store when the cupboard was completely bare. I managed to get in the car twice a week, though, to meet with my therapist, trying to see through my tears as I drove along Ventura Boulevard to her office. I noticed a couple on the street holding tightly to each other. A kid, both arms tattooed, was riding his skateboard. A homeless vet was holding up a piece of cardboard with writing on it, asking for money. A chic-looking woman was waiting for the WALK sign, and I imagined, no, I was sure that they all felt better than I did. They were acting like life was normal, anxiety was not wracking them like it was me, and I envied them for being anything or anyone other than me. I had become like the girl who cried at business meetings when she was the only woman in the boardroom. I was a modern-day version of Greek Niobe, destined to weep until the end of time. I was student Myrtle in the Harry Potter tales who had died in the girls' loo at Hogwarts and lived there forever in spirit, eternally weeping. How would I write books, do interviews, and make money?

"Just drown," I kept hearing Matt repeat in my mind, even when I decided that I couldn't be saved. I wasn't afraid to drown anymore. I was *ready* to drown. In fact, I was praying to drown. It was the only reasonable thing to do, or maybe the only available thing to do—the only exit door in a room otherwise locked, keyless, and completely devoid of love, hope, or compassion.

I couldn't muster it. The compassion for myself, I mean. Not much here to love, I figured, since I was a slobbering, broken mess, living alone, no boyfriend or husband, no children, unable to taste food and in dread of getting on a plane to go back east and visit my aging mother. My friends were willing to listen to me and try to help, but after a while, I stopped calling them. My extended sorrow and grieving had to be wearing thin. Or so I surmised. The possibility of hearing the blandness of a voice at the other end of a phone, barely tolerating me, was so terrifying and shame inducing, I didn't want to take any chances.

During my long ordeal, I tried a multitude of different antidepressants and antianxiety medications, most of which brought me more pain. I would swallow something, wait for it to start working, and throw in the towel after a week or two, needing to recover from the damage the wrong meds were causing me. I would finally find the right combination with the help of a brilliant psychopharmacologist, but I didn't know that then. I told myself that if it went on forever, at least it was within my power to take my life. I'm not saying I was suicidal. I wasn't, but I sometimes stemmed my anxiety by pretending that there was an end in sight, that I was about to take the pills, run out in front of the bus, eat the poison, or pull the trigger. I knew, however, that I wouldn't do that, not to myself or to my friends and family. Not to my mother, who was busy dying herself. What kind of a daughter would steal her mother's thunder while she was doing the immense job of dying and letting go after close to a hundred years of hanging on?

"Just drown" was the only directive that made any sense or at least that I understood and thought I could do. So I drowned. And I drowned. And I kept on drowning.

And then one day, with a smart doctor, the right pills, enough self-love, and a ton of therapy, the images that were making me cry stopped. I awakened from a restful nap that day, stunned to find myself dry-eyed and breathing more deeply than before. I went stock-still for a moment. Was this real or was I actually asleep, crying, pounding with anxiety, dreaming that I wasn't? Was I finally allowing in enough breath to function without the terrible images parading through my mind that brought forth the searing anxiety and the never-ending tears? I searched my mind. The images were gone. I had worked my way through them, so I got up and wondered how it would feel to walk around the house without dragging a box of snotty Kleenex with me.

I pulled myself out of bed. I had no idea what time or day it was, and as I walked to the bathroom, I noticed that I was hunched over at the waist like a ninety-five-year-old woman, walking slowly, staring at the ground, and amazed that I had been delivered from my misery. I suddenly saw the sham of it. While my mother had made it through close to a century, I was dying to my own future, as if I had forfeited any growth or joy that might be in store for me, skipping to the part where all I could feel was the pain and isolation I was projecting onto my mother. Hell, for all I knew, she was having a really good day right then, smiling, laughing, resting in soft and peaceful memories of better days and love affairs. Or not.

There was no way to know, and in a sense, it was none of my business whether she felt well or ill, whether she was satisfied or disappointed. I stood straight up, placed my weight on my strong, powerful dancer legs, sniffed in the snot that was choking me, swallowed it, and walked upstairs and into the kitchen. My mother was not me, I was not my mother, and I needed to let her go back home, the only place where she really wanted to be anyway. All things must come to an end, including our lives, and the apparent bottomless well of tears and anxiety has to run dry one day. That is the nature of existence, whether we like it or not, and I now realize that while it felt like my tears were imprisoning me, making me red-faced, swollen, and ashamed, in truth, they had saved me.

"May I be happy," I said out loud.

I took a carton of orange juice out of the refrigerator.

"May I be at peace."

I poured the sweet fruit juice into a glass.

"May I be free from suffering."

Finally, for the first time in a year and a half, I was.

Chapter Twelve

THAT DREADED THING

Old age is like a plane flying through a storm.

Once you're aboard, there's nothing you can do.

— Golda Meir, former prime minister of Israel

A few days ago, I was in my house searching upstairs and down for my iPhone, limping because my hip was sore, calling my cell phone with my land line, unable to remember if I had turned the ringer back on, with two deep frown ridges forming between my eyebrows while I looked for my glasses, which were on my head, doubling as a hairband. I wasn't stoned or drunk. I was simply in a hurry to get to the chiropractor to adjust my spine so my hip would stop hurting when I walked.

I sorted it all out. I found my glasses and put them on, grabbed my iPhone that was chirping to me from the kitchen, replaced my cordless phone in its charger, and reminded myself to breathe and relax my face. But I was stunned that I was doing that dreaded thing I had vowed never to do when I was young: aging.

When I was in my twenties, my friends and I were fond of ingesting psychedelic substances that transported us to magical realms that seemed to exist beyond time and space. In those altered states, we felt ageless and accepting of everyone, including each other and ourselves, exactly the way we were. No bad or good. No judgments.

Way back when I was still doing such things, a group of my friends and I took psilocybin mushrooms at one of my favorite haunts in Ojai, California. At the end of a long dirt trail, a natural waterfall cascaded into a rocky pool, reflecting prisms that bounced through the sunlight. But as lovely as it was, my mind was busy passing judgments on everything and everyone, especially myself. That was when I had a vision of a judge in dark robes presiding over court proceedings, sitting at his bench and banging a gavel. "That's good," he declared. "That's bad." Over and over again, he was judging every thought I had.

In my magical psychedelic state, I managed to step inside my vision and face the judge head on. "I have an idea," I told him. "You're doing a great job, but why don't you take a nice long recess, have a brandy in your chambers, and I'll call you when I need you?"

I watched him rise, slightly disgruntled, and exit the courtroom, leaving green and purple light trails behind him as a deep calm settled over me. My mind went quiet, and I was able to focus on the drops of water splashing onto the ground and the sunshine lighting up the rock faces that rose majestically on either side of the waterfall. The quality of the sound was electrifying. I watched and listened for a while, serene and content, breathing and resting easily in my body. Then, out of the corner of my eye, I saw the judge slinking back into the courtroom, gavel in hand, ready to recommence his declarations as he headed for the bench. I stopped him. "Not yet," I said.

"I thought I heard you calling me," he said. "Are you sure you don't need me?"

"I'm sure. Go back to your chambers and have another brandy."

"But who'll do the judging?"

"No one. It'll be OK. I'll let you know when I need you."

And my mind went quiet again.

At the end of these psychedelic journeys, each one different and in some ways strangely the same, when the high wore off and my friends and I came back down to earth, we dropped into restfulness and recovery, feeling like we had journeyed beneath the veil of physical reality and carried a sense of timelessness back with us across the worlds.

After inhabiting realms without borders or boundaries, we believed that if we wanted to retain our youth, we could simply do it, just like that, by deciding to do it. But that kind of thinking set us up for failure, and we took on judgmental attitudes, just like the judge in my vision, blaming our parents when they showed signs of aging that we decided were bad, unnecessary, and avoidable. On our quest to stay young, several of my friends got face-lifts or filler injections in their brows and lips that were meant to make them look younger or fresher, but I didn't think it worked.

I decided early on that I would refrain from face-lifts, and I wasn't attracted to having fillers like Restylane or Botox shot into my face, partly because the idea of having needles in my face made me uncomfortable but mainly because I didn't like the way women looked afterward. I decided I would keep my spirit young instead and accept the wrinkles that showed up, and I did—until a few years ago, when I noticed the puffy skin that suddenly (or so it seemed) had appeared beneath my eyes. I couldn't imagine that I hadn't seen it before, since in my current evaluation, it was the only thing visible on my face. "I don't really mind my wrinkles," I told a friend. "I call them 'smile lines,' but the bags under my eyes make me look old and tired. I guess I should see a plastic surgeon, but aren't the good ones booked up until next year?" I suddenly couldn't wait that long.

A guy I knew, a mover and shaker in the film business, picked up the phone and dialed a plastic surgeon who had worked on countless movie stars. "Hello?" he said. "Jennifer Aniston told me to call you. I need to make an appointment for a friend." He listened for a moment and said to me, "How's tomorrow at three?"

I got into my car the very next afternoon, sans makeup as I had been instructed, on my way to Beverly Hills to see one of the top plastic surgeons to the stars. When I walked through the door, I was instantly intimidated. The outer office, shaped in a pleasing curve, looked like a lobby in an exclusive resort, and his assistant was so beautiful, I wondered why I should even bother. When she ushered me to the inner office and sat me down in a large corner room with windows on two sides, I felt so self-conscious, I was moved to tell the most beautiful assistant in the world, "Someone told me not to wear any makeup, so I didn't."

"That's good," she said, a radiant smile on her perfect face. "He's an artist, and he sees your face as an empty palette."

The upshot was that after Van Gogh had looked closely at my empty palette (his own face looked unnaturally tight, especially around his hair line), he said that noses, not eyes, were his specialty, and he gave me the number of a different doctor, an eye man. I felt like he was rejecting me, but I contacted my friend, who made a call similar to the first one, using Susan Sarandon's name this time. I got an appointment for two days later. When the second doctor, also located in Beverly Hills, looked me over and referred me to a third doctor, a female, who specialized in undereye surgery, I felt doubly rejected and was too embarrassed to call back my friend. I'd heard that these surgeons worked on anyone who came calling, whether they needed it or not. Was I that much of a lost cause?

After I got through debasing myself, I picked up the phone and told the receptionist I was being referred by Kate Hudson (I had the game down by now) and got myself an appointment that afternoon. This doctor looked at me through her super-duper magnifying light for a while, studying the skin under my eyes. If I had been stark naked, I couldn't have felt more exposed. Finally, she pushed the light off to the side and said, "If I remove the bags under your eyes, your face will look sunken in. Your under eyes aren't really puffy," she added. "Your eyes have just sunk back because you're aging. Go buy yourself a pair of large glasses that'll cover the offending area."

I was relieved she hadn't asked me how Kate was doing, but I'd had enough. It was clear that while everyone else was out there getting tight eyes, huge stand-up boobs, puffed-out cheeks, and exploding lips, no matter how much name-dropping I did, I couldn't pay anyone to work on me. I made a decision to stop looking in the mirror, save my money, and just get over it. And I did. It was mostly psychological, I had to admit, when a few days went by and I stopped noticing the bags that had been so prominent when I was hoping a plastic surgeon would take me on.

Today I'm relieved that no one agreed to operate on me because from what I've seen, one simple tweak seems to be a gateway drug to an endless array of surgeries and injections that are never enough. It's like painting one room in your house—the others start to look shabby in comparison. I realized that I couldn't postpone the inevitable, and if I didn't want to be surgically transforming myself constantly over the next thirty years, I'd better get comfortable with the woman in the mirror.

I had a good role model, although she was obsessive in the other direction. My mother thought that doing anything to her face was a waste of time and money, and she never even had a facial. It helped that she was so beautiful. My father used to call his wife "a good-lookin' tomata," but she squirmed and shook her head when anyone complimented her. I decided to fashion myself after her, not the refusal to take compliments part, but the part about accepting what was happening to my face. I'd always been told I looked like her, so I vowed to "act" younger. Each time I saw my mother searching for lost objects, like her purse or her keys, I judged her for it and vowed to do things differently. I would have duplicate keys made when I got older, I promised myself. I would check my head first for my glasses if and when I lost them. I'd stop frowning because it would make permanent lines on my face, and I would remember to stand up straight and walk like I meant it.

It never occurred to me that the elderly were stooped over and took forever to get out of their cars because of debilitating back or hip pain, and forgetfulness was something they simply couldn't avoid. And so, while I'd been running around the house, frustrated, frowning, stressed out from my search, and anxious to get to the chiropractor that morning, I was breaking several of the vows I'd made about holding onto my youth.

For my mother's ninetieth birthday, my sister and I traveled to Hartford, Connecticut, where she lived, and took her and several of her friends out for dinner. When I got back home a few days later, I received a note from her:

Andrea dear,

It just hit me that I have grown old—ninety years old. You provided such an exciting birthday celebration that I forgot to bemoan my advanced age. Didn't even think about it.

Mom & Me

A teacher of Shakespeare and a ready conversationalist, when my mother hit her nineties, she began stumbling over her words when she tried to explain things, like how she felt and what her mornings were like, partly because talking about feelings had never been her strong suit, but also because expressing herself wasn't easy anymore. She was frustrated, aware that certain things couldn't be comprehended until you were there. Like aging. However she might have attempted to articulate it, there was no way I could get it; she knew that, so she kept saying over and over, "You just don't know what it's like. You just don't know what it's like."

She was right. I didn't know what it was like, and I won't know unless I'm destined to live for ninety-six years like she did. There is a grief in aging as we mourn the person we used to be, but we can't explain it to someone younger. No matter how good a person is at descriptions, there are some things, like exploring psychedelic realms and growing older, that can only be understood by direct experience.

For those of us raised in Western societies with Western belief systems, aging is almost impossible to accept. And then my generation has the added obstacle of the Peter Pan–type vows that we would never get old that we made in our youth. "I won't grow up. I don't want to go to school," Peter Pan sings out on Broadway, flying weightlessly over the rooftops, and we all delight in it, products of a society that loves to declare, "Forty is the new thirty" or "Fifty is the new forty." What does that even mean? I once saw a cartoon of a middle-aged man standing in front of his mother's grave. The caption read: *Don't worry, Mom. Dead is the new eighty.*

I thought back to when my mother was young and agile, when her mind was crisp and she met each day with strength and vigor. An English and Latin teacher, she would sit beside my father in the living room at the end of each day, reading the newspaper as she stopped to cut out discount coupons that she kept in her purse. She swore up and down that she was not a creative person, but the ways that she found to save money proved her unequivocally wrong.

When I was young, I thought that all bath towels were white and had names of hotels on them: the Sheraton, the Hilton, the Hyatt. Whenever the family went on vacation or spent a night in a hotel, our bags, which were modestly full when we arrived at our destination, were bulging on the way back home. In fact, the Cagans returned home from a hotel stay with everything that wasn't nailed down, including pillows and bathrobes. Even the chambermaid's carts weren't safe. When the room girl made a quick visit to the garbage shoot, several Kleenex boxes went missing. A turn of her head and rolls of toilet paper vanished. Under the deafening sound of her industrial vacuum cleaner, bars of soap, miniature shampoos, and plastic shower caps disappeared.

I remember my parents arriving at my home in Los Angeles once with a brown paper bag that held four drinking glasses. "Where did you get these?" I asked them suspiciously, certain they'd been taken from their current hotel. There was no other explanation for the shoddy brown paper bag gift wrapping.

"You should never ask where gifts come from," my mother chided me. "It's rude."

My parents didn't consider themselves thieves, but according to them, they weren't pushovers either.

"Why are we taking all this stuff? I don't think it's right," Jill grumbled one day when we were dragging our overstuffed suitcases to the elevators. No bellboys for this family. My mother refused to waste money on tips when we were perfectly capable of carrying our suitcases ourselves.

"We take what's coming to us," she snapped. "Everyone does."

"Well, I don't think it's right either," I chimed in.

"Just wait until you're making your own money, young lady," my father scolded me as we heaved our swollen suitcases into the elevator. He always took my mother's side; they were a united front, which for Sam was a lot easier than going against the tide.

"We paid a pretty penny to stay in this hotel," my mother added. "They expect it. The stuff won't even be missed; they buy in bulk."

End of discussion. My father looked irritated, but he kept silent. When he traveled alone, he never took anything, but not because he considered it wrong. He simply couldn't be bothered. My mother, on the other hand, was unstoppable, an infinitely patient mastermind at getting something for nothing, and the rest of the family were shamed and guilt-tripped into going along with her.

"Don't upset your mother," was the ongoing mantra from my childhood, and I learned it well, along with, "Always watch out for Number

One. Nobody else will." Everyone in the family followed the rules or we suffered the fate of disapproval, isolation, and exile, as my mother dreamt up endless methods of doing whatever it was cheaper and better. For her, life was a constant challenge in compromise, which shaped me also, but in a different direction. While my mother felt it was worth expending any amount of energy for the purpose of conserving money, I developed the opposite credo of spending any amount of money to conserve energy. Different sides of the same coin.

I must point out here that on my mother's part, it was not a matter of need. My father made a good living, but saving a buck was her passion. It didn't matter to her that in the final analysis, things didn't balance out, like spending the extra fifty cents on gas to drive the extra ten miles to save twenty cents at the cheaper gas station. Or exhausting and annoying the entire family by waking us up at five o'clock in the morning to drive to a neighboring city to catch a cheaper flight when there was an accessible airport only a few miles from our home.

Getting us up before the crack of dawn made us grouchy as hell, and Jill was usually the one who spoke up. "I just don't understand this family," she moaned. "It isn't normal, getting up in the middle of the night. Nobody is awake in the whole world. We could have slept for another two hours."

"You can sleep on the plane," my father said. "Look at your mother. Nobody's more tired than she is, and you don't hear her complaining."

By the time we boarded the plane, the family was at war. Add to that my mother's fretting about the cost of airplane travel and the "exorbitant" amount they charged for parking fees, and we had saved a grand total of about ten dollars—if we weren't actually in the red. Charlotte passed out as soon as the plane took off—she was exhausted from scheming around the almighty dollar—and she never felt rested until just before we repeated the whole process on our return. But the aggravation was worth it to her. Ten dollars was nothing to sneeze at, she reminded us. She viewed her thrift as practical and down-to-earth, and at the same time, her religious devotion to conservation served as an infinitely creative outlet to exercise her imagination.

When my mother did her grocery shopping, she shamelessly held up the line at the checkout counter, digging into her purse, pulling out her coupon collection, and meticulously poring over each one, smoothing the curled-up edges, searching for the ones that matched the particular items she was buying that day. I stood beside her, distressed by the seething anger spewing from the long line of impatient shoppers behind us who resented how slowly she was moving.

"Hurry up, Mom," I pleaded. "People are getting impatient."

"They can wait," she'd say with a shrug. "I know I have a coupon in here for frozen peas." She carried on at her own pace, picking out the appropriate coupons and tucking the rest safely back into her purse, protected by two red rubber bands.

Rubber bands made my mother's life secure. They held notepads and shopping lists together, bagels and lamb chops, graham crackers and candy bars, English muffins and ancient pieces of chocolate cake. In the freezer alone there were thirty or more rubber bands, neatly crisscrossed over plastic wrap, wax paper, and aluminum foil, harboring refugees from bar mitzvahs, like smelly cheeses and smoked salmon, gefilte fish and miniature meatballs. The rubber bands had to be removed and stored (she never threw them away, even after they'd lost their elasticity) before anything could be defrosted, toasted, roasted, or simmered. Whatever might need corralling in my mother's world was secured by a rubber band, and sometimes two, to keep in the maximum amount of freshness. Even if it wasn't perishable.

Rubber bands showed up in the most unexpected places, loitering around doorknobs, lurking in glove compartments, hanging off of gear shifts, clinging to dresser drawers, or hiding in the bottom of my mother's purse. When the screw-on lid of a jar was stuck, instead of calling her husband for more muscle power, my mother would reach for a rubber band, wrap it around the stubborn lid, and using the rubbery surface for resistance, she twisted sharply until it separated from the jar with an angry pop. It never failed. Like mace or an alarm, when my mother went for the rubber, we knew she meant business.

In all the years that I lived with my parents, we had an occasional dearth of pencils, Scotch tape, paper clips, and staples, but rubber bands were always there in a never-ending stockpile. I knew where the thick blue ones came from. They were wrapped around broccoli in the supermarket. We ate broccoli a lot; perhaps that was part of the appeal. The thin light-brown ones held together particularly large mail deliveries. It was clear how these had arrived. But the bulk of them, the multicolored balls of rubber on my mother's bedside table, in the kitchen junk drawer, or on my father's desk, appeared mysteriously. I never saw them as an item on my mother's shopping list, so I figured my father must have pinched them from the supply closet at work along with reams of paper and ballpoint pens that also showed up from out of nowhere. I never asked my parents about it, but it was clear that the rubber bands had never been purchased.

After my father died in 1991, I had been writing for a living for some time when my mother came to Los Angeles to stay with me and attend one of my book signings.

Book Signing

After she left, I opened the freezer to find that everything in there had been wrapped in tinfoil with two crisscrossed rubber bands. Like Zorro leaving the sign of the Z, my mother left rubber bands in her wake, and I had no idea where in my house she had found them.

She became mostly housebound after that trip. She never returned to California again, and my sister and I began traveling to see her. As the years passed, everyone kept saying how great it was that my mother was so old. Good genes, they'd say, smiling and winking at me, suggesting I might also be lucky enough to live into my nineties. But after witnessing my mother's aging trials, it didn't look like living into one's nineties was a prize. With longevity came enormous vulnerability, as my mother found herself unable to perform the simplest of tasks, which she had easily accomplished years earlier. It looked to me like getting old was a massive challenge, and her body didn't seem to be up to the task.

My mother contracted macular degeneration at the advanced age of ninety-two, and although she never said as much because she was not inclined to grumble, I imagine she found losing her sight to be extremely unfair. She'd had poor hearing for most of her adult life. Wasn't that enough to have to deal with? It seemed that as long as my mother could read, she could endure just about anything, but when her eyesight began to fail, and she could no longer lose herself in a good book, it was as if her protection had been stripped away. Her increasing inability to see words on the page was one of the few things she ever complained about, and it made me feel helpless and frightened as I projected how terrible life must be without sight. I kept searching for a solution for her, from large print books to electronic readers to Books on Tape, for her devastating problem that devastated me right along with her.

We had no success. The range of available material in large print was limited, especially for my mother, who had read everything from the complete works of William Shakespeare to the biographies of Madeline Albright and Liz Taylor. It was going to be difficult to find a book in large print that she hadn't already read or that would hold her interest. And then she couldn't even see the large print after a while.

"Did you try reading with the Kindle I sent you?" I asked her. "You can make the letters really big."

"It didn't work," she said, explaining that if she made the letters large enough for her to see, there would be only a few words on each page. A person couldn't read a book like that and enjoy it. And there was the added difficulty of learning which buttons to push and when. She had never taken to computers, and she wasn't about to start now.

"What about Books on Tape?" I asked her in a pleading tone. I had done years of volunteering for Recording for the Blind and Dyslexic. She agreed to try listening to books instead of reading them, but she didn't take to it. "I don't like it," she announced after a friend brought over the equipment and got her set up with a novel or two.

"What don't you like?" I asked her. "It's like someone reading to you. Can you hear it OK?"

"Yes, I can. The headphones work fine. But I don't know what to do with my hands."

My suggestion that she hold a book as if she were reading it was summarily rejected with a flip of her wrist, and she refused to talk any more about it. Jill and I knew better than to continue a topic after the wrist flip, because if we did, she would just stare straight ahead and go silent, as if we weren't even there.

I'd heard about battles between aging parents and their children over the car keys, but my mother gave them up all on her own when she was eighty-eight. It was right after she took out several mailboxes in front of the local post office. She couldn't figure out why she had put her foot on the accelerator instead of the brake. She knew she had gotten away easy; she was haunted by a newspaper article about an elderly man who had hit seven people, killing several of them, when he mistook the accelerator for the brake in the parking lot of a farmers' market. When my mother hung up her keys for good, a few of her friends actually encouraged her to keep on driving, mailboxes be damned! They went on to say that her post office accident had been a fluke, and she needed her independence, but she refused to get back behind the wheel. Jill and I were grateful, but while she easily relinquished her car keys, she never embraced Books on Tape.

During the last year of her life, she was plagued with bouts of insomnia, attacks of diarrhea, and falling down. We got calls in the middle of the night, and so did some of her caregivers, who belonged in a sitcom. They didn't hail from a professional nursing service, which was probably why they were so colorful. My mother drew them in, one by one, finding people she could pay under the table, and as well-meaning as they all were, you really do get what you pay for. They entered into a battle of wills, each trying to outdo the other, vying to be considered number one in my mother's eyes. The head honcho. As they scrambled around to win her favor, uncontrollable arguing ensued among them as they had verbal battles in the lobby of my mother's building and in doctors' waiting rooms. They fought about who had committed the mortal sin of smoking in the car, who was feeding my mother the wrong food, who should take which shifts, who left early and arrived late, who would go pick her up when she fell down, and on and on. At first I was the mediator, listening to their complaints and trying to help them get along. But soon my sister had to bear the brunt of it because I descended into a state of anxiety attacks and depression that I couldn't overcome for many months, while my mother's health continued to fade and deteriorate.

My own health had improved a great deal, and the anxiety attacks were over when my sister and I flew into Hartford, Connecticut, on September 2, the day before our mother's ninety-sixth birthday. I was starting a writing project that I had to put on hold, and Jill was taking time off from work and from finishing her latest mystery novel because we thought that this would be our mother's last birthday. When we arrived at her condo to find her withdrawn into herself and not speaking, we were sure of it. No actual ongoing illness was claiming her. Her heart was erratic but not failing, and her brain was still firing, albeit a little more slowly. She had cancer, but she'd only been diagnosed a week earlier, and so far she had minimal pain.

The upshot was that she was dying of old age; her body was slowly deteriorating like a used-up machine, this part rusting, that part cracking, this part leaking, that part stopping as her organs were systematically losing their ability to perform their designated jobs. One of her less tactful doctors said that her bad stomach was in the early stages, and one day it would stop working altogether. I had exploded at him on the phone, chiding him for allowing my mother to leave his office once with a bleeding sore on her leg. All he said was, "Oh, it wasn't that bad," and he hung up.

Despite all of this, my mother had remained undaunted. But the cancer diagnosis had wrung all the fight out of her. Her trusty gaggle of caregivers who were by her side night and day, swatting at each other and holding each other up, all at the same time, told us that when she learned about the cancer and realized the kind of future she was facing, that was the last straw. She reportedly had said, "I'm through here. It's time for my girls to take over." And she withdrew. With the exception of a word or two here and there, she stopped talking and started preparing to make her exit.

Among the many decisions my sister and I had to make, I am still haunted by our resolution to tell our mother that she had cancer. A close friend of mine whose dad, the same age as my mother, had contracted prostate cancer, told his family that if he ever got the big C, he preferred not to know. It was easy to honor his wishes since he was an avoider, he never asked questions, and apparently the cancer was moving very slowly, not causing him any discomfort as yet. To him, no news was good enough, but he was a completely different kind of person from my mother. He had been content throughout his life to know as little as possible about any sorts of hardships, especially those he had foisted on others, while my mother was a stoic New England woman who faced her troubles head on and never felt sorry for herself. Or anyone else, for that matter.

She didn't want us keeping secrets from her, and I had debated, both internally and with my sister, whether or not we should let her know about the diagnosis. No matter the news, she wouldn't be opting for any kind of treatment. She was much too frail for that, so it was conceivable that we could have kept it under wraps. But in the end, the decision to tell her won out. She had always wanted and expected the truth. If we kept it from her now, how would we explain her stomach pain of which she had been complaining lately? If it got worse, which it was sure to do, she would suspect it anyway. In fact, she already did.

When I finally told her, she went quiet on the other end of the line, taking it in. "Why now?" was all she said, something I never understood and neither did Jill. Perhaps she had reached a stage of acceptance and was ready to carry on the way she was. Whatever she meant, there were no further discussions about it since we were scheduled to fly there in less than a week. We figured we could talk about it then if she wanted to.

We never got the opportunity to discuss anything with her because she stopped talking on her birthday. I remember walking into the condo where my mother had lived for forty years, twenty with my father and twenty more on her own after his death. I inhaled that familiar musky mold smell from the humidity mixed with the overwhelming scent of old things. I put my purse down on the extraordinarily uncomfortable couch beside the upholstered chairs whose bases were built low and hard. If you sat down on one of them, you had a hell of a time getting back up, even if you were young and agile. My mother had talked about getting rid of them for years, but just like the terrorists in Guantanamo Bay, they were never released.

My mother was a hoarder—not the kind who bought everything she could get her hands on, but rather the kind that never threw anything away. I like to avoid making blanket statements using the words "never" or "always," but she always had been the quintessential packrat. Her double storage spaces in the basement of her building held everything she had ever owned, like five ancient toasters; half a dozen broken, latched, hard-sided suitcases; and three dinosaur-era typewriters, all of which no longer worked and were beyond the possibility of repair.

In her kitchen, she held onto broken and chipped dishes and stained towels and dishrags. Jars with a mere scraping of jam languished in the refrigerator, and cracked TV trays were taped up and unevenly stacked in the corner beside the stove. She kept old manila folders together with paper clips, and she refused to throw away pencils with blunt leads (she didn't own a pencil sharpener) or pens without ink that couldn't be refilled. She kept price tags that had been removed from clothing that she had given away years earlier, and in the medicine cabinet was an empty deodorant bottle that I'd thrown away once during a visit and she had retrieved from the garbage. She kept expired aspirin (they're still good, she said, you just need to take a little more), threadbare wash-cloths, tattered bath towels, broken mirrors, and old tote bags without handles. At first glance, there was order in her condo; each item seemed to have its designated place. But if you looked deeper, under the clothes in her closets, on the top shelves of the linen closet, at the back of her drawers, and in eroding cardboard boxes that were piled on top of each other in the corners of every room, the stuff was all there like it always had been, and as long as she could still draw breath, none of it was going anywhere.

Jill and I spent the four days following my mother's ninety-sixth birthday at her bedside, stepping around boxes, ministering to her every need with various caregivers and a couple of hospice workers who were like angels sent from heaven. I derived an unexpected satisfaction when I began to massage my mother's arms and legs as she lay still, breathing deeply and not looking directly at anyone. During most of her life, she had shunned being touched. A few years back, when I went to caress her forehead in a moment of heartfelt emotion, she had shrunk away from my hand. It had hurt me, and so had her hugs as she put one arm around me and kept the other on her chest, the palm facing outward, pulling me in and pushing me away at the same time. The quintessential mixed message.

But once she had withdrawn and stopped talking, she visibly relaxed when I touched her. I took full advantage, reading her nonverbal signals as to whether she liked it or not. She sometimes moaned, whether it was due to pain or not, we didn't know, but her breathing seemed to relax whenever I placed a hand on her body, satisfying my lifelong desire to hold her hands and touch her face. At one point I noticed she was clutching something, and I gently opened her fingers. It was a handkerchief that had belonged to my father; she was holding it close by her side as she was preparing to leave this world and join him in the other one, and I softly closed her fingers back around it.

The day before she died, some time in the late afternoon, a dark gray mushy substance with no smell began to expel from her mouth and nose. It was projectile, and those of us who were caring for her took turns using a suction machine in her mouth, extracting the viscous fluid so she wouldn't choke on it. In all my work with the dying, I had never seen that phenomenon before, and neither had the hospice workers who came several times a day to check on us. I thought maybe she was regurgitating her organs. I have learned since that it was her lymph, but at the time, no one was sure, and I remember suctioning that terrible stuff for hours on end, barely able to stand up, thinking, *It's OK if she's on her way out, but I'll be damned if she's going to choke to death!*

I drew strength from the fact that I wanted, no, I demanded, a gentler death than that for my mother, one in which she floated peacefully out of her body, not in the midst of gasping for breath and choking. I wanted peace for her, and I did everything I could to arrange that, the last gift I would ever give her.

During the early hours of the morning of her death, the fluid stopped secreting, the suctioning was no longer needed, and we all sat there, wrung out, sweaty, exhausted, and crushed. When Jill and I headed back to our hotel to get two or three hours of sleep, we made peace with the possibility that our mother might die while we were sleeping. But she was still there when we returned, breathing shallowly but in a peaceful state. Finally. The drama was over, and she was quietly inhaling and exhaling. She'd had nothing to eat or drink for three days except small drops of water we had put on her tongue so she wouldn't die of dehydration, a painful way to go, and squirts of liquid morphine, a purple solution that stained her lips and quieted her moaning.

I was on the phone in the next room, speaking softly to a girlfriend, when someone came in and told me it was time. My mother's breathing had slowed dramatically, and all of her caregivers who had asked to be called when the time came were gathered in her room. Jill took one of her hands and gestured for me to do the same. I took her other hand, and each time she exhaled, we thought it was over—until she would sharply inhale again. I looked around her room, noticing the half-full bottle of purple oral morphine on the bedside table, the now-idle suction machine, the hospital bed remote, boxes of latex gloves, lemon tongue hydrators, adult diapers, the torn hem of a curtain, the broken slat of a venetian blind that separated the sunlight into long, jagged, horizontal shadows.

When my mother exhaled her last breath, we all waited, holding ours until her lower jaw dropped, her chest stopped moving, and Jill and I began to sob like abandoned children. Kurt, one of the hospice angels, said a prayer over her soul. Elaine, the other hospice angel, cleaned her up and tied a scarf around her jaw, holding it closed, and slowly everyone left the room.

All alone, I sat on the chair at the side of my mother's body. It was clear that her soul had departed, and I could feel something hovering in the room, a presence, a shadow, a lightness that filled my chest when I inhaled. In that moment, I silently told her everything I wanted her to know. Someone paused at the door, saw me there, and walked away as I forgave my mother and myself for all that had ever come between us. I thanked her for allowing me and assisting me in following my dreams, and I blessed her on her journey. Then I stood up, walked over to her bed, stroked her forehead one last time, took the handkerchief she'd been holding for the last four days, and put it in my pocket.

A few hours later, I stayed in the living room and watched while the morticians rolled my mother's body out of the house. They had warned the small group gathered there that they were about to wheel her body out the front door of the home where she had lived for the last forty years. If we wanted to miss this event, they told us, we ought to step out on the patio until they were gone. But after all that we had been through for the past four days, watching a gurney being wheeled past me with my mother's body covered was almost a relief. And so I watched, dry-eyed, as she crossed the doorframe for the very last time. It was over. Her body had stopped working.

Later that night, Jill and I walked into the condo that had become ours. We'd never had much affection for our parents' home, and we each picked up an item, a shredded key chain and a broken dish, and chucked them into a wastepaper basket. We looked at each other, and without a word, we started tearing through the condo in a mania, tossing everything we could get our hands on, doing what we had wanted to do for decades. Rushing around like we had gone mad, we threw away hundreds of plastic bags, a ton of junk jewelry, torn towels, obsolete hearing aids, dead batteries, unused adult diapers, a dozen umbrellas with broken ribs stashed in a standing urn in the entryway, a leg brace, a bunch of empty wallets held together with rubber bands and paper clips, old shoes missing their soles, their heels worn down, tarnished forks with crooked tines, knives that could no longer cut, stained threadbare dish towels, expired medicine bottles, empty containers of Ajax, and broken detergent dispensers. We tossed everything we could get our hands on into jumbo black plastic garbage bags, which we dragged outside the condo and down the hallway. We began to throw them all down the trash chute.

When we were nearly through, I stood at the trash chute for a few minutes while Jill gathered the last few items from the condo that were destined to go and threw them to me. I caught them, one after the other, and stuffed them all down the chute until it got completely backed up. When I told Jill to stop, that we'd broken the trash chute, we fell to the ground laughing hysterically, rolling on the floor in the hallway, almost peeing in our pants. We were letting go, emptying and flushing and removing and dumping and surrendering, all at the same time.

The mortuary that had buried my father did the same for my mother. She had pointed to the ground the last time we'd visited my father's grave and said wistfully, "That's where I'm going to be, beside Daddy." There was no fear in her voice—there was almost a longing—and I only hoped I would feel the same way when it was getting close to my time. Maybe that was a gift that aging offered, unconditional acceptance of the life-and-death cycles and the ability to face one's end without fears or regrets. It seemed to me that my mother had attained that kind of acceptance, moving toward her exit from this world steadily and fearlessly.

I expected that my mother's body was safe, that she was well out of it by that night, but just in case she felt lonely or frightened during her transition, Jill and I hired a Jewish cantor to sit beside her casket in the mortuary the night before her internment from eight in the evening to eight the next morning, singing psalms to my mother, watching over her soul, and keeping her company. I fell asleep in my hotel room that night, riding the waves of the beautiful tenor voice that I swore I could hear, comforted in the knowledge that even in death, I had not left my mother alone.

Chapter Thirteen

GURU FUCKERS

Let each man take the path according to

his capacity, understanding, and temperament.

His true guru will meet him along that path.

— Sivananda Saraswati

I've met a number of people, probably more than my share due to the nature of my work, who think they have all the answers. A client of mine appeared on a TV talk show many years ago, claiming to be a "spiritual relationship expert." Couples seated on the stage described their relationship and marriage woes, and her job was to use her higher powers to solve the problems of featured guests, the studio audience, and telephone callers. With each question, the camera zoomed in on her as she told everybody what was so and what wasn't, what they should do and what they shouldn't, what worked and what didn't, all according to her alleged deep understanding of spirituality.

I thought about the terrible burden she was carrying. Imagine having to "know" unequivocally how to unravel the universal conundrum of how men and women could get along when times were tough. She never said, "I don't know. Give me a minute to think about that." Instead, she cannonballed her answers, quick and direct, pat and obviously rehearsed, overconfident and didactic, failing to mention that even as she sat there telling people what to do, her fifth marriage was on the skids.

Joining her on my colorful list of "people who have all the answers" are a clairvoyant/psychiatrist, a life coach/psychic, a self-declared enlightened seminar leader, a horny tantric guide, a guru pedophile, a thousand-year-old entity channeler, an astrological soothsayer, an anorexic nutritionist, a sadistic chakra point holder, a past-life regressionist, a tarot card/palm-reading witch, and an auric massage therapist who claimed that her obesity was the result of having healed so many people with serious ailments. "This isn't mine," she told me, grabbing a layer of fat around her belly.

"Whose is it?" I asked her.

This happened more recently, but these kinds of assertions were nauseatingly common during the sixties and seventies, when spiritual arrogance was on the rise. So was "guru fucking." They went hand in hand since one required the other. The expression "guru fucking," by the way, is not necessarily literal. Sometimes it is, but in general, it describes people who hold a teacher's or a guru's value above their own, offering him their undying devotion, all their money, their body, and their firstborn child. Again, I'm not being literal, but a host of gurus from India and other foreign lands saw a lot of self-gratifying action during the "New Age," grabbing at everything they could get their hands on, all in the name of helping others get closer to God.

"I'm very spiritual," I've heard people say, "and I know you better than you know yourself, so let me tell you what to do." Arrogance is always annoying, but I find spiritual arrogance to be shameful, damaging, and at times, criminal. Examples come to mind, like motivational speaker James Arthur Ray. He served two years in jail when several people, supposedly under his guidance, died in a sweat lodge in 2010. And can we ever forget Reverend Jim Jones? He "convinced" more than nine hundred of his followers, some who volunteered, others at gunpoint, to drink Kool-Aid laced with cyanide so they could move beyond this existence into an Eden-like afterlife. They died with their tennis shoes on. Go figure.

On a lighter note, but repellent nonetheless, there was and still is nothing new under the sun about teachers claiming ultimate knowledge, preying on unsuspecting women, and garnering wealth by inserting both hands into someone else's pocket. In the sixties, however, New Age claims gave these people a handy way to speak about their actions in an elevated kind of jargon as they considered their points of view to be higher forms of spiritual learning.

I once broke up with a boyfriend who had the jargon down when he propositioned a number of my girlfriends behind my back, offering his body and sexual prowess as a tool for them to release their negativity. The only authentic part of his overture was offering the use of his tool, which he was more than willing to give freely. To my horror, two of these women took the bait. When I got wind of it, I crossed them off my list of friends and asked the offender to leave the premises since I owned the house. He packed up and took off, kicking and screaming, telling me I was making a big mistake and quickly finding a channeler who encouraged him to have sex with as many women as he wanted.

"You're for the many, not for the few" was the message he allegedly received from the great beyond. He felt the need to repeat that message to me, assuming I'd take him back once I understood that his infidelities were being supported by an all-knowing thousand-year-old entity. When I refused to let him back in, he adjusted quickly, moving in with two bisexual women who didn't mind if he shared their bed. He started what he called a "tantric practice," offering vaginal massage (I kid you not) for women who had been sexually abused, all in the name of spiritual healing, all in the space of about a month. He actually got a number of takers. Way to go, dude, and speedy at that.

I complained bitterly to a therapist I knew that this man needed to be shut down, that he was offering something to abused women that would only reabuse them. She agreed with me, but she told me that legally he couldn't be stopped. He wasn't licensed, so there was no board to suspend him. The only way he could be shut down was if one of his victims blew the whistle on him, which was unlikely. Abused women are not particularly good at standing up for themselves or at recognizing a predator for what he is, especially one who has his indiscretions neatly tied up with a heavenly bow, the epitome of spiritual arrogance.

Not that it was all bad back in the day. Some authentic and wonderful teachers from the East showed up and offered meditation, prayers, and healing to whoever was ready to take the next step in his or her spiritual development. Refusing to toe the line and accept the rigidity of our parents, the youth movement that started in the sixties, of which I was a part, shunned the status quo as we experimented with psychedelic drugs, expanding our minds and hearts. In order to explore the worlds beyond the one that previously had appeared solid and set in stone, we ingested these mind-altering substances to "see" that the illusion of solidity was just that, an illusion, as we watched molecular structure break apart, dance, leap, and quiver right before our eyes. When we ascended into altered states, we merged with our friends of all races and nationalities as we looked into each other's eyes and saw ourselves looking back. We understood that there was no separation, and we retained this understanding when the drugs wore off.

Once we had seen "the light," the fact that we were so small and inconsequential, and at the same time inexorably connected in the larger scheme of things, compelled us to search for meaning in the bigger picture, a picture over which we were learning that ultimately we had no control. At the time, seeking a haven in a hostile world that was warring with itself was more than a whim or a way to justify our doing drugs. It was a necessity for us to find our niche and our purpose in a world that made no sense. What better way was there than turning to spiritual teachers who claimed they could teach us how to reach powerful highs without the drugs?

Since we were authentically looking for answers, it was a travesty for a male "teacher type" to promise women that sex with him, even if he was an aging old coot with no hair and bad teeth, had a good chance of resulting in instant enlightenment—for her. Oddly, though, they maintained that it only worked if she was relatively good-looking. In other words, the unspoken message was that plain or unattractive women need not apply. Since beauty is in the eye of the beholder, a few women teetered on the edge of acceptance, not necessarily fair of face, but their very large breasts, perfectly rounded butts, or massive bank accounts made them highly attractive and eligible for entrance into the inner circles. For the most part, however, exotic-looking, long-haired, high-cheek-boned fairy princess and model types with curvy figures, tight asses, full rosy lips, ample breasts, and a penchant for doing as they were told were the main targets. Barefooted, dressed in low-cut tie-dyed T-shirts and long, colorful transparent skirts, women flocked to these conniving men for advice and healing in whatever form it was being offered.

I pondered these dichotomies a great deal when practices like crystal healing, herbal remedies, and aroma and color therapy were coming to the forefront. In each of these systems, I encountered talented, wise people who truly cared about others and wanted to free them from suffering, alongside shysters who used these same methods to seduce their disciples. Over the years, I have been approached by representatives of the light and the dark, the East and the West, true believers and controlling types, the real deals and wannabes who have asked for my help in writing books about their individual methods of healing. And I have to say that although I've met some brilliant healers in my travels, people who were humble, nurturing, kind, and very effective, the know-it-alls and the would-bes overrode them in sheer numbers alone, with preposterous claims about their omnipotence.

Back in the eighties, when the AIDS epidemic was terrorizing the masses, a woman once told me, "I can cure AIDS."

"So get out there and do it," I said. "Why are you wasting your time sitting here with me?"

That kind of sums it up, and I guess it's still going on as I recently refused to edit a book for a young upstart who boasted that anyone could become instantly enlightened if they hung out with him, even though wise men and philosophers had dedicated lifetimes to achieving this revered state of being and were still seeking. *Why wait?* he told people. *Don't be a sucker. Come and get it now.* It begs the question: Does having your name on a book validate you and make you more substantial than you really are? These days anyone can self-publish anything from a diet that might kill you to an aerobics method that could cripple you, from how to learn a language in your sleep to how to work out and get results without moving any part of your body an inch in any direction.

Like most of my friends, I dabbled in a number of spiritual pursuits when I was in my twenties. I practiced yoga; Later I read *The Center of the Cyclone, An Autobiography of Inner Space* by mind/brain pioneer John Lilly; I also read *A Course in Miracles*, a self-study curriculum for spiritual transformation; and I practiced several different types of meditation, including Transcendental Meditation (TM), which was introduced to the West by Guru Maharishi Mahesh Yogi, famous for catching the Beatles' attention.

A boyfriend of mine had been practicing TM for years when I met him back in the seventies, and he offered to set me up with his friend Tom, a certified TM teacher, who would initiate me into this method. I showed up at Tom's house so he could relieve me of several hundred dollars and give me my secret mantra that I was never to utter aloud, a word in Sanskrit, the sacred language of Hinduism.

Tom, a good-looking guy, and I sat and chatted for a few minutes. I felt oddly uncomfortable as he asked his much younger wife to bring us water and then escorted me to the back bedroom closet to whisper my mantra in my ear. I thought it was overkill to be hiding in the closet. Who would overhear us? But what did I know? I got my Sanskrit word (he didn't make a pass at me) and we headed back to the living room to meditate together for my first twenty minutes of TM. Just before we started, when his wife asked him what he wanted for dinner that night, he looked at her askance and told her to "shut up and meditate." That did it for me. I handed him the cash, but I couldn't abide a man who insulted his wife. I only practiced TM once after that, so I guess my mantra was never fully "activated." Maybe he ought to give it to someone else, I thought, since I had hardly used it.

I had seen the TM founder, Guru Maharishi, on television, and he looked wise and all-knowing with his inviting eyes, salt-and-pepper beard, long white robes, and floral necklaces. But with people like Tom doing the initiating, something was clearly getting lost in the translation.

I heard about a number of gurus in my day, but I never followed one, thank goodness, which is why I still have my home, my bank account, and my own opinions. I was privy, however, to stories from friends who were not so lucky about some of the secret, sacred rituals of the most famously revered gurus. One supposed master who arrived here from India had settled in the West with large groups of devotees who gifted him with Rolls Royces, Rolex watches, and their life savings. He presented himself as celibate while he handpicked "certain" women (pretty ones with large breasts) to dance topless for him at hush-hush spiritual gatherings in his private quarters several evenings a week where he brushed his white-robed body against them, touching here and stroking there, gifting them with his "special" blessings.

His right-hand man, an American who quickly latched onto the guru to enjoy the spoils, cruelly broke up marriages, luring the newly single women into group sex (he was the only male) supposedly in order to make these women more powerful and independent. I met an American Indian chief who claimed to lead groups of followers to sexual ecstasy in sacred tantric rites while he watched and "helped" the women reach orgasm. And I met two other men, leaders of ancient sects of spiritual worshippers, who reportedly traded wives (some of them had more than one) for a night or two as a neighborly gesture of goodwill and cooperation, a practice that was considered beneficial and healing—for the wives, of course.

In my opinion, with or without a sexual context, the very idea of leader/follower or *guru/chela* in Sanskrit terms, suggests a closed system in which two people engage but are not considered equal. Certain gurus in India believe that no one can reach enlightenment without a living teacher, perhaps someone like them, which in my estimation sounds like a good insurance policy to remain relevant in their job descriptions. Such living teachers, by the way, are not necessarily sexual predators, although some reportedly are, and they are not necessarily healers, either, although once again, some of them are. Where would they stand, I wonder, in the case of my predatory ex-boyfriend who valued the alleged wisdom of a discarnate entity over that of a living human being?

The concept of healing, in all of its varied shapes and forms, has been much debated for centuries, and opinions vary as to what it really means and who is actually responsible for the results. Is the source of healing power the healer or the patient? Or a combination of both? Or someone or something else altogether? Does the expression "we create our own reality" mean that we should feel guilty if we become ill? That we somehow brought it upon ourselves? If so, why did a number of powerful spiritual teachers die from cancer? What happens when realities clash, when you and I define healing differently? Is getting better the only goal? What if someone finds peace before she dies? Is that considered a success because she healed her soul and found peace in her heart or is it a failure because she died?

These kinds of questions were circulating during the early eighties, when I met a woman who introduced me to a unique healing world. Up to today, after nearly a dozen trips to the Philippines where I witnessed countless healings and miracles by faith healers, after writing a book about it, promoting it, lecturing, and spreading the word as to what I saw firsthand, I still haven't found an effective way to clearly explain it or defend it. I expect I never will. In fact, it took me years to accept what I saw with my own eyes, and even then, my beliefs kept wavering until I embraced the fact that even though I wholeheartedly believe in science, certain happenings surpass the logical, scientifically constructed ideas on which most of our beliefs are formed.

For me, it started years ago when I spent a few days at a private spa near San Diego with pools of healing waters rich in minerals set at different temperatures that were open all day and night. There was an overpriced restaurant that served healthy fare and there was a spa menu that offered a variety of healing treatments including shiatsu, Swedish and deep tissue massage, natural mud baths, salt scrubs, scalp conditioning, and cleansing facials to clean out the pores, tighten the skin, and encourage collagen and new tissue growth. I had just ended my first marriage when I booked a room at this spa and scheduled a facial with a woman named Lois, who was considered much more than a facialist. She was reputed to be an energy balancer, a spirit refresher, and an all-around healer extraordinaire.

I admired the hand-painted mural on the walls as I headed down into the spa a few minutes before my treatment was scheduled to start. When Lois stepped into the lobby of the treatment center and smiled at me, I went over and took her hand. She was about twenty years my senior, and as wild as her eyes looked, her touch was warm and comforting as she led me down a partially darkened hallway. Since the treatment rooms were underground, there was no way to tell if it was night or day as we entered a room with a sink filled with fresh mineral water, an altar with a burning candle, and a massage table. The light was low, and when I removed my robe and lay down on the massage table, Lois covered me with a sheet and a light blanket, wrapped my head in a fluffy towel, put cool, moist cotton balls over my eyes, and turned on her facial light to take a good look at my skin.

She gently washed my face with hot mineral water, and in a pleasant voice, melodious and calming, she told me, "You have some blackheads on your nose, not too many, so we'll just get rid of them."

I thought that was a good idea, and her touch was light and feathery as she quickly and painlessly cleaned out the pores of my skin. She cut open a gooey leaf of a fresh aloe vera, which she smeared over my entire face, and she went on to apply a lightly scented freshener on top. She was smooth and sure, and when she began to cover my skin with a tightening mask, handmade from powdered herbs and water, her voice was low and her movements were measured and light as air. She applied the mask all over my face and neck, dabbing a little extra over trouble spots, directing me to concentrate on my breath and to envision a beautiful environment that felt safe and protected. She left the room for about ten minutes while the mask dried, and I listened to my breathing, deep and steady, as I traveled in my mind's eye, floating and hovering. I could hardly hear her as she stole back into the room and placed hot, wet towels on my face to break up the mask, turn it into a moist lotion, and wipe it away.

For the last step, she moisturized my skin, told me I was renewed, and invited me to open my eyes. She turned on an overhead light, and when I sat up, my attention was drawn to the wall beside me on my right. There was a photograph hanging there of a slight man with short black hair wearing a short-sleeved *barong* (a traditional Philippine white shirt) with his hands *inside* a woman's belly, covered up to the second knuckle. It was she, my facialist, who lay on the table in the photo, the man's hands buried in her stomach as she smiled for the camera.

"What's that?" I asked her, my eyes glued to the photograph.

"It's psychic surgery," Lois said quite matter-of-factly.

"Who is he?"

"That's Alex, a Philippine faith healer. I had a stomachache, and he took out something."

"What do you mean, he took out something?"

"He removed some dark energy."

I continued to stare at the photo. "What is he doing?" I asked her. "It looks like his hands are inside your stomach."

"They are. That's psychic surgery," she repeated.

"How did he get his hands in there? Did it hurt? Did you feel better when he was through?"

"It didn't hurt at all, and I felt much better."

I studied her eyes, trying to evaluate if she was lying or just plain crazy. Neither seemed to be true as she stared at the photo with me. "I originally went to the Philippines to interview these healers for a magazine article. They're fantastic. Do you want to see more?"

I nodded, and she pulled a photo album out from under the massage table. She sat beside me and began turning the pages, showing me more photos of Alex and similar ones featuring other healers.

"People don't put their hands inside flesh. These pictures can't be real," I said.

"I know they can't," she agreed, "but they are. I know they weren't photoshopped because I saw the healings with my own eyes. I took most of the photos myself."

"How do they explain it?" I asked.

"They don't. They're religious, they call themselves *Espiritistas*, and they say it's the work of the Holy Spirit."

That was a lot to stomach for a New England–raised Jewish girl. "I don't understand," I said, shaking my head. "Was this your first trip there?"

"No, it was my third."

"Are you going again?"

"Yes. In a few months. I love the healers, especially Alex. He's funny and smart."

I pulled my attention away from the photos. Enough was enough. Lois directed me to look in the mirror and notice my aloe vera glow. I definitely looked different, but it was hard to say where it had come from—the facial, Lois's healing hands, or the photographs that had shocked me so much. I bought some of Lois's facial scrub "with rounded grains that won't damage the skin," and I went on my way as she welcomed in her next client.

I took Lois's card and returned to see her over and over. She became a beacon for me, since I'd recently left my husband and I needed a non-judgmental mentor who would help me find some healthy excitement to replace the insane lifestyle I was leaving behind. And I needed to talk about psychic surgery. Lois and I had endless discussions about it. I sometimes stayed over in the spare room in her house, and we would talk late into the night and again the next morning over coffee before she went to work.

I was on my way back home from her house one weekend, the winds were high and gusting, when I realized that if something like this was going on in the world, I had to go see it for myself. That was the only way I would know if it was real or a scam that was so well executed it had fooled someone as sharp as Lois. It definitely would not fool me. I was too grounded and realistic.

A few months later, I sat on a plane beside my mentor, enduring a seventeen-hour flight in coach to see what the hell was going on in the Philippines. I had traveled extensively throughout the United States when I was in the ballet, I had performed in South America and Europe, and I had lived in Monte Carlo and Brighton, England, but I had never seen the Far East.

Manila airport was complete pandemonium when we arrived at 6:00 a.m. local time. I broke out into a sweat the minute I walked into the terminal; the humidity was off the charts, and the cigarette smoke turned my stomach. We retrieved our suitcases and were waved through customs. When we made our way outside, as many as five short, dark-haired men rushed us, fighting each other to lure the blond-haired American giants to their taxicabs. Lois chose one, I followed her into the backseat of the cab, and we drove off, heading toward the Manila Midtown Hotel. When I cracked the window, a stream of hot air assaulted me, carrying the smells of bitter diesel fumes and sweet palm fronds burning in the coconut fields.

Traveling with Lois was eye-opening and somewhat aggravating. I had never been around anyone who was so relaxed, which made me more anxious than I already was. Airplane travel, bad mattresses, jet lag, and foreign food seemed to have no effect on her. She slept her way through the entire flight there, and once we arrived, she instantly shifted into the next time zone with no insomnia. And she had the digestive system of a goat. She could eat anything, and she never got sick. I, on the other hand, didn't sleep a wink when I was flying, dropped into heaviness in the middle of the afternoons, lay awake on sagging mattresses at night with jet lag, and I was sick to my stomach a lot of the time. I became incredibly annoyed after a week of Lois's waking up each morning, stretching, and announcing, "I feel great!" And I didn't like her telling me I needed to "raise my consciousness" when I complained of nausea and stomachaches from exotic food my body didn't know how to digest.

But beyond my silent inner kvetching (Lois wouldn't tolerate listening to it), I spent each day in shock and amazement as I met the famous Philippine faith healers who specialized in miracles and performed the impossible on a daily basis. Over the next couple of weeks, sleep was hard to come by between the oppressive heat, tropical bugs, and the things I saw that I could not reconcile.

The day after we arrived, we took a taxi to Alex's house, the healer in the photo I had seen, and we found seats in his backyard chapel located just outside his healing room with glass windows. Starting at 8:00 a.m., the benches, which were arranged like pews, began to fill up with people until it became standing-room only. A minister stood at a podium at the front of the designated area, preaching to the congregation in Tagalog, the native language, which someone interpreted for me. He was telling them that Alex was not the source of the healing power. It was the Holy Spirit, and if they wanted a positive outcome, they should keep that in mind and thank the Holy Spirit, not Alex, for whatever happened. I was not oriented in Catholic beliefs about Jesus and the Holy Spirit, but it was easy to overlook since they prayed in their indigenous dialect, and I couldn't understand a word. I just sat there for a long time in the damp heat while they prayed, studying people with all kinds of illnesses, some superficial and hardly noticeable and others more serious that had taken their toll by turning people's eyes and skin yellow.

When it was time for Alex to start seeing patients, he walked into his healing room and gestured for Lois and me to come and stand on either side of him, an honored place to be, where we would be able to see everything he did. When the first person laid down on the massage table, I watched Alex scan her body with his eyes. In the next moment, he placed his hands on her stomach, and his fingers disappeared inside her body. He pulled out something bloody and stringy-looking and held it up, and my brain exploded. The woman's face remained calm and unstrained as Alex showed everyone what looked like a dark blood clot, his fingers stained red.

"She have no more stomachache," he explained in broken English, smiling and discarding the darkened tissue into the bowl. Then he splashed his hands in a sink full of water that was behind the massage table and dried them on a towel. "How about you?" he asked me.

I shook my head vigorously. "No, I'm fine," I said.

"Good," he said agreeably as he turned to a man who was already lying on his table. It didn't seem to matter if someone was rich or poor and who or what they worshipped. During the healing sessions that I attended every other day for two weeks, no one was turned away. If a patient had money, that was fine. They took the cash. If someone had no money, a handful of rice, a couple of papayas, or a few fresh fish would suffice. Or in some cases, nothing at all.

While the peasants and farmers from the barrios showed up regularly because they couldn't afford a doctor, foreigners also gathered, hailing from all different countries, many who had been told there was nothing a Western doctor could do for them any longer. I talked to a number of French, German, Italian, and Scandinavian citizens, and although I wasn't there long enough to follow up on the long-term effects of the healings, many were back for the third and fourth times, which meant they were satisfied and wanted more.

I was endlessly engaged, I couldn't get enough of it, and I saw a few dramatic demonstrations. A woman who apparently couldn't move her legs for years was carried to the table, and she walked away about ten minutes later. When a delirious child was placed in front of Alex, after a few sweeps of his hands, she got up on her own steam, focused and alert, smiling and looking fine. I'm aware that it sounds like I'm describing an old-time revival meeting where a minister scams the people and takes donations as someone throws their crutches or glasses away, but it didn't feel showy, and Alex was no preacher. He quietly went about his business until it was over, working anywhere from two to four hours at a stretch.

Overall, there was a sense of wonder and a lightness in the air that I felt whenever I was in Alex's presence and particularly when he worked. I stayed off the table, remaining an observer for the first two weeks, until the beginning of the third week. Lois and I were about to travel north for a week into the mountains to a resort city called Baguio, and I got a roaring bladder infection, complete with burning urine and constant visits to the bathroom. I felt awful, and Lois coerced me to get on the table and let Alex work his magic. I figured I had nothing to lose because no one on Alex's table had died or experienced any pain. I laid down, and as my fear surfaced, I said a short prayer even though I was not in the habit of praying.

I closed my eyes. I felt Alex's hands graze the lower part of my belly right above my bikini line, and there was some pressure, like it feels when your gums are numb from Novocain while the dentist works on a tooth. I let go and relaxed, there was no pain, and in a moment, Alex held a stringy-looking piece of tissue in front of me. He screwed up his nose as if it had a bad smell, laughed, and tossed it into a bowl that Lois was holding. By the time I had retied my drawstring pants, pulled them up over the pink mark his fingers left, and sat up, the infection was gone, and it didn't return.

I had become a believer, and when Lois brought me to several other healers up in the mountain regions, I learned to discern a charlatan from a master by the atmosphere surrounding each of them. They all had their own chapels where prayers were offered before sessions, and I noticed that I felt uplifted in some of them and heavy in others. One healer in particular who removed a few gaudy, expensive rings before he worked strutted arrogantly and made strange flourishes with his hands. I couldn't make out what he was doing, and I didn't like being there. His shirt had long sleeves, and he didn't let anyone stand beside him. I didn't trust him. It seemed like he was doing sleight of hand, and he treated his patients like an audience, performing and being noticeably affected by their reactions. In the Philippines, just like anywhere else, there were authentic healers as well as the impostors who went along for the ride, shamelessly cashing in on the real work that real healers were doing.

I can't possibly sum up all that occurred during my month-long stay without turning it into a book, which I actually wrote several years later, *Awakening the Healer Within*, combining three of my trips.

My First Book

I was drawn to return many times to the Philippines, twice more with Lois, and then I took a number of trips there on my own to continue my research and to learn what I could from a host of different healers that I met along the way. I felt a genuine connection with the place, and I was enthusiastic about returning, but each time I arrived at the airport to board my flight, I cried my eyes out before I got on the plane.

It was partly because I had no affection for Manila. The pavements were so badly cracked, I had to watch my feet when I walked down the crowded streets, and if I stared down too long, I'd bump into someone. The city reeked of sewage, the air was oppressive and stunk of diesel fumes, huge tropical bugs were everywhere, restaurants had faulty air conditioning, and taxis swerved in and out of the oncoming lanes, putting themselves and their fares in mortal danger. But beyond these physical deterrents, more threatening to me was the research I was doing, which shocked my system regularly, placing in question my most primal beliefs, as basic as the nature of matter. The longer I stayed, the more lonely and isolated I felt, yearning for home. But when I got back home, so few people believed the stories I told them, I felt isolated and a little bit crazy, and I couldn't wait to return.

Among the healers I met who lived in various cities and on the more remote islands, each seemed to have his or her own strength and specialty. A male healer specialized in eyes, and a woman who lived in a town several hours away from Alex was particularly good with ulcers. Her five children joined the congregation at her chapel for morning prayers, where they enjoyed meeting the foreigners who gathered around their mother. A Canadian man loved the children, and I remember the irony when he showed them the disappearing thumb trick. While their mother was burying her hands in a patient's stomach a few feet away, they were riveted by this man's silly parlor trick in which he pretended to separate his thumb into two pieces and then put it back together again.

When I wrote my book about my Philippine experiences, I tried to find a book agent who didn't laugh me out of his or her office. I had never written a book before, only articles and poetry, but I turned to my journals to help me describe people and events that no Westerners had ever seen. I found a smart editor who helped me shape my stories, but as hard as I tried, I couldn't find an agent who believed what I had written. I remember getting severely reprimanded on the telephone by a local agent for even attempting to write such a book. "Everybody thinks they have the greatest topic on earth, and they think someone will actually give them money for it," she chided me.

"We have to believe in our books or we would never write them. Thank you for your time," I said through gritted teeth, and I slammed the phone down.

I once threw the manuscript into a closet after a particularly painful rejection, and there was another time I considered tossing my computer through the panes of glass on a set of French doors. Resilience was hard to come by in the face of so much rejection, but I soldiered on, and one day, three years after I finished writing the book, the miracle happened. I got a book deal with a New Age imprint of Simon & Schuster called Fireside Books, from a female editor with an open mind and a desire to circulate information about alternate healing methods. And then I found an agent who was willing to negotiate the deal for me. I did it backward, getting the publisher first and then the agent, who didn't really care about the topic since I had already sold it.

Long after the promotion of my book, I kept returning to the Philippines. It wasn't just the healers that drew me. I had a unique opportunity to immerse myself in a foreign culture, and it was a constant delight to be the only Westerner, tall and blond, among the Filipinos, short, dark, and compact, who embraced me like one of their own. I made a total of ten trips to the Philippines over eight years, spending a lot of time there with a healer who lived near Alex who told me he could teach me to perform psychic surgery. I wanted to learn, as I fantasized saying "I told you so" to people who had ridiculed me and told me I had been duped. I wanted to show nonbelievers that I'd been telling the truth all along about what I'd seen and what the healers could do, and I made a commitment to myself that no matter how hard and expensive it was to keep returning, I would not stop my research until I had either learned to do psychic surgery myself or lost interest. The latter happened, but not in the way you might think.

Chasing the phenomenon of psychic surgery had guided me to a beautiful group of talented people who, for the most part, cared about others and had great compassion and kindness. But I learned what healing truly was from a different group of Filipinos who were highly educated and spoke perfect English. They knew all about psychic surgery and faith healing, and they didn't endorse it or reject it. They were beyond such arguments and reactions. While I listened to their personal healing experiences, I came to realize that when a person lies down on a psychic surgeon's table and says, "Fix me," or when any healer says, "Let me fix you," they are both missing the point.

A smart, wonderful man known for his extensive research on faith healers, took me around the city to meet healers and to see strange phenomena that had no explanations. I called him "the most skeptical believer" I had ever met, which delighted him. And then, another of my friends there who was particularly well spoken told me, "Being healed by a phenomenon may be exciting, but it has nothing to do with personal awareness. If someone says they healed you, they are lying. And if you say you healed anyone, then *you* are lying.

"In my earlier stages of healing," he explained, "I was caught in an ego trap. I had a few techniques within my grasp, and I walked around with spiritual arrogance, a holier-than-thou attitude. I said I was serving humanity, but I wasn't coming from my heart. I have since learned that real and effective healing can only happen through self-awareness and humility. Healing is a personal search, a personal awakening. We are learning to heal for ourselves, not for others. And while we want to feel better and help our friends feel better, we are not goal oriented. What is important is that we have not separated ourselves. We are connected to the whole and to other people. That is where healing comes from—a lack of separation, a true and indestructible connectedness."

I recall my final trip to the Philippines in 1994, when I said good-bye to the wonderful people I had met. I knew I wouldn't be returning. I had followed my instincts, and there was no longer any draw for me once I was willing to give up the phenomenon, go deeper within myself, and awaken to who I was and how I wanted to live. I had dropped my ambition around wanting to be a faith healer myself, because I was doing it for the wrong reasons. I had learned all I needed to know about the numbing effects of chasing a phenomenon and exhibiting spiritual arrogance. I had seen a lot of it, I had engaged in it myself, and I had returned, time after time, trying to learn to heal other people, while my new friends were quietly and masterfully encouraging me to heal myself.

In the end, I understood that while a phenomenon had drawn me and scintillated my senses for a decade, I was not destined to emulate these people. I was there only to love them and learn about life from them. In turning away from my quest for false power, a deeper humility and understanding of true healing in all of its glory was my priceless reward.

Chapter Fourteen

Baby Boomer Blues

The sixties are gone,

dope will never be as cheap,

sex never as free,

and the rock and roll never as great.

— Abbie Hoffman (1938–1989) political/social activist

We baby boomers are in a pickle. We're glad to get senior discounts at the movie theater, but we're pissed off when the kid behind the counter doesn't look surprised. We can finally afford the sexy stiletto heels we always lusted after, but now our hips and feet hurt like hell the day after we wear them. We love our iPhones, but we're leery about using Skype and FaceTime because we think we look wizened on the screen. We have mixed feelings when someone tells us we look great "for our age," resenting those three little words, wishing we could turn back time and know as much as we do now.

In a world where youth is celebrated and aging is rebuffed, how can we embrace our sags and wrinkles? If the pop idols and movie stars who died so young were around today, what would they be doing, and how would they look? Can you imagine Marilyn Monroe with swollen lips from Restylane injections? Jim Morrison writing poetry about rehab? Janis Joplin asking, "What did you say, man?" and turning up her hearing aid? James Dean, a deadbeat dad with a beer gut, an angry ex-wife to support, and a brood of children to raise?

That constant look of surprise on baby boomer faces is much more than bad Botox. We're facing a load of challenges we never anticipated. Most notably, we're stunned and disappointed that we're aging, as if we had the power to do anything else. When we were young, my friends and I swore so adamantly that we would never get old, I think we actually believed it, and now it's devastating to wake up in the morning with aches, pains, and facial lines that weren't there before. My arms are suddenly too short to hold a restaurant menu far enough away to read it. I can't see small print, I need my electronic reader to be backlit, and I can't read the hands on the dial of my fancy designer watch that I reluctantly shelved and replaced with a cheaper, larger, more practical digital readout so I know what time it is.

These days, everyone seems to have a personal story about dental implants (we're outliving our teeth), joint replacements (I have two bionic hips, and I consider myself part robot), hair plugs, cataracts, or the latest hearing aids that are so transparent and fit so well into your ears, you can hardly see them. Our continuing health and vitality are all about spare parts: having old ones removed, getting new ones, and trying to refurbish and make the best of what still works. And we're plenty freaked out about it. We seem to be suffering from a strange epidemic called Baby Boomer Blues, and the only cure is something we dread: growing too old to care. But when you consider how my generation imagined the future when we were coming of age and compare it with what we actually got, it's a wonder any of us can function at all.

- When we were young and carefree, we vowed never to trust anyone over thirty, and here we are, in our sixties.
- We can't reduce our stress by "turning on, tuning in, and dropping out" like we did before, à la Timothy Leary, because our aging bodies can't handle the drugs.
- We used to take LSD to uplift our moods and feel better about the world. Now we take Prozac.
- We touted the psychedelic drugs of our era as mind expanding and heart opening. Now we're doing everything we can to stop our children from using them.
- We judged anyone who didn't have long hair, and today a lot of us are going bald.
- We strove to overcome racial prejudice and become "color blind." Now we all need glasses.
- We women grew the hair on our legs and underarms because we wanted to be "natural." Now we're having it waxed and lasered off, all over our bodies.
- We believed "love is all you need." Now we get Botox and plastic surgery and lie about our ages because we obviously think that love is not enough.
- We used to practice "free love." Today herpes and AIDS have made us slaves to condoms.
- We used to live in communes with "extended family." Now we isolate in private rooms, our heads perpetually stuck in a maze of electronic devices.
- We used to fall in love by gazing into each other's eyes. Now we have technological romances with people we've never met.
- Our slogan was "make love, not war." And to this day, our country has perpetually been at war.
- The parents we reviled and rebelled against are living into their nineties. We're forgiving them for whatever we thought they did to us, caring for them, and helping them die with dignity. And we have to acknowledge that we're next in line.

What the hell happened? What we thought and what we got seem to be diametrically opposed. These days, my fabulous hairdresser's hot husband is fashionably bald, more women than I can count are getting facial fillers and nips and tucks, a large number of us are taking antidepressants, smoking pot leads to coughing fits and paranoia, and lovers who fall into bed together without condoms or at least a rundown on their partner's sexual history are in the minority and considered uncool.

Back in the sixties, my friends and I believed we were immortal as we took pride in being young and strong, creatively on fire, sexually liberated, righteously arrogant, politically rebellious, teeming with hope, and certain that love was all there was in our glorious and enviable future. "Were the sixties really all about free love?" members of other generations ask me from time to time. "Were there really orgies and love-ins? You were so lucky to be growing up at a time when sex was free."

Maybe. But these days, we have herpes and AIDS, and the bad boys who used to turn me on feel like pesky mosquitoes biting at my ankles, while the din of loud music gives me a headache. "A couple of decades ago," a friend told me, "I would never have gone for the man I just married." Where we used to seek out excitement and drama, now we want steadiness in our jobs, our relationships, our families, and our homes.

A few years back, I was collaborating on a self-help book at the home of a prominent motivational speaker, a woman in her midthirties who was obsessed with talking fast, achieving, and being productive. She so rarely stopped moving, she gave new meaning to the expression "ants in her pants." It was a task for her to sit still for the hour or so that we worked together each week. One afternoon, as the sun was setting in its pastel glory over the Pacific Ocean, she asked me quickly and breathlessly, "What do you see in your future? What do you want for yourself next? What are your hopes and dreams?"

It was clear to me what I used to want: travel, exciting men, hot sex, exotic food, and new mountains to climb. That was then. I thought a moment, watching the gulls soar and swoop in front of the plate-glass window of this woman's sumptuous Malibu estate. I had already traveled extensively, my career was on course, I had a home that I loved, I'd been married and divorced twice, I was open to meeting someone new, but I'd made peace with living alone for the most part, and I preferred food that was fresh and simple. "Peace," I said. "I want peace."

She gazed at me wistfully, clearly disappointed by my answer, and asked me, "Is that all?"

I smiled and nodded. I understood where she was coming from because I had been there too. How could I explain to her that my prior dreams and hopes for the future had been replaced with a yearning for contentment, and that one day it would most likely happen to her too?

I recently had lunch with Marianne Williamson, a friend and editorial client who is a lecturer, best-selling author, and was a political candidate for Congress. We hadn't seen each other for a while, and after we hugged and sat down to eat, she said, "Well, Andrea, these are the women we've become. What do you think?"

Her declaration took me by surprise. I thought I was pretty much the same as I always had been, but when I really thought about it, somewhere along the line, a switch got flipped that changed the way I felt about life and what I wanted for myself. It's not that I feel old and tired these days. I don't. It's about my commitment to being present in the moment and realizing how much beauty I missed when I was rushing around, addicted to drama and measuring my worth against how much I could produce in the shortest period of time. When did we start basing the validity of our lives on how much we could get done? What about monks who meditate in a cave for decades? Are they wasting their time and energy? Or have they embraced the idea that "do no harm" is being productive enough?

My parents, who were perpetually busy "doing," were lost during the few vacations we ever took as a family. They called themselves "lazy bums" when they sat and read a book in the daytime or sunbathed or took a dip in the pool or dropped into an afternoon snooze. They had harsh judgments about anyone who believed in slowing down and smelling the roses, and they were diligent about passing those attitudes on to my sister and me.

One time, when I had finished writing a book that had a very tight deadline, I was exhausted and really needed to rest my mind, but it was hard to do since I didn't think taking life easy was a viable or valuable option. I was on the phone with my mother the day after the book was submitted, and when she asked how I felt, I told her I felt good about the book, but I was having difficulty adjusting to my free time. "It feels strange," I told her. "I guess I need to learn how to relax and get comfortable doing nothing." A few days later, a letter from her arrived in my mailbox. In her elegant penmanship featuring perfect serifs at the ends of her letters, she told me, "I force myself to do at least two unpleasant tasks every day. It keeps up my discipline."

I wondered if one of them was writing me that letter. I knew all about discipline and being productive. I was an ex-ballet dancer, and I was all too familiar with an array of self-help books, many of which I helped write, about how to do and achieve more while obsessively checking off items on one's to-do list, filling up the calendar, accomplishing a load of difficult tasks, showing up at the hippest night spots, making lots of money, buying lots of stuff, and taking on the world. Advice on feeling peaceful and content in the world that everyone was so obsessed with taking on and conquering, however, was nowhere to be found. How could I possibly relax and find contentment if I was obsessed with "doing"? Along the same lines, how could I accept aging when a new and burgeoning race of people my age and younger were cropping up that I dubbed "the Plastoids"?

Talk about being in denial about aging. These people who are shopping, dieting, and living among us think they're in disguise, that they've taken years off their faces, gotten rid of all their cellulite, and that they fit in. I think they're kidding themselves. In many cases, the skin on their injected faces looks waxen, their eyes are so wide open it appears that blinking takes effort, their lips are swollen into distortion, their crooked smiles are so disconnected from their eyes that they look like the Joker in *Batman*, and their stomachs and thighs look like they were ironed flat. With very few exceptions, their waists are tiny, while their breasts can get so large they end up needing back surgery.

The Plastoids as a race are wrinkle- and food-phobic. They barely eat at all, and being skinny is a state much revered. I actually met a male Plastiod once (they're rare, but they do exist) who invited me to dinner at a raw foods restaurant. When he picked me up in his Maserati, I joked that the back end of his car looked fat and he took offense. On the whole, they're ultra-sensitive about everything and they mostly gather in larger cities where they try to blend in with the general population, until (this is one of their common characteristics) they finally decide that everyone else should look like they do.

I had lunch with one of them, a potential book client, and while I was trying not to stare at her unnaturally upturned eyes and her hornet-stung lips and make her feel like an outcast, I noticed she was staring at *my* face like *I* didn't belong there, her eyes focused on the area just above my nose. When I finished telling her in a spirited way about my latest writing project that was challenging me creatively, she raised her arm, pointed her French-manicured finger right at my face, aiming directly between my eyes, and said in a thick Australian accent, "Botox." As in, she thought I needed some, but it sounded like she was either hexing me or blessing me with some sort of sacred aboriginal word.

She was profoundly wrinkle-phobic (she'd actually had her knees done), and I hardly knew what to think. They say that beauty is in the eye of the beholder, and I realized that the lines above my nose and on my forehead were deeply disturbing for her, so I felt I needed to explain myself. "I'm kind of scared to get injections in my face," I said, skipping over the knees altogether. My explanation clearly did not compute, because without missing a beat, she said, "You'd be really pretty if you just got a little bit of Restylane above your lips, just enough to hide those crevices where your lipstick bleeds through."

She couldn't have used a kinder voice, and she reminded me of an episode of the original *Twilight Zone,* in which a woman was recovering in the hospital after undergoing plastic surgery. We didn't see faces at first; hers was wrapped up like a mummy, and we only saw the hands and heard the voices of her attending doctors and nurses, who were kind and sympathetic, especially after they unwrapped her face and realized there was no change in the way she looked. There was nothing they could do for her. When the camera lens finally zoomed in on the poor woman's unwrapped face and those of the doctors, the patient was absolutely gorgeous while her attendants were hideous-looking creatures with lumpy foreheads, uneven eyes, and painfully swollen cheeks and lips, a cigarette hanging out of the side of someone's repulsive-looking mouth.

I have to admit I feel resentful as I get older, not about aging itself, but rather that society considers my wrinkles and lines unsightly and expects me to hide them so no one will know how old I am. One of my clients, a former rock-and-roll legend who refuses to get Botox, Restylane, or any form of plastic surgery, called me on my fiftieth birthday and sang out, "Welcome to the half-century club." She completely ruined my day, and I decided to keep my age a secret.

But the truth about my age is no secret. At the beginning of 2014, every health network across the country bombarded me with piles of snail mail and e-mail, touting their supplemental and prescription Medicare plans, obviously aware that I was old enough to be eligible. I signed up for Medicare and Social Security—no reason not to—but if I stick to my plan and forego injections of filler and/or plastic surgery, maybe I'll be one of the few elderly people who retain their original looks. Perhaps science will want to study my face or put my photograph in a time capsule to show future generations of Plastoids how humans used to look before the youth-oriented technologies took over and became mandatory. Or maybe they'll find out that fillers and plastic surgery cause some lethal kinds of diseases, and I'll be among the few remaining women on earth.

I blame these attitudes for a large part on technological advances, which make these physical alterations accessible, affordable, and in some cases, a must. But while I'm stubbornly against the technology that can alter my face, I am gung ho when it comes to technological advances in communication. I was one of those crazy people who stood in line for five hours several years back to get the latest version of the iPhone, vowing every fifteen minutes to walk away from the line and abandon my quest to be one of the first to get my hands on that enviable electronic toy. I even got reprimanded by a guard when I sat on the floor for a moment, tired from standing in one place for so long. Apparently, sitting was against the rules. But I hung in there, forming a kind of camaraderie with the other people in the line. There was a short scuffle when I was just about to get into the store to place my order and pick up my reward. It was getting late in the day, and some people behind me in the line were afraid the store would close before they got their booty. I just made it, thank goodness, because if I had walked away empty-handed, I would have felt like even more of a loser than I already did.

My generation are "in betweeners" when it comes to electronic savvy, a little bit dumb about the latest technical shortcuts, options, and available apps. But I'm doing my best. Like a good little technocrat, I speak to a robot named Siri who hangs out in my iPhone (I ask her trivia questions), I text my friends and clients (although a lot less than some of the younger generation), I play Words with Friends, and I upgrade my devices whenever new operating systems become available. "It's so easy to use," a tech advisor lies to me each time I order something new. "All you have to do is plug it in and it'll just work." It never does, but I'm still an avid Amazon Prime customer. I like buying online and waiting for my stuff to arrive (I'm fascinated by the possibility of drone delivery), but I draw the line at the one Internet offering that seems to pull in the most people over fifty— online dating.

My friends keep goading me to do it. I know that lots of people meet their mates this way and have good marriages (apparently meeting a guy in a bar is passé), but for some reason, online dating is abhorrent to me. First of all, I never expected to be single at this age, and when I stare at a long list of available men and their photographs, they all blend into one highly undesirable guy. But in truth, the bottom line is that I just don't trust myself when it comes to choosing men. I'm told that the conventional wisdom is to e-mail back and forth before you meet the guy to see if you have anything in common. But even so, I might end up with someone who doesn't even exist. It happened in 2012 to footballer Manti Te'o, a linebacker with the San Diego Chargers.

When he was twenty-two, Manti Te'o became the poster child for being victimized by an online hoax when his story went viral on YouTube. He had fallen in love online and shared hours of phone calls with a woman named Lennay, whom he had never met. His heart broke when she was allegedly diagnosed with leukemia, and then it broke again when she allegedly died in a car accident on the same day his grandmother died. It turned out that his grandmother really had died, but Lennay hadn't because she never existed in the first place. A mean-spirited Internet user had a crush on the athlete and created a woman named Lennay out of thin air. He faked her voice for hundreds of hours of phone calls and got so angry when Manti Te'o seemed to be losing interest, like a jilted lover, he decided to kill off his alias in a speeding car.

This kind of humiliating and heartbreaking experience would never have happened if Mr. Te'o hadn't blindly accepted technology without questioning its veracity. Back in the sixties, Timothy Leary warned us, "Think for yourself and question authority," and now we can adapt it to, "Question technology." It would be best not to trust someone until you've seen him or her with your own eyes. Or at least Skyped with the person.

Although Skype is a medium that I use for work because it's necessary in my career, I was hardly a kid when the Internet was born, so it didn't come naturally to me. And my parents grew up in a different world altogether. Their brains were hardwired to writing longhand and using typewriters instead of computers. To them, an electronic reader was a sorry substitute for a book. It was much too complicated to learn how to use it, it didn't smell like a tree, and it had a battery that constantly needed recharging. So while we have advanced beyond our predecessors, we baby boomers will always be a step behind the next generation, who grew up with their heads stuck in a Game Boy or an Xbox. To them, texting is the new talking, and I'm sure their brains are mutating into a brand-new configuration. I'll never forget the look on my nephew's face when I explained to him that not only did we not have computers or cell phones when I was growing up, we didn't even have answering machines. If you needed to talk to someone, you phoned her. If she wasn't available, you stayed home and kept trying.

Whether you're twenty, forty, sixty, or eighty, however, it feels like time itself is speeding up. We simply can't look at it in the same way, now that athletes best each other by one one-hundredths of a second, the New York Stock Exchange measures trading results in nanoseconds, we formulate nuclear energy in rads, and unless you're a rocket scientist, forget about helping your kid with his math homework. The only way to cope with all of this is to return to something we learned when we baby boomers were coming of age: Stay in the moment.

"Be here now" was a golden expression for people in my generation, when Richard Alpert, a.k.a. Baba Ram Dass, coined the phrase. A Harvard professor and therapist known for his extensive mind-expanding experimentation with LSD, Alpert traveled to India in 1967 to explore his spirituality. He was given the name Ram Dass, which means "servant of God" by his guru, Maharaj-ji. His book, *Remember, Be Here Now*, published in 1971, was considered a counterculture bible, and those of us with a spiritual bent embraced the concept. "Be here now" meant that we needed to stop projecting into the future or the past so we could enjoy a grounded experience of living in the moment. But like so many expressions that become clichés, it seems a bit simplistic and narrow in its scope today when you really contemplate the subtleties.

Being here now doesn't necessarily produce the best results when you're considering things like a quick affair with a girlfriend's boyfriend or hooking up with someone else who is not particularly good for you. What about when you crave junk food because you're hungry—right now? Or when you want to "shop till you drop," but you don't have the money for what you want here and now so you put it on plastic? "Be here now" could easily be interpreted as permission to go for whatever you want at any given moment, whether or not it's the right thing to do. How about allowing yourself some time to think through a variety of options?

Then you can choose one that's good now *and* in the future, something that might be based on a past experience that worked out well.

For me, the modern-day Buddhist-inspired expression "be mindful" replaces "be here now" with more grace and wisdom, as I do my best to alleviate suffering, mine and that of anyone else I know, attempting to infuse my day-to-day life with light and hope for positive transformation. I believe that any creative expression, whether it's written, painted, danced, sung, composed, or anything else, must contain the possibility of transformation and expansion for it to be of value. In my opinion, a stark painting of the dark is uninteresting, hopeless, and meaningless unless somewhere within it a hint of the emergence of light is at least suggested. But I'm not referring to trivialities. On the day that I write this, some supposedly respectable TV news anchors are doing a series of ongoing segments called "Love Your Selfie." While jumbo jets are dropping out of the skies, wars rage in the Middle East, and ebola is becoming a global threat, the news anchors of major TV networks are taking photos of themselves (selfies) and showing viewers how to build a more positive self-image in order to like what they see in the mirror. In a world filled with so much negativity, warring, and tragedy, shouldn't the idea of learning to love yourself be left to therapists and fashion consultants?

It seems that the Buddhist ideal of "living mindfully" is the only way to embrace an unjust world that seems to be governed by thieves and acrobats who are stealing our nest eggs and dropping the ball at every turn. How can they care so little about the unnecessary suffering, violence, and tragedy that define the daily comings and goings of so many people? The first of the "four noble truths" in the Buddhist teachings is that there is suffering in the world, a philosophy that I have trouble embracing. In fact, the mere act of trying to accept suffering as a reality causes me suffering because I am forced to give up the childish notions that "everything will be all right" and "she lived happily ever after." As I fret about why people have to suffer, and I search futilely for a way to change it, I see that I have no answers. Neither does anyone else, and I know this because I've asked around. I've had the good fortune to write books with some of the greatest movers and shakers of my time, including movie idols, rock stars, news anchors, and expanded spiritual thinkers, and they all agree that the older they get, the more confounding life becomes. "Aging is a form of madness," actor Olympia Dukakis told me.

"Why are Cher and I the only two people who admit how much we hate getting old?" said Grace Slick. So I don't expect to get any definitive answers about the meaning of life before it's my time to check out, and contrary to what I used to believe, that day will come.

Whether it happens with a loud bang or a dull thud, the time will come when all of the baby boomers have left the building, and our philosophies, rituals, and favorite toys will fall under the categories of "quaint" and "outdated" like typewriters, answering machines, and ice-cube trays. And still, the questions will remain and people's lives will revolve around trying to find solutions that hover just out of reach. It would be nice to be remembered for something that mattered, for bringing hope and light into a world gone mad. Or maybe it was always this way, and each of us tries to solve our small piece of the puzzle and leave behind an impression that will bring a smile to a loved one's face. The truth, however, is that how people remember me and my musings when I'm gone is none of my business. I can only hope that when I'm no longer around, people will think for a moment and say about me, "She didn't have any answers, but she sure had some great questions."

Epilogue

We become the stories we tell ourselves.

— Michael Cunningham, *A Home at the End of the World*

When I told my mother some years back that I was going into therapy to help me sort out a few things, she said, "I'm not the type for therapy. It's not my cup of tea. I'm just not that interested in myself."

Barring the extremes of succumbing to narcissism or self-punishing judgments, I wonder what could be more interesting, rewarding, and just plain useful than an archeological dig into what makes us tick. For me, it has been a fulfilling and astonishing exercise to recall and put down on the page the wondrous, curious, funny, and often tragic stories that exist within my larger story, the path that my life has taken. I have shed the sheet of invisibility and moved out into the open, and now there is no turning back.

When I turned sixty-five, I decided I had lived long enough to get my story out. But how? I can't draw a decent stick figure, so I can't paint it. I don't perform *tour jetés* anymore with my titanium hips, so I can't dance it. I don't have a voice like a lark or a nightingale, so I can't sing it. And the extent of my music-making skills is keeping the rhythm on a tambourine, so I can't play it. But I can write it, something that pleases me to no end, something I intend to keep doing until my time runs out. And so, this is my book that has yearned to be written for many years, and this is my time to write it.

When I started, I wondered if I had done enough, met enough fascinating characters, and been enough places to write an interesting memoir that would hold a reader's attention. Now that I've finished it, I am astonished at the abundance of memories that have risen to the surface and literally begged to be indelibly inked on these pages. I have felt breathless in narrating my story, laughing and weeping all by myself, truly amazed at what has shown up on these pages, at all that I've done and the places I've been, at times moved to tears by my courage and determination, and at other times ashamed of my fears and bad choices. But I stand behind all of my choices, viewing them as living lessons that I have needed in order to keep this life moving forward. I know I can't physically alter what I've done in the past, but with more understanding and deeper compassion for myself, I can see how I've been affected and transformed by everything that has happened along the way. And now I can make better and more fulfilling choices.

I feel good about how my life has turned out, and still I ponder the provocative idea of alternate realities, wondering what might have been if I had taken a different road than the one I took. What if I had said yes, when I actually said no? Or vice versa? What if I had gone to the right instead of the left or made friends with different people than the ones I chose? Undoubtedly things in my life would have been different, but the longer I live, the more I have come to see that I couldn't do everything. I had to pick and choose and make decisions that would take me where I needed to go.

I have paused at a crossroads at various times in my life, and whether I was clear, confused, embittered, enthusiastic, fearful, brave, or some of each, I had to make a choice or stand still, the latter being a virtual impossibility in the scheme of things. As many of our great poets and songwriters have reminded me, and I paraphrase: If we're not busy living then we're busy dying, and life happens while we're making plans for a future that most likely will never come to fruition. "Man plans; the gods laugh" is a saying that I hope will never disappear or lose its meaning.

For now, this book is complete, but my story, like all of our stories, is ongoing and will only end when I do. When my life on earth is over, whatever or wherever that will be or how it will look, my story will either be lost for all time, returning to the dust from which it was originally fashioned, or it will be taken up by someone else, who will interpret it according to his or her ideas and memories. When I'm gone, what my friends, acquaintances, readers, and adversaries remember about me and about what I did and said and how I affected people along the way will be determined by them, not by me. How they think of me in the future, if they do, will be skewed by their own interpretations, and there is nothing I can do about that, as I will be gone, and they will live on without my ability to correct them, influence them, or change their minds. But for now, my story belongs to me—one more thing, like my body, my friends, my family, and my possessions, that I have borrowed along the way but will be required to let go when I die.

As I read back through this book, I have made a rational and well-thought-out decision to embrace my story and love it because doing anything else would be a waste of time. I regret some of my choices, imagining, for example, that being a wife and mother would have made me less lonely than choosing the life of a career woman who has had adventures out in the world. I regret that I have so often treated myself with less respect than I treated others. And I regret the many times I swallowed my words, afraid to speak up and tell the truth about what I felt, wanted, or needed, a disease that so many women in the world share with me.

All of that may be true, but I can say without reservation that I have consistently done the best I could, with myself and with others, and what's done is done. I can't change what I can't change. When one of my best friends was dying of AIDS, he was drowning in self-judgments, chastising himself for having been promiscuous and predatory and ending up with a sexually transmitted disease that was killing him. Then, one day, he let go of all the self-blame and self-recrimination. I asked him how he had managed it.

"I did a lot of things I wish I hadn't," he told me. "I chose some unsavory people, and I acted in unbecoming ways, but I forgive myself. I may have been looking in the wrong places, but I understand now that all along the way, wherever I went and whatever I did, I was only trying to find love."

It's the same for me. I've chosen the wrong partners, I've taken risks that put me in danger, and I didn't always find the most loving way of relating to other people. But in the end, I was trying to find and give love, and I did it the only way I knew how.

Like Popeye says, "I yam what I yam."

Like chanteuse/rock star Grace Slick told me, "If something was supposed to be different, it would be."

And like the Dalai Lama says, "Change your mind; change the world."

In my life, I have covered the extremes. I've been a lonely child and a baby boomer, a warmonger and a pacifist, a hider under the covers and a go-getter, a wannabe and a jet-setter, a beach bum and a ballerina in pink, a desert rat and an island dweller, an unhappily married woman and an ecstatic lover, a failure and a successful writer, a battered woman and a high priestess, a self-hater and a self-defender, a scavenger hunt item and a loyal sister, a mean-spirited gossip and an open-hearted healer, and now, the author of my own memoir.

This is my story, my truth, that was yearning to be told.

That was up to me.

Do with it, think of it, and speak about it as you will.

That's up to you.

ACKNOWLEDGMENTS

My undying gratitude goes out to the following people:

Pamela Kawi, for her loyalty and expertise throughout the writing, editing, and designing processes and for imagining my beautiful cover when it didn't exist.

To Olympia Dukakis, who taught me to honor my words, my story, my femininity, my strength, and my eternal ancestry.

To Andrea Geffner, who showed me how to believe in myself, to boldly face my history, and to change my mind about how to live my life.

To Gaines Hill and the staff of CreateSpace, who worked with me diligently and with great kindness to help me create the space I had in my mind.

My thanks also go out to Jill Cagan, Juliet Green, Jerry Mandel, and John Densmore.